GRAND PRIX
BRITISH WINNERS

**A swamp and the sprawling city of Buenos
Aires form the backdrop as Revson's
McLaren chases the Ferrari of Ickx in 1973.**

GUINNESS PUBLISHING

GRAND PRIX BRITISH WINNERS

MAURICE HAMILTON

The use of the banking in 1960 brought the disapproval of the British but they turned up the following year, only to be thrashed by the 'sharknose' Ferraris. Phil Hill leads the way during the ill-fated 1961 Italian Grand Prix.

First published in 1991 by
Guinness Publishing Ltd
33 London Road
Enfield Middlesex

This book is a product of FORSTER books

Designed by Graham Mitchener

Text copyright © 1991
by Maurice Hamilton

Illustrations copyright © 1991 as credited

Typeset by First impression

A catalogue record for this book is available
from the British Library

Printed and bound in Great Britain by
Butler & Tanner Ltd, Frome, Somerset

'Guinness' is a registered trademark of
Guinness Superlatives Ltd

ISBN 0-85112-505-0

Contents

Introduction

The idea for this book came about one wet winter's afternoon while Christopher Forster and I watched horses gallop by at Plumpton. The purpose of the day's racing was supposed to be a moment of relaxation following the publication of our previous effort, *British Grand Prix*. But, inevitably, the subject of what to do next arose. A history of the various foreign Grands Prix seemed a very attractive idea but it lacked a necessary ingredient for the British market.

As we talked, the runners and riders were declared for the next race and I was immediately struck by the formal nature of the announcement. Among their number were famous names such as Richard Dunwoody and Peter Scudamore yet they were brusquely referred as 'R. Dunwoody' and 'P. Scudamore'. No gushing adulation and public relations hype here, I thought; just the pleasant business of the day. Rather like Grand Prix racing used to be.

The discussion moved on to how Formula 1 had changed from the days when Mike Hawthorn became the first British driver to win a world championship Grand Prix in 1953. And that led to the thought that many casual followers of the sport today knew very little about either Hawthorn or his friend, Peter Collins. Indeed, it's a sign that the years are slipping by when people ask about Jim Clark, a particular hero of mine when I camped at the British Grand Prix in the Sixties.

Forster became agitated and voluble – a sure sign he feels a good book coming on. Discarding a punter's cap for his publisher's hat, he suggested I write about the 13 British drivers who had won a championship Grand Prix; that way, I could link them with the story of 13 different Grands Prix. *Grand Prix – British Winners* was a runner from that moment on.

There are a couple of points I would like to mention. Some names fall easily with certain Grands Prix; for instance, Graham Hill and Monaco are linked forever by his five wins in the Principality. Stirling Moss is also associated with superb drives at Monte Carlo and, indeed, the Nürburgring, but it has not been possible to make the most obvious connection in his case, the choice being limited by other drivers having won only a few races.

Germany, therefore, goes to Tony Brooks; a worthy combination nonetheless. And so the equation moves on, Innes Ireland and Peter Gethin accounting for the US and Italian Grands Prix because of their single victories in those respective events. Which explains why Nigel Mansell, for example, is bracketed with South Africa – not the first race that springs to mind in Nigel's case, but an interesting one even so.

With regard to the drivers, I set out in the space available to provide a resumé of their careers and give an indication of their characters and the regard in which they were held. In other words, I have attempted to answer the question: 'What was Jim Clark really like?' For this, I have had to weigh heavily on the opinions and recollections of others and balance them with my own views.

Reading through the text which follows, I have come to realise that personal feelings show clearly between the lines from time to time and, while that was not the original intention, I make no apology for it. I suppose it was rather naïve on my part to believe such an emotive and enjoyable subject could be tackled in any other way. You may not agree with certain assessments but my hope is that the book is the livelier for them.

I would like to mention several people who gave invaluable help: Stephen Spark for combing through my words with his usual painstaking grammatical efficiency; Graham Mitchener for a delightful artistic touch; David Phipps for swiftly providing a wide-range of photographs; Eoin Young for unearthing so many useful books and allowing me to delve into his wonderful archives at Motormedia and use so many previously unpublished photographs; Christopher and Jo Forster for their usual encouraging abuse down the telephone when I showed signs of running out of steam; 'Lofty' England, Esler Crawford, Nigel Snowdon, Denis Jenkinson, Edgar Jessop, Nigel Roebuck and Alan Henry, and other friends and colleagues for their help in various ways.

We each backed a winner or two at Plumpton that day, Chris and I, and it would be nice to think that the idea for this book was one of them. I hope you agree.

Maurice Hamilton
Rudgwick
West Sussex
June 1991

Mike with a wind-blown look after being unable to resist having a run over the Hog's Back in an 8C-2300 Alfa Romeo. The picture was taken by Denis Jenkinson in 1958 outside the Hawthorn family garage in Farnham.

Hawthorn in the Squalo Ferrari on his way to
victory in the 1954 Spanish Grand Prix on the
Pedralbes circuit, Barcelona.

MIKE HAWTHORN

It had been raining heavily during the morning of Thursday, 22 January 1959. It was six months since Mike Hawthorn had won the French Grand Prix for the second time, and just six weeks since he had announced his retirement from motor racing. He had stepped down after winning the world championship and now he was undertaking the heavy schedule of social responsibilities conferred on the holders of such a prestigious title.

Hawthorn had a lunchtime appointment in London. He set off at a brisk pace on the 38-mile journey, the British Racing Green Jaguar 3.4 swiftly climbing onto the Hog's Back, a fast stretch of road which runs along the ridge of high ground between Farnham and Guildford. Hawthorn knew this piece of Surrey countryside intimately. He had covered it many times on a motorcycle while commuting to work at Dennis Brothers, the commercial vehicle manufacturer with which he had served a four-year apprenticeship.

His time had largely been spent working on motorised mowers but Hawthorn frequently managed to create havoc when entrusted with driving the machines from the assembly bays to the paint shop. Bored with that, Hawthorn one day climbed into the cab of a lorry and took it for a run across the yard.

Unfortunately, he met the foreman *en route* and the subsequent heavy braking succeeded in noisily depositing the vehicle's bonnet panels, lying loose on the back, at the supervisor's feet. Hawthorn did not receive his cards and that fact, plus the nature of the indiscretion itself, says much about his boyish charm.

Much had happened since he left Dennis Brothers. His father, Leslie, a motor racing enthusiast and a bluff, outspoken man, had done all he could to encourage his son's progress at the wheel. Mike's first car was a Fiat 500, followed by an 18-year-old Riley Nine, a reflection of Leslie Hawthorn's penchant for the Riley marque. This particular car was as robust as the rest of them, although because the front doors were held

shut by a piece of string, the young driver had to gain access via the rear and climb over the seats; that was just part of life's rich pattern as far as Mike was concerned.

With Dad being a regular competitor in club events, it was not long before Mike found himself coming under starter's orders. In 1950, he took part in his first competition, the Brighton Speed Trials. For this blast along the prom against the clock, Mike had an 1100 cc Riley Ulster Imp. He won his class. And Dad finished second in the 1500 cc class at the wheel of a Riley TT Sprite. The die had been cast; there would be no looking back for John Michael Hawthorn.

The following year, he took part in 12 meetings, the most significant being at Dundrod in Northern Ireland. Dundrod was made up of eight miles of country roads on a plateau to the north of Belfast. Natural hazards took many forms: earth banks, telegraph poles, stone walls, narrow bridges. Hawthorn had entered a ten-lap handicap race supporting the main event, the Ulster Trophy for Grand Prix cars. There were a number of influential people present – and they saw Hawthorn win impressively.

This race, though, would hint at a problem which would affect Hawthorn's performance in the future. The stiff cart springs on the Riley, doing their best to cope with the numerous bumps endemic to this circuit, had given Mike's insides a terrible beating. The following evening, he passed out. The application of a cure – whisky and hot milk – could not hide the fact that his internal organs, particularly his kidneys, would not take kindly to such punishment in the future. It would, at times, severely limit Hawthorn's performances but, when you are 22, and with everything to play for, such early warnings seem irrelevant.

Hawthorn was back at Dundrod 12 months later, this time to take part in the main event. He had moved into Formula 2 (considered to be the final stepping stone to Grand Prix racing) at the wheel of a Cooper-Bristol, a neat and extremely nimble single-seater which allowed Hawthorn to exercise his impressive natural flair.

During practice, there was a spot of bother with the water pump. Since there was not enough time to have a spare shipped from England, Hawthorn called upon a local major, who owned a Bristol road car, and asked if he could borrow his pump. The major did not hesitate.

But the trouble did not end there. The following morning, while driving the racing car to the circuit (then customary procedure, of course), a leaking head-gasket appeared to put the race out of the question. A swift visit to some nearby cottages, however, culled numerous tins of Colman's mustard and the contents were dumped into the radiator in order to stop the leak.

Hawthorn led for a while but further mechanical trouble meant he had to accept second place: no matter, his first race in a Cooper-Bristol earlier that year had brought victory at Goodwood (even though Hawthorn had been up most of the night before practice working on the car) and now he was poised to take part in his first Grand Prix, the Belgian at Spa-Francorchamps. He finished fourth. That, though, was probably not half as exciting as the effort required just to reach Rouen-les-Essarts and the French Grand Prix a few weeks later.

Engine repairs in Paris had taken longer than expected. Hawthorn describes what happened next in his book *Challenge Me the Race*:

'They finished the car late in the afternoon and we had no lorry to get it to Rouen; I said "Fair enough, I'll drive it there". So we started up the engine, it was getting quite late by that time, I leapt into this single-seater racing car and drove off through Paris all the way to Rouen. It was a wonderful drive. Tony Hume, Archie [Bryde, owner of the Cooper] and his wife drove in Archie's Bentley and I followed in the Cooper. Wherever we went, the police held up the traffic immediately and waved us through and the people in the villages cheered us on. A wonderful sight. We eventually arrived in the dark, it was absolutely pitch black. We had no lights on the car, open exhausts, no

Englishman joining this emerging team made a couple of lines in the back of the weekly magazine *Autosport*.

There would be no shrinking from jingoistic duty in July 1953, however, when Mike Hawthorn scored his first Grand Prix victory, at Reims, in France; a remarkable performance by such a comparatively inexperienced driver when pitched agains Fangio, one of the greatest exponents of the game.

The wave of euphoria lost its momentum the following year. Ferrari – and everyone else – were eclipsed by the return of Mercedes-Benz, while Hawthorn's season appeared to lurch from personal crisis to personal crisis.

He was badly burned and spent several weeks in hospital following a crash at Syracuse. Back at home, the national newspapers accused Hawthorn of deliberately avoiding the call-up for National Service by remaining abroad.

In fact, he was doing nothing of the sort. He had always declared himself available but, in any case, he had been granted indefinite deferment because of his kidney trouble. He was nevertheless surprised, and not a little hurt, by the vicious press campaign.

In the midst of it all came news that his father had been killed in a road accident, leaving his mother with the task of running the family garage in Farnham. Then, with utterly tactless timing on the morning of the funeral, a policeman arrived on the doorstep to serve summonses in connection with a minor incident in which Hawthorn had touched a parked Post Office van.

Having helped his mother sort out the family's affairs, Hawthorn went to Spa for the Belgian Grand Prix, where fumes from a loose exhaust pipe brought him to the point of collapse. A win in Spain was a small consolation at the end of a desperate season.

It was not much better in 1955. Rather than turn on his heel and raise two fingers to the British and their habit of denigrating their heroes, Hawthorn chose to leave Ferrari and join Vanwall as the British team began to show promise. But that was as far as it went. The green cars were slow and

mudguards, no lights, no insurance, no anything ...'

He retired from the race. But it didn't appear to matter after such an eventful journey.

Everything seemed so relaxed then. When Hawthorn went to Monza for the Italian Grand Prix, Tony Vandervell, the engine-bearing magnate who would later run the Vanwall Grand Prix team, casually mentioned that he had been chatting with Enzo Ferrari and suggested that, if Mr Ferrari could see his way clear, it might be nice for young Hawthorn to have a test drive.

This was arranged, with similar informality, and Hawthorn duly noted that it 'certainly was a lovely motor car'. He agreed to drive for Ferrari in the non-championship Modena Grand Prix. Just like that!

Unfortunately, this seemingly laid-back approach was to catch Hawthorn out. When he arrived to start practice, Mike found that his car was not quite ready. So, rather than do nothing, he asked if he could complete a few laps in his Cooper. No one seemed to mind.

Hawthorn forgot, however, that the brakes on the Cooper were no match for those on the Ferrari and he tried braking as late with the green car as he had done with the red one. The ensuing shunt was a major affair.

Hawthorn spent some time in hospital, his racing finished for the season. And yet Ferrari were still keen to sign him for 1953. After careful deliberation – 'I was hoping there might be another British car which would give the Ferraris some competition' – Hawthorn joined the team, just two years after making his competitions' debut on Brighton prom. The news of an

11

Hawthorn, dressed and ready for action in his bow tie and green windcheater, listens intently at a drivers' briefing before the start of the 1956 British Grand Prix. Left to right: Salvadori, Scott Brown (head bowed), Da Silva Ramos, Hawthorn, Schell and Manzon.

unusually unreliable and, just to rub it in, Stirling Moss was doing great things for Mercedes-Benz.

Hawthorn did, however, win at Le Mans. Yet even this victory was clouded in the worst possible manner. During the early stages of the race, Hawthorn, driving a Jaguar D-Type, was waging a furious battle with Fangio's Mercedes-Benz. As Hawthorn was making his way towards the pits for a scheduled stop, the Mercedes-Benz of Pierre Levegh struck the back of an Austin-Healey driven by Lance Macklin just after Macklin had pulled out to pass Hawthorn's slowing car. The Mercedes-Benz became airborne and flew into a spectator area, killing more than 80 people.

Mercedes-Benz withdrew but the race continued, to avoid panic and to leave the roads clear for emergency vehicles. Hawthorn was persuaded to carry on by Raymond 'Lofty' England, the Jaguar team manager.

England had become something of a father figure to Hawthorn and Mike had need of him, particularly when the newspapers judged him to blame for the accident. He was to be exonerated completely by an official inquiry, and photographs show clearly that Hawthorn's actions were perfectly correct.

'At the time,' recalls England, 'I had to get him back into the car. He had overshot our pit and the rules said he had to do another lap – come round again – before we could work on the car in our pit. He did what he was told and there was no problem with Mike. He was quite a sensitive chap in some ways, but perfect to work with.

'The thing about that drive, prior to the accident, was Mike was showing once again that he was the equal of Fangio. He did it three times during his career: in the 1953 French Grand Prix, at Le Mans in 1955, and later that year at Dundrod.'

The latter, in fact, was a fine example of Hawthorn's resilience in the aftermath of Le Mans. In some respects the Jaguar was not as quick as the Mercedes-Benz, yet Hawthorn used the D-Type to hustle Fangio during a classic drive on a classic circuit. He retired eventually but the thrill of the

chase brought some relief during a gruesome year. Unfortunately, that particular race, the last to be held for cars at Dundrod, brought further grim news as three drivers died as a result of injuries received in various accidents.

'Three of my closest friends and several acquaintances,' wrote Hawthorn, 'have been snatched away in accidents and I have been caught up in the greatest disaster in the history of motor racing. I only hope that 1956 will have something better in store.'

Hawthorn did not help himself by joining BRM. He turned down an offer from Ferrari because he wanted to drive Jaguar sports cars – a sign of the importance of this class of racing at the time. In 1957 Ferrari agreed to his terms and Mike returned to Maranello, only to find that the red cars were uncompetitive when compared with the Maseratis – and the Vanwall, driven by that man Moss.

Hawthorn, however, had struck up a wonderful rapport with Peter Collins, yet another happy-go-lucky character from the same mould as Hawthorn. They drove alongside each other at Ferrari in 1957, and again in 1958 after Mike decided not to retire.

Even though Hawthorn won only the race at Reims, consistent finishes meant he was in the running for the championship. It developed into a straight fight with Moss, with everything depending on the result of the final race at Casablanca. Moss won and set the fastest lap (for which one point was awarded at the time) but, by finishing second, Mike Hawthorn became the first Englishman to win the world championship. Then he decided to retire.

It was the right decision. Motor racing on an international scale was losing some of its appeal for a man for whom enjoying life was a top priority. A few months before, at the Nürburgring, he had seen Collins crash to his death, the Englishman becoming yet another statistic in a year which had accounted for another Ferrari team-mate, Luigi Musso. Then, at Casablanca, a popu-

lar young Welshman, Stewart Lewis-Evans, had suffered severe burns. Hawthorn flew back to England with him and was deeply distressed when Lewis-Evans succumbed to his injuries a few days later.

In many ways, such a comparatively brief sojourn at the forefront of the sport fitted Hawthorn's dashing image. He usually wore a bow tie, even when racing, and would go to great lengths to join 'the lads' for a pipe and a pint at the pub after a race. He was the archetypal English sporting hero, with his flaxen hair and jutting good looks; he would not have been out of place 15 years earlier in the bar at Biggin Hill, a breathless Spitfire parked outside. He had, at the age of 29, much to live for and it was anticipated that he would play an important part within the sport and the motor industry.

That was just what he was doing that day in January in 1959. Hawthorn was due to judge a competition in aid of the Invalid Tricycle Association at the Cumberland

Hotel in London. He planned to have lunch with his fellow judges Billy Butlin, Viscount Lewisham and Frank Farr, editor of *Power and Pedal*.

He was not late, but he was pressing on as he crossed the Hog's Back and began the descent towards Guildford and the Dennis factory. He overtook a Mercedes-Benz 300 SL driven by Rob Walker, a former racing driver and friend of Hawthorn. As he went by, Mike nonchalantly waved two fingers, the Jaguar sending up plumes of spray.

Not long after, Walker watched, and thought nothing of it, as the Jaguar went into a slide; Mike could deal with that easily. But the green car continued to slide and Walker, to his disbelief, realised it was out of control. The Jaguar shot across the road, careered onto a verge and smashed sideways into a tree, totally uprooting it and almost bending the Jaguar double in the process.

A report later stated that the skid marks measured 133 yards long and the road at the

point of the accident was 60 feet wide with traffic bollards in the middle. At the inquest, the accident was attributed to high speed on a wet road.

Walker stopped and ran back to the scene. At first he could not find Hawthorn. Then he discovered that Mike had been flung into the back of the car, where he lay face down with severe head injuries. A doctor on the scene said death must have been instantaneous.

'It was an absolute tragedy,' says 'Lofty' England. 'He absolutely loved life. And he was one of the best drivers around; I have no doubt about that. He was capable of giving superb performances and he had the ability to overcome any deficiencies in the car. His only problem was that he was not terribly fit because of this kidney problem. I'm sure he could have coped very well with racing as we know it today, even though it is a money-making business. He would have been a sponsor's dream. But he was never

interested in money and yet he would do anything you asked. I would ring up and ask him to come up to Coventry for an apprentices' dinner and he wouldn't hesitate. He wouldn't expect to be paid and he would be tremendous company. He was a wonderful chap.'

When they removed his car from the roadside at Guildford, the front end had almost been wrenched away from the rear. It was unrecognisable. The front number plate had been torn off, but the badge bar was intact and on it was the insignia of the British Racing Drivers' Club; nothing else.

The badge summed him up. Mike Hawthorn was British through and through, he was a racing driver in the true sense of the expression and he was just the sort of chap you would expect to see at the day's end, living it up in the club, win or lose. It was an appropriate epitaph to a short but remarkable story.

The French Grand Prix

The French have always had their say. Whichever pages of motor racing history you may choose to turn, there is always a distinct whiff of garlic mingled with Gallic chauvinism. The down-turned lower lip and imperious closing of the eyes; the shrug that says 'I understand your argument but I have not the slightest intention of doing anything about it': these badges of office have been worn by Grand Prix racing's custodians with an easy manner which suggests they invented the sport.

The trouble is, they did. Such was the influence exerted by the French at the turn of the 20th century that their principal race was simply known as 'The Grand Prix'. Further descriptive comment was considered superfluous, and it remained that way until the First World War.

Even when the French Grand Prix became part of championship series in 1950, it was still considered to be one of the premier events on the calendar. Certainly, it was to settle for a period in a grand location on public roads near Reims and it was here in 1953 that motor racing produced a battle of epic proportions.

There was little doubt that victory would go to either Ferrari or Maserati but, with these two Italian teams fielding four cars apiece, the precise result was difficult to predict. Mike Hawthorn, having joined Ferrari that year, was very much the junior when ranked alongside his team-mates, Ascari, Farina and Villoresi. The Englishman was scarcely the favourite, particularly when Maserati had Juan Manuel Fangio among their number. But, as this race unfolded, it emerged that Hawthorn was the only one capable of taking the battle to Fangio. Winning against such a seasoned master would be something else again, however.

Hawthorn had one thing in his favour: Fangio had lost the use of first gear. Normally, such a failure would not amount to much of a handicap but, at Reims, the very slow hairpin at Thillois called for first gear to power the cars onto the finishing straight. Even then, it seemed the slightly more powerful Maserati would have the edge.

The race lasted for close on three hours. It was a battle of the most incredible intensity as the two red cars raced wheel-to-wheel for much of the way. Hawthorn could study the master at close quarters. By the time the final laps beckoned, Hawthorn understood the Maserati's strengths and weaknesses – including the fact that Fangio was in gearbox trouble.

At the start of the final lap, Hawthorn led across the line, but Fangio moved ahead on the long run to Thillois. Hawthorn knew it was now or never. Taking his courage in both hands, Hawthorn braked later than ever, scrambled down the inside of the Maserati, took a tight line, pointed the car towards the finish and floored the throttle. Fangio was beaten – and gracefully conceded to this youngster 18 years his junior who possessed such outrageous talent and audacity.

The 1953 French Grand Prix immediately went down as one of the greatest races of all time. Or, at least, that was the way the locals saw it. Small wonder that many Frenchmen continue to see their Grand Prix as a cut above the rest. This is merely maintaining a national trait which infuriated the rest of the motoring world as long ago as 1906.

When the first French Grand Prix was held that year, French manufacturers dominated the entry list. This was proof of the home nation's pre-eminence, although some of the jingoistic outpouring in the local press took some believing. A passage in *Petit Parisien* was a case in point. It said:

'If we win the Grand Prix, we shall let the whole world know that French motorcars are the best. If we lose it will merely be by accident, and our rivals should then be grateful to us for having been sufficiently sportsmanlike to allow them an appeal against the bad reputation of their cars.'

This nicely balanced little commentary had been singled out by *The Motor*, and the very fact that the British publication had taken the trouble to do so gives some indication of the depth of bad feeling which was abroad at the time. Suspicion was rife that France's motives were less than sporting.

France had rightly considered itself to be the cradle of motoring competition. The first-ever time trial had been run between Paris and Rouen in 1894, Count de Dion's winning steam car covering the 79 miles at 11.6 mph. After that there were a number of point-to-point events, most of them starting from Paris, but the Paris–Madrid race in may 1903 proved to be the nadir, a succession of fatal accidents bringing the event – and the idea of further city-to-city races – to a premature end at Bordeaux.

Attention switched to the Gordon Bennett Cup races on adequately policed 'circuits' made up of public roads. These races had been established to encourage the participation of the burgeoning motor industry, and one of the rules, permitting only one team to represent each country, was designed to allow the various national industries to compete on equal terms.

The French, with the largest number of manufacturers, did not like this. It cramped their perceived superior style, not to mention the chances of an otherwise sure-fire domination of the results.

The French suggested a change to the rules and the format. Rather than limit the entry to one team per country, the nations in question could enter a number of cars depending on the size of their respective automobile industries. Thus France, to no-one's surprise, allowed themselves 15 cars, whereas Britain and Germany were restricted to six cars each; Austria, Belgium and the like to three cars apiece.

This high-handed legislation was not well-received outside France and the entire affair descended into chaos. France said they would not play any more and exercised their sanction by refusing to organise the event in 1906, as was their right as host nation since a French car had won the 1905 race. That was the end of the Gordon Bennett series. More down-turned lips and shrugging of shoulders in Paris.

Out of the disorder came proposals to run a Grand Prix, or Grand Prize, under the auspices of the Automobile Club de France

(ACF), the body which had been formed to take charge of all motoring events in the country. Thus, the first French Grand Prix came into being in 1906, although the ACF later caused some historical confusion by counting the earlier city-to-city events as Grands Prix, in a futile bid to establish the French Grand Prix as the oldest race in the world.

There is no doubt, however, that the French Grand Prix was the single most important race in the world and, as such, it attracted 34 entries in 1906.

The race was colossal in every respect. The circuit, very rough in parts, was mapped out across 60 miles of roads to the east of Le Mans and the distance was fixed at 12 laps, or 769.36 miles. It would take two days, the cars being removed to a *parc fermé* overnight after the first six laps. At the start of activities on the second day a 'well-rehearsed horse' would haul the cars from the *parc fermé* to the start line, where they would be fired up and work could commence on a given signal, the precise time being established by finishing positions the previous day.

As a plaque at the Hungaroring, near Budapest, now celebrates, the race was won by Ferenc Szisz, an Austro-Hungarian, although that did not prevent the French from calling him François Szisz since he was at the wheel of a Renault and had once been a mechanic to Louis Renault himself. The total time taken was 12 hours, 14 minutes and 7 seconds, Szisz averaging 62.88 mph. Felice Nazzaro finished 32 minutes behind at the wheel of a Fiat, with Clement taking third place in a Clement-Bayard, so French honour was at least partially satisfied.

Nazzaro won for Italy the following year, the race having been moved to a circuit near Dieppe that was both shorter, at a mere 47 miles, and more suitable (it was tar-sealed for its entire length). Like Le Mans, this was also roughly triangular in shape but, in response to criticism, racing was restricted to just one day, albeit a fairly long one, the winning Fiat taking 6 hours 46 minutes to cover the ten laps.

That race was considered to be such a success that precisely the same format was used in 1908. There was just one shortcoming as far as the French were concerned: they didn't win. In fact, they failed to make it into the top three, a Mercedes finishing first with cars from Benz taking the next two places.

The French laid half-hearted plans to run their Grand Prix again the following year but, in view of the potential threat of being embarrassed further, little was said. The race was quietly forgotten until 1912, when Georges Buillot triumphantly carried the day (or days, for the race was once again spread over two) in a Peugeot.

He repeated this performance the following year when the race was shifted to a simpler and shorter (19-mile) circuit south-east of Amiens. The ACF was keen to move away from the northern half of the country, however, so for the 1914 Grand Prix a 23-mile circuit near Lyon was chosen.

This also coincided with a change in the technical regulations which restricted the weight of the cars and the engine capacity. In effect, designs were moving away from the towering pieces of cathedral-like architecture to the sleeker lines of a more svelte racing car. Technically, there was sophistication thanks to the adoption of four-wheel braking. The standard of racing improved dramatically as a result.

After six hours, the leaders were split by 14 seconds, but a well-organised challenge by Mercedes during the closing stages saw the German marque score a one-two-three at the expense of a battle-worn Peugeot team. Despite the ultimate disappointment this had been a thrilling contest between exciting cars, but the advent of the First World War brought a temporary halt to the enormous technical strides being made by the manufacturers.

After hostilities ceased, it took a year or two for racing to get under way. When, in 1921, the French Grand Prix was run at Le Mans (a new variation incorporating two roads running into the outskirts of the city), an American by the name of Jimmy Murphy had the audacity to come over and win

it. His handling and performance of his Duesenberg left the competition standing and, when Murphy raised his arm in triumph, the victory was received in virtual silence by the crowd. Nazarro won at Strasbourg the following year, but 1923 will be remembered, in Britain if not in France, as the year in which Henry Segrave won in a Sunbeam. It would be another 32 years before Britain would achieve similar success in international motor racing.

The 1924 French Grand Prix, run at Lyon, was notable for the first appearance of the now celebrated Type 35 Bugatti and a victory for the comparatively new Bugatti marque.

In 1925, an artificial track was used for the first time, the race switching to the 7.76-mile venue at Linas-Montlhéry, 15 miles south of Paris. This consisted of a banked oval combined with a long road reaching down to a hairpin and then returning to the banking. It represented a major improvement in facilities, but Montlhéry got off to a terrible start by claiming the life of Antonio Ascari in that race in 1925.

Racing was heading towards a confused state as the technical regulations were changed frequently, often to no positive effect. One such change (a reduction to 1.5 litres) came just as the French Grand Prix was shifting to a totally symmetrical – and completely featureless – autodrome at Miramas. The entry of just three cars were all Bugattis.

It was becoming evident even to the French that this was no longer 'The Grand Prix' but a part of a European series. Generally, though, the standard of racing was in decline and a 16-mile circuit, using well-surfaced roads at Comminges, deserved much better than the sports car race which claimed to be the Grand Prix in 1928.

A return to Le Mans the following year saw the introduction of a link road which cut off the hairpin in the town itself. William Grover or, 'Williams' as the Englishman was known, led from start to finish. Another change of venue in 1930 took competitors to Pau, although not onto the streets used for annual classic today; the

1930 race used a triangle of roads to the east of the town. In 1931, it was back to Linas-Montlhéry where Louis Chiron and Achille Varzi shared the winning Bugatti in a race lasting ten hours, an unusual feat in many respects since it was rather like Alain Prost and Ayrton Senna agreeing to share the same car in 1989.

In the midst of a generally depressing standard of racing, however, came the introduction, in 1932, of a circuit which would have a far-reaching effect on the history of the French Grand Prix. The signal was given to the Automobile Club de Champagne to hold a race on the roads near Reims.

Once again, it was a familiar triangular format: very fast and not particularly demanding. But the attraction of Reims was the location; fields of golden corn bountiful vineyards, excellent Champagne and equally commendable cuisine. And, almost inevitably, the French Grand Prix would be run in brilliant weather. The press, as you might imagine, loved the place.

With the distribution of the final results in the press room came a bottle of the best bubbly for each media representative. The parties that followed are legend. So too are the stories concerning the escapades of the drivers, the plush Lion d'Or being the hotel in which Harry Schell, on the morning after a Grand Prix, found his Vespa coupe parked on the landing outside his room. The manager, so the story goes, was not best pleased. Neither, in later years, was the driver of a Mini-van, owned by the Cooper team, when he arrived to find his vehicle had been manhandled into a space between two trees. It was a perfect fit and he could move neither forward nor backwards.

Champagne would flow freely throughout the weekend and it was not unknown for the odd hack to become tired and emotional as the sun belted down on the press tribune on race day. As likely as not, though, the activity on the track kept everyone on their toes, the flat-out blind around this circuit providing a thrilling theatre for feats of derring-do.

The French Grand Prix (as opposed to

the Grand Prix de Marne which had previously been run at Reims) was won by Tazio Nuvolari's Alfa Romeo in 1932. There followed a spell at Montlhéry but the return to Reims in 1938 and 1939 coincided with the days of German supremacy, the silver cars from Mercedes-Benz and Auto Union providing an awesome sight as they swept across the golden horizon at an average in excess of 100 mph.

Lyon hosted the Grand Prix in 1947 as the racing teams attempted to pick up the pieces after the Second World War. Apart from a visit to Comminges in 1949 and the introduction of occasional races at Rouen, Reims would be the popular choice during the next two decades.

Major alterations by the AC de Champagne in 1953 included the introduction of an improved pit area and a new link which by-passed the hairpin in the village of Gueux. And, to mark the occasion, Fangio and Hawthorn laid on one of the greatest duels ever seen at this, or any other circuit.

Mercedes-Benz chose to make their return to Grand Prix racing at Reims the following year, the streamlined cars sweeping the competition aside as though they had never been away. Hawthorn won again in 1958, but the day was significant for other reasons.

His team-mate, Luigi Musso, had been killed while attempting to keep pace with the Englishman through the long right-hander after the pits and Musso's death had a profound effect on Fangio, who finished fourth. Returning to the circuit on the Monday morning to sit quietly among the debris of a weekend's racing, the five-times world champion thought about his future. He had decided during the previous day's race that it would be his last and the subsequent news of Musso's death, yet another in a sad season, merely strengthened Fangio's resolve to finish competing in a sport he had served with such dignity.

The Grand Prix weekend at Reims was always a memorable occasion, not just because of the ample supply of liquid refreshment but because the organisers provided a feast of motor racing to go with it.

19

Apart from practice for the Grand Prix, Saturday would be set aside for a Formula 2 race, followed by a 12-hour sports car event starting at midnight.

It was not unknown for drivers to take part in the sports car race and then prepare themselves for the rigours of a three-hour Grand Prix. Speed, however, was becoming a problem as the question of safety became more pressing in the 1960s.

When Jack Brabham won 10,000 francs for his victory in 1966 (the first man to win a Grand Prix at the wheel of a car bearing his own name), that would be the last occasion the French Grand Prix would visit Reims. The safety work necessary to bring the circuit into line with contemporary thinking was excessive, even for the wealthy AC de Champagne. In some ways it was good that Reims was not butchered by chicanes and the like since this would have removed the circuit's heart and soul. Reims had had its days of slipstreaming glory and stunning hangovers.

Besides, there was always Rouen-les-Essarts, a road circuit but of a totally different character. First used in 1952, the original 3.17 miles ran through a wooded valley to the south-west of the cathedral city. In 1955, it was extended to 4.06 miles, but the key to this track remained the thrilling downhill sweeps to the cobbled hairpin bend at Nouveau Monde. Along most of its length, the circuit boasted high grass banks which provided perfect vantage points. Rouen-les-Essarts was enjoyed by drivers as well as spectators but, like everywhere else, it had its darker moments.

Rouen-les-Essarts was used for the French Grand Prix on just five occasions. Alberto Ascari, as was his wont in 1952, totally dominated the first Grand Prix there for Ferrari; Fangio laid on a consummate display of car control with the winning Maserati 250F in 1957; Dan Gurney won in 1962 and 1964; and, in the wet in 1968, 22-year-old Jacky Ickx simply drove away from the opposition in his Ferrari. That race, though, will be remembered just as readily for the death of Jo Schlesser, the Frenchman crashing heavily in the air-

cooled Honda, a new car which many believed was not yet ready to race. The stigma, however, was attached to Rouen thereafter and the Formula 1 teams never went back.

The year before, the Grand Prix had moved to the Bugatti circuit at Le Mans, a half-hearted combination of the pits straight and Dunlop Curve on the track used for the 24-hour race, followed by a zig-zag return leg through the car-park at the back of the paddock. A handful of spectators turned out to see Jack Brabham win and, thankfully, the idea of holding the Grand Prix there was never mentioned again. In any case, a vastly superior alternative had been found in the mountains of the Auvergne.

The 5-mile road circuit above Clermont-Ferrand, climbing magnificently around the Puy de Charade and the Puy de Gravenoire, had everything . . . except decent facilities. The pits were crammed onto the side of a hill, but the drivers loved the dipping, twisting nature of the circuit itself. The only complaint concerned the sharp stones lining the track, one of which did for Chris Amon when the subsequent puncture robbed the Matra driver of a certain and well-deserved win in 1972. Given that this was a driver's circuit of the highest order, it is fitting that the list of winners at Clermont-Ferrand consists solely of Jim Clark, Jochen Rindt and Jackie Stewart.

The problem was, however, that the establishment of the Charade circuit coincided with the new awareness of safety. It was clear right from the start that the natural hazards could never be adequately covered; that the track was shrinking as car performances increased. The 1972 race was destined to be the last, news which was

The extension loop had yet to be added at this point on the rear of Dijon-Prenois when the French Grand Prix came to Burgundy for the first time in 1974.

made even more depressing by the bland nature of the substitute which had been found near Toulon.

By building the Circuit Paul Ricard on a flat, dusty plateau – the only flat dusty plateau in an otherwise rugged and richly endowed region – M Paul Ricard proved to the world that his greater talent is in inventing alcoholic beverages. The most attractive aspect of his race track was its location, high above the coast near Bandol. That appealed to many but, for the first year at least, most of the locals preferred to stay on the beach instead of choosing to watch Jackie Stewart win a fairly straightforward race for Tyrrell in 1971.

The track, at least, was considered to be safe. That won it the necessary approval even though the layout, with the Mistral Straight measuring more than a mile, presented the drivers with little in the way of a challenge. That changed as the speeds continued to rise and the 'S de la Verrière' a left–right sweep beyond the pits, became a place for the very brave. Ironically, that corner would heap trouble upon the circuit in 1986 when Elio de Angelis lost his life during testing.

Immediately the circuit length was slashed as the cars turned right before Verrière and joined the Mistral Straight halfway along its length. Now, apart from the almost flat-out-in-top-gear Signes corner at the end of the straight, there was nothing to get excited about. And that was usually reflected in the races.

The facilities, though, have always been excellent, a suite of air-conditioned offices above the pits providing solace from the heat for officials and press. With commendable foresight M Ricard also provided a first-class runway close by. The Circuit Paul Ricard was the epitome of the Eighties term 'racing facility'.

Of a more basic nature, but more appealing as a result, was the track at Dijon-Prenois, scene of the Grands Prix in 1974, 1977, 1979, 1981 and 1984. This place had a lot going for it, not least the gastronomic pleasures offered by the region and the bountiful supply of great wines from the Burgundy vineyards.

The circuit itself, rising and falling through the woods behind the the paddock, offered a serious challenge even though, in its original guise, Dijon was considered to be too short. An extension in time for the 1977 race fixed that and the Grand Prix itself proved to be a thriller as John Watson's Brabham-Alfa Romeo refused to pick up the last drop of fuel, thus handing victory to Mario Andretti in the closing lap. Poor Watson was utterly dejected, having driven brilliantly throughout the afternoon.

Two years later and the French pride knew no bounds as Jean-Pierre Jabouille gave the Renault turbo its long-awaited maiden victory. But this almost went unnoticed thanks to an unbelievable dispute over second place as René Arnoux and Gilles Villeneuve raced side-by-side, sometimes on the track, sometimes off it, both thoroughly enjoying the clean intensity of their battle. In the end, Villeneuve's Ferrari beat Arnoux's Renault by a whisker. And neither of them cared!

Alain Prost scored his first Grand Prix win here in 1981 but, as the years went by, the circuit began to lose some of its charm. Money needed to be spent on improvements, but, more than that, zealous officials performed their duties with an officiousness which was out of keeping with the region. Indeed, the harassed and angered crews of the teams' motor homes expressed their displeasure on departure one year by emptying the holding tanks of their vehicles by the management's doors. Perhaps it was as well for all concerned that the Grand Prix never returned, although the feeling was that a challenging and attractive venue was being wasted.

As for Paul Ricard, its future seemed secure but, in motor racing, the only certainty is that nothing is certain. As the 1990 French Grand Prix reached its well-organised conclusion, moves were afoot to take the race to Magny-Cours, near Nevers, the following year. The Magny-Cours circuit and, more to the point, its surroundings, were thought to be unsuitable; there was a hint of scandal in the air.

Those associated with Paul Ricard were quick to point out that France's Finance Minister was the mayor of Nevers and, by chance, French President François Mitterrand was once president of the region in which Magny-Cours is situated. Whatever the reason, it was argued that since the French Grand Prix had already visited 16 different circuits, one more was not likely to make much difference.

Even so, there was concern that Magny-Cours would have serious shortcomings, political expediency outweighing the practicalities associated with hosting one of the world's most important and prestigious motor races. Each time the subject was raised with those responsible, however, the response was always the same: downturned lip, closed eyes, and that familiar Gallic shrug of indifference. It was always thus in matters of the French Grand Prix.

His last victory. Collins simply left the
opposition standing when he led every lap of
the 1958 British Grand Prix at Silverstone.

In his later years Enzo Ferrari's press conferences were fairly rare but the questions would have a familiar ring to them. One of the favourites concerned the many drivers who had passed through his hands: which, if any, did he hold in high regard? And, just as inevitably, the answer would be the same.

Ferrari would mention Tazio Nuvolari. And then at some stage, he would talk about Peter Collins. 'A great driver,' he would say, 'and a generous gentleman.'

Certainly, Collins could not begin to be measured against such a heroic figure as Nuvolari. The initial reaction was to suppose that Ferrari had mentioned the Englishman purely for the benefit of any members of the British press who happened to be present. But the tribute was genuine enough. Peter Collins did hold a special place in Enzo Ferrari's affections for two main reasons.

Enzo's beloved son, Dino, had died on the day before the 1956 French Grand Prix and, of the five Ferrari drivers present – each wearing a black arm band as a mark of respect – it was Collins who won the race.

Collins only ever won three Grands Prix and he never became world champion for Ferrari, nor for anyone else. And there was the rub; the second reason for Ferrari's considerable sentiment. It was the method of his failure to win the title in 1956 which endeared Peter Collins to the 'Old Man'.

At Monza that year, Collins had compromised his slim chances by agreeing to hand over his car to Fangio during the race so that the Argentine might claim his fourth title. Enzo Ferrari had never forgotten such a generous act. It is a story of sportsmanship which has since been polished and improved with the passing of time.

In fact, as in all things connected with Grand Prix racing, there is more to this than meets the eye. It is perfectly true that Collins did not hesitate or complain when asked to abandon his car, but the truth is that he was rather relieved since he did not yet feel ready to take on the pressures which came with the office of world champion. That, as far as he was concerned, was not

strictly what motor racing was all about. The considerate action at Monza in September 1956 summed up Peter John Collins in more ways than one.

His career is not particularly well documented, which says much about its comparative brevity and Peter's reluctance to dwell at length on his chosen profession. And yet motor sport played a part in his life from the age of 17, when he joined the growing army of racers in their simple but effective rear-engined 500s.

In 1949, he won the 500 cc One Hundred Miles race at Silverstone and a 500 cc race at Goodwood, two results which prompted one contemporary journal to note: 'This promising young racing driver, who is the son of Mr P A Collins, MBE and Mrs Collins of Shatterford near Kidderminster, has already made his mark on the racing world.'

Two years later, while driving a works JBS, Collins won at circuits as diverse as Gamston, Silverstone and Dundrod. But he was still in the 'half-litre' class of racing car, a category which had its drawbacks if Collins wished to progress. While enjoying the closeness of the racing, Peter found his driving development cramped by the short races, the sub-standard size of the cars and, paradoxically, their responsive handling and good road-holding. The answer came when John Heath's HWM team offered Collins a season of Formula 2 in 1951.

At the time, these 2-litre cars were racing in Europe, frequently playing the supporting role at major international meetings but, more often than not, providing the main event on the streets of some town in France, Belgium or Italy. In the Grand Prix de Sables d'Olonne, for example, Collins finished second behind the Ferrari of Luigi Villoresi, a result which did as much for his reputation as this school of racing was doing for his driving.

Perhaps the most important development at this point in his career was the offer of a works drive with Aston Martin. This took him around the world, and for several years he would be a mainstay of the team. Winning the Tourist Trophy at Dundrod in 1953 and finishing second at Le

Mans (with Stirling Moss) in 1956 were high points in an association which showed great promise but was frequently bothered by mechanical problems.

It was at Goodwood, however, that Collins won numerous races. By and large, he did not like airfield circuits, their straightforward nature stifling a driver's style and fostering, as he called it, a 'trick cycling' technique. But the perimeter track at Goodwood at least had some character and Collins won the Goodwood Nine Hours in 1952, finished second the following year and third in 1955, each time sharing the wheel of an Aston Martin.

He also savoured victories there in powerful single-seaters, most notably the 4.5-litre Thin Wall Special, in effect a modified Ferrari and a forerunner of the Vanwall Grand Prix car. Collins was chosen to drive the Vanwall in its first world championship Grand Prix at Silverstone in 1954 and, the following year, he raced a Maserati 250F, entered by the Owen Organisation.

By now Collins had come to the attention of Ferrari, not least because of an impressive drive in the Targa Florio, a race for sports cars on the wild and rugged roads of Sicily. Sharing a Mercedes-Benz with Stirling Moss, Collins had been presented with an eight-minute deficit and a battered car after Moss had left the road. Collins not only made up for lost time but he handed back the 300SLR to Moss with a one-minute lead.

Earlier that year, Collins had won his first Formula 1 race, the International Trophy at Silverstone, the victory meriting a cover photograph in *Autosport* depicting Collins drifting the Owen Maserati 250F through Copse Corner. On 30 December 1955 the same magazine carried the following announcement, tucked beneath a longer item advising readers of the riveting news that the Crystal Palace circuit was to be extended from 1.39 miles to 2.4 miles:

'It is now confirmed that Peter Collins, 24-year-old British driver from Kidderminster, has signed with the Scuderia Ferrari for the 1956 season. He will thus become a

Collins drove brilliantly with the battered
Mercedes-Benz 300 SLR during the 1955
Targa Florio. Moss, his forehead still covered
with tape as protection against flying
stones, enjoys the moment of victory
with his co-driver.

team-mate of Juan Fangio, Eugenio Castellotti, Olivier Gendebien and Luigi Musso in the "prancing horse" équipe in the next year's Grands Prix and will also drive sports Ferraris in between commitments with the Aston Martin team, thanks to David Brown, with whose team he has prior engagements in major sports car events.'

It was a low-key printed prelude to what would turn out to be quite a year for Peter Collins, although at first it seemed he was destined to be an also-ran in every sense.

The season started badly when he collided with a tardy back-marker in Argentina. At Silverstone, during the International Trophy, Collins was called in to hand over his car to Fangio and, when exactly the same thing happened again a week later at Monaco, Collins appeared to be playing second fiddle even more than Moss had done while driving alongside Fangio at Mercedes-Benz the previous year.

Collins had been lying second at Monaco, 32 seconds behind Stirling Moss's Maserati, when team orders were applied, yet he accepted it without question. Collins referred to himself as the 'junior employee' and this, he said, was merely part of the process of racing with a driver for whom he had nothing but the greatest respect.

Collins spoke French fluently and he used this to help communicate with Fangio and establish what would become a warm relationship, one which had, as its basis, a simple ground rule. In an interview at the time, Collins described the straightforward terms of racing with Fangio. 'If you find yourself ahead of him,' explained Collins, 'you don't have to decide whether you'll let him pass. He'll pass you whether you like it or not.'

That unspoken rule became irrelevant during the Belgian Grand Prix when Fangio retired – as did the leading Maserati driven by Moss – and Peter Collins won his first Grand Prix. It was a splendid place to score his maiden victory, one for which the element of luck was outweighed by the fact that Spa-Francorchamps had been made treacherous by prolonged rain.

When they moved on to Reims for the French Grand Prix, Collins found that his success made little difference to the pecking order within Ferrari. Fangio was still the top dog and, even though Collins had claimed pole position, Fangio duly moved into the lead.

The Lancia-based Ferraris were not the best-handling cars but they had sufficient power to deal with a fast circuit such as Reims, and it was predicted that they would have the race to themselves.

Fangio stayed in front until a split fuel pipe brought a lengthy pit stop. Collins then passed Castellotti and they were ordered to hold station, Collins going on to win again. With the British Grand Prix next on the calendar, there was serious pre-race publicity talk of the Englishman winning the championship.

That appeared to take a dive when his car retired with no oil pressure but – and this was a sign of the changing times – Alfonse de Portago was called in to give his car to Collins. He duly finished second to Fangio, thus keeping his championship hopes alive.

Fangio, however, was into his stride now and he led all the way at the Nürburgring, Collins eventually spinning off in de Portago's car, his own having run into mechanical problems. That meant the final race at Monza would settle the championship, the positions being:

Fangio	**30**
Behra	**22**
Collins	**22**
Moss	**18**

A win for Collins could possibly give him the title since Fangio could only increase his score by winning outright; a driver had to rely on his five best results from the seven races. When Fangio's steering broke, his chances appeared slim, particularly when Musso declined to give up his car, forsake the lead in front of his home crowd and lose the important Italian National Championship.

It was at this point that Collins came into the pits and jumped from the car. Fangio climbed on board and swept off in pursuit of Moss (Musso having retired). Fangio finished second, which was enough to give him the championship.

The British press could not believe their luck. Here was the perfect underdog story – and a willing participant at that. It was assumed throughout the eulogies that Col-

lins could have won the championship. Certainly, that would have been the case had he not been stood down at both Monaco and Monza, but it is debatable whether his actions on the final day alone had scuppered his chances. He needed to win at Monza and his pit stop had not been purely for the purpose of handing over to Fangio. Col-

lins's car was in need of a fresh rear tyre and it seems unlikely that he would have caught Moss.

In any case, he still saw himself as the 'junior employee' at Ferrari even though his performances in 1956 had warranted a more serious title. There is no question that Peter Collins could drive as quickly as the best of

them but, when racing was done, he liked to retreat with his wife, Louise, to their boat *Genie Maris* a 70-foot ketch moored at Dartmouth. There, Collins enjoyed nothing better than deluding unwanted guests by pretending he was merely a deckhand. Indeed, he looked the part at times since his background as an automobile engineer (he spent three years, on and off, as a Ford trainee at Dagenham) allowed him to strip and rebuild the engine and electrical gear on the ketch.

Peter was spending less and less time working with the family transport business in Worcestershire, confining himself to board meetings and such like. But that did not prevent him from driving commercial vehicles when the opportunity arose. Denis Jenkinson tells the story of a drive to the British Grand Prix at Aintree. Pulling up at traffic lights in his Porsche, Jenkinson was startled by a torrent of lorry driver's abuse being hurled his way from the lofty cab of a lorry alongside. Looking up, Jenkinson was relieved to find it was Collins having fun while delivering the vehicle, *en route* to Aintree. And that was one of Peter's shorter journeys. In 1955 he drove an AEC special-bodied van loaded with Aston Martins bound for the Geneva Motor Show.

Collins enjoyed the lighter side of life although, at times, his *joie de vivre* sometimes seemed forced when he found himself in Mike Hawthorn's ebullient shadow. At Goodwood one year, Collins turned up with a child's bucket and spade because, as he pointed out, they were not far from the beach. When he insisted on bringing the implements into the pits, John Wyer and the Aston Martin management were hard-pressed to see the funny side.

But there was no question that life was anything but quiet when Collins and Hawthorn were together and their friendship and cameraderie found new limits when Mike joined Ferrari in 1957, the Englishman moving in to replace Fangio who had gone back to Maserati. In fact, Peter and Mike would need a keen sense of humour as Ferrari went through a dismal season, third places in France and Germany being the high-points in Collins's year.

Help was at hand in the shape of the Dino 246, a delightfully nimble car which, after some early-season development work, would bring Ferrari back to the forefront in 1958. And in between, Hawthorn and Collins were busy driving Ferrari sports cars, Peter sharing the winning Ferrari with Phil Hill in Argentina and at Sebring.

Collins used the Dino to win the International Trophy at Silverstone, his path to victory doubtless being helped by the sight of his mate, Hawthorn, standing by the finishing line waving a pint of beer each time Collins passed during the final laps.

When it came to the more serious business of Grands Prix, however, a win for Hawthorn at Reims, coupled with consistent placings elsewhere, had put Mike at the head of the points table. The British Grand Prix followed and Collins immediately vowed to help his team-mate win the championship, the plan being for Peter to force the early pace in the hope that the rival Vanwalls would blow up. And if his Ferrari also failed in the course of this offensive then, said Collins, so be it.

True to his word, Collins took charge of this race. And there was nothing desperate about his driving either. It was one of those days when he could do no wrong and it seemed right and proper that he should win the race with ease, particularly when engine trouble meant Hawthorn was not in a position to capitalise on Peter's willingness to let his pal into the lead. Mike, in fact, took second place and it was the perfect result, the two men absolutely delighted as they accepted their laurels.

After much celebrating, Peter and Louise headed for Kidderminster, where they were to find a Georgian-style house in which to settle come the day Peter stopped racing and returned to the family business. Having paid a deposit, they then set off for the Nürburgring and the German Grand Prix.

The drivers stayed in the Sporthotel opposite the pits, a handy location which allowed Hawthorn and Collins to relax by lounging around in their dressing gowns until it was time to prepare for work. On race morning, Hawthorn joined Peter and Louise for a late breakfast in their room, boiled eggs, toast and jam being washed down with copious amounts of tea.

Throughout the weekend, Collins had been struggling with a recently acquired wooden puzzle, made up of interlocking pieces, and he continued his attempts to put it together as the start time drew near. Finally, to his great delight and the relief of all and sundry, he managed it. Now he could go racing.

Even though Peter's win at Silverstone had strengthened his chances for the championship, he continued to insist on helping Mike. Come the race, though, both Ferrari drivers found their cars were not running sweetly – Hawthorn had a clutch problem while Collins had engine trouble – and they could do nothing about Moss in the Vanwall. Eventually, Moss retired but, almost immediately, Tony Brooks moved forward, first passing Hawthorn and then Collins.

Peter hung on to the Vanwall as best he could and, going through the dip at Pflanzgarten, the Ferrari ran wide, two wheels mounting a small grass bank. At first, it seemed it would be a harmless incident and, just as Hawthorn was formulating some choice words for his team-mate, the Ferrari suddenly flipped over the bank, flinging Collins from the cockpit. Hawthorn was distraught. What should he do? Stop or carry on? In the event, he pressed on and, as luck would have it, his car broke down on the far side of the circuit. Mike then spent the remainder of the race trying to find out about Peter, affectionately known as 'mon ami, mate'.

The news, as always on these occasions, was confused. Some said he was unhurt, others claimed he had broken an arm, one or two gloomy reports spoke of grave injuries. Eventually, Hawthorn discovered that Collins had been taken to Bonn. He had serious head injuries. By the time Mike reached the hospital, his dear friend was dead.

Peter Collins was buried during a private ceremony in Worcestershire. A few days later, on 10 August 1958, a memorial service was held at St Mary's Church, Stone, near Kidderminster. The small church was packed. The vicar spoke of Collins's courage and his dignity, his capacity to act with great modesty as a true sportsman in such a public arena. Enzo Ferrari must have approved whole-heartedly of those words.

The Belgian Grand Prix

There are many milestones in the career of Juan Manuel Fangio but one of the most memorable occurred on 5 June 1955. On that day, King Leopold III presented Fangio with the Royal Belgian Automobile Club Cup, to be held in perpetuity in recognition of his third victory in the Belgian Grand Prix.

Fangio considered it to be one of the most prestigious trophies he had ever won, not least because it meant he had truly conquered the Spa-Francorchamps circuit, a magnificent combination of public roads sweeping through the Haut Fagnes region in the foothills of the Ardennes.

Such recognition also meant his name joined those of previous winners engraved on the trophy, names such as Nuvolari, Caracciola, Farina, Wimille and Ascari; distinguished company, to be sure, but none of them had won three times at Spa-

In the beginning. Antonio Ascari heads for the bridge at L'Eau Rouge during the first Belgian Grand Prix in June 1925. Ascari's Alfa Romeo led throughout the 6 hours and 43 minutes of racing on rough roads at Spa-Francorchamps. Note the circuit leads towards a hairpin located beyond the bottom right-hand corner of the picture.

Francorchamps. That's what made the 1955 Belgian Grand Prix even more memorable in Fangio's estimation. And, had the differential on his Ferrari not seized the following year, Fangio would have made it four.

Instead, however, the name 'Collins' was added to the impressive list on the trophy. It was the first Grand Prix win for the Englishman and he could not have chosen a more impressive place to do it.

Peter Collins had begun to come of age in 1956. Having served his apprenticeship, a contract with Ferrari that season marked his elevation to the major league and, at once, Collins proved himself capable of running with the best. At all times, though, he was second in line to Fangio, as had been proved at Monaco when Collins had been ordered to hand over his car once Fangio's had broken.

Collins fully accepted the situation and he travelled to Spa-Francorchamps in the full knowledge that the same thing might happen again. In the meantime, though, he would continue to enjoy life out of the cockpit and then simply give of his best once in the car. In any case, he was scarcely the favourite to win, a situation which suited him admirably since he did not relish such pressure.

Most of the predictions for the 1956 Bel- gian Grand Prix favoured either Fangio or Stirling Moss, now in a works Maserati. Sure enough, Fangio put his Ferrari on pole, five seconds faster than Moss. Collins was on the outside of the three-car front row. Ahead lay 36 laps, a total of 315 miles. Fangio had averaged 126 mph during his pole-position lap; this was not a Grand Prix for the faint-hearted. And, for good measure on race day, it was raining, an all-too familiar feature at Spa-Francorchamps but one which might give Moss the edge over Fangio.

Moss shot into the lead with Fangio in pursuit but, after five laps, the Ferrari was in front and gradually edging away. The

rain had stopped and, as the lap times reduced, Collins moved into third place ahead of his team-mate, Castellotti. Collins then began to take two seconds a lap from Moss, the Ferrari driver establishing a new lap record as he did so. All the while, though, Fangio was pulling away and he sliced 1.3 seconds off Collins's record lap. Now it was a question of whether or not Moss could maintain his second place, never mind challenging for the lead.

That discussion became academic after the tenth lap. Cresting the rise at the exit of L'Eau Rouge, Moss and the Maserati went out of control as the left-rear hub fractured and sent the wheel bouncing into the valley

on the right. Moss was fortunate not to end his race in a similar fashion, the 250F grinding to a halt on the grass verge, a few feet from the edge.

Not that it bothered Moss. Quick as a flash, he was out of the car and running back to the pits. At the same time, a Maserati mechanic was dispatched in the opposite direction to signal Cesare Perdisa to stop and hand his car over to Moss. The Italian did as he was told and the car was barely at a standstill before Moss was on board, anxious to better his new-found sixth place. It was a lot to ask since there was no doubt now that the race, barring mechanical misfortune, belonged to Fangio.

The reigning world champion seemed unstoppable but, on lap 24, he smelled burning and became aware of sparks flying from beneath his car. Fangio began to brake and, just as he was about to come to a standstill, the rear wheels locked, leaving two lines of rubber on the road. The differential had seized. And, with this having happened at Stavelot on the far side of the circuit, there was no opportunity for Fangio to claim another car by returning to the pits and exercising his option as the senior driver.

Collins, now in the lead, was as safe as he would ever be and he continued to produce a virtually flawless performance. He had been passed by Moss as the Maserati driver unlapped himself on his way to third place and a championship point for fastest lap. In between the two Englishmen was Paul Frère, the Belgian scoring what would be his best-ever result in a Grand Prix. And, like Collins, he could not have asked for a better stage on which to demonstrate his ability.

To finish in the top three at Spa-Francorchamps was an achievement worth remembering. But to win there was, as Fangio pointed out, something else again. As things would turn out, the 1956 Belgian Grand Prix would mark the Argentine driver's last appearance at the circuit.

The very first Belgian Grand Prix had been held 31 years before. A group of

enthusiasts had dreamed up the idea of holding a race along a series of roads that more or less linked the villages of Francorchamps, Malmédy and Stavelot. The town of Spa, some six miles distant, did not figure in the actual circuit but the organising club was based there and Spa was known by the well-to-do thanks to its natural spring water. Since Francorchamps was the village nearest to the pits, the name Spa-Francorchamps was adopted when a motor cycle Grand Prix was held in 1921, followed by a touring car event in 1924 and a Grand Prix a year later.

The circuit was roughly triangular in shape, with two hairpins and a tight corner at its extremities. The attraction, though, was the majestic location as these narrow, tree-lined roads draped themselves around a valley for a distance of just over nine miles.

The start presented an unusual feature since it was on a steep hill, with the pits on the right and a permanent wooden grandstand slightly askew on the left. At the bottom of the hill, the road swung to the left and crossed L'Eau Rouge by means of a narrow bridge before rising along a short straight towards a hairpin. This would be bypassed in time for the 1939 Grand Prix, resulting in a steep climb to the right immediately after drivers crossed L'Eau Rouge.

After levelling briefly, the track continued to climb, sweeping right and left through the trees, each corner being fast but blind. At the circuit's summit, Les Combes, the road swung to the left and headed into more open countryside, falling as it did so towards a very fast right and left at Burnenville, followed by a tighter right at Malmédy.

Then followed the Masta Straight, as daunting a piece of road as you will find anywhere, mainly because it was not straight for its entire length, not by any means. Half-way along came the Masta 'Kink' which was a left and then an equally distinct right, with buildings on either side. Once that had been successfully negotiated, it was flat out once more towards Stavelot which was at the bottom end of the circuit.

Originally there was a hairpin here but that was soon bypassed by a banked right-hand sweep which led cars onto the final leg and a climb through quick curves at Carrière and Blanchimont. At the point where the imposing stone clubhouse came into view on the inside of the circuit, the road swung left and headed down a short straight towards La Source, a tight right-hand hairpin which led the cars onto the downhill pit straight once more. In all, it presented a daunting challenge which thrilled and frightened the drivers in equal amounts.

In 1925 the surface was exceptionally rough and the seven starters faced 54 laps (502.74 miles) of this punishment. Under the circumstances, it was a miracle that two cars survived, both Alfa Romeos, with Antonio Ascari having led from the start to the finish, some 6 hours 42 minutes and 57 seconds later.

The Belgian Grand Prix was not contested again until 1930, victory going to the Bugatti of Louis Chiron after a mere 371 miles. The following year, though, it was serious stuff as 'Williams' and Conelli shared a Bugatti during a race covering 820 miles. Tazio Nuvolari, having stormed out of the Scuderia Ferrari team of Alfa Romeos not long before the 1933 Belgian Grand Prix, rubbed salt in Enzo's wounds by winning at Spa-Francorchamps in a Maserati. The following year, René Dreyfus averaged 89.95 mph in his victorious Bugatti, but already there was rumbling from across the border as the mighty Mercedes-Benz and Auto Union teams began to make their presence felt. Indeed, according to one report, they were both scheduled to take part but withdrew in protest over attempts by the Belgian customs to levy duty on the German teams' special fuel.

In 1935, they arrived in force and proceeded to dominate. Indeed, Mercedes-Benz had the questionable luxury of two of their drivers, Rudolf Caracciola and Luigi Fagioli, squabbling over the lead as Fagioli ignored team orders. In the end, Fagioli quit in disgust and Caracciola continued a brilliant comeback as he recovered from the dreadful injuries received at Monaco in 1933.

There was no Grand Prix in either 1936 or 1938 (the Belgians preferring to run 24-hour sports car races instead) and, thanks to most of the leading drivers competing in the United States at the time, Rudolph Hasse scored an unexpected victory for Auto Union in the year in between. In 1939 the Grand Prix was back on the schedule despite the growing unease throughout Europe over the activities of Adolf Hitler.

The German teams were there in strength, of course, but on race day, 26 June, the outcome was uncertain because of heavy rain. Caracciola, the supposed master of these conditions, spun off and eventually the Mercedes-Benz of Richard Seaman moved into the lead. The Englishman had scored a splendid win at the Nürburgring the previous year and then finished second in the wet in the Swiss Grand Prix, and was ready now to further his reputation. But, when the rain stopped and the track dried in some places but not in others, Seaman appeared to throw all caution to the wind as he went faster and faster. With Caracciola out, Seaman was determined to show he was more than a match for the great man in such treacherous conditions.

Coming to the end of lap 22, Seaman lost control at Club Corner and slid sideways into a tree. The violent impact at the side of the cockpit broke Seaman's right arm and knocked him unconscious. But it also broke a fuel pipe and, with Seaman having made a pit stop a few laps before, it was not long before gushing fuel caught alight on the hot exhaust. By the time Seaman had been pulled from the blaze, he had suffered serious and extensive burns. He died that night at a hospital in Spa. Hermann Lang, Seaman's team-mate, was in no mood to celebrate a victory for Mercedes-Benz.

The intervention of war brought activity of a more unpleasant kind to the Ardennes and when racing resumed in Belgium in 1946, a street course in Brussels was mapped out. The Frenchman Eugène Chaboud won the 73-mile race at the wheel of his Delahaye. Spa-Francorchamps, resurfaced and modified, was back in use the following year, Jean-Pierre Wimille giving Alfa Romeo victory. Louis Rosier took the honours with the lumbering but economical Talbot-Lago in 1949 after the more fancied opposition had to stop twice to refuel. Just as significant was the first appearance at Spa-Francorchamps of Juan Manuel Fangio.

He retired his Maserati from that race, but in 1950 he was a member of the all-conquering Alfa Romeo team and in Belgium Fangio disputed the lead, much to the indignation of the haughty Farina, before going on to win. He looked like making it two in a row at Spa until a lengthy pit stop cost time and Fangio had to give best to his team-mate, Farina.

In 1952, Alberto Ascari won almost everything in sight with his Ferrari and the Belgian Grand Prix was no exception. By 1953, however, Maserati were offering a decent challenge, Fangio and Froilan Gonzalez enjoying a fine tussle for the lead until both six-cylinder cars broke down. Fangio took over the car of the local driver Johnny Claes and was lucky to avoid serious injury when he left the road at Stavelot while avoiding a car which had spun on oil. The result was a repeat of the previous year.

Fangio lapped at an average of 115 mph while on his way to victory in 1954, this being his last outing in a Maserati before the Mercedes-Benz team returned to Formula 1. The silver cars were ready to dominate at Spa-Francorchamps the following year, Fangio giving Stirling Moss a first-hand demonstration of high-speed motoring as he headed towards his appointment with King Leopold III and that splendid trophy.

It was the turn of Peter Collins in 1956 but, due to financial problems, the Belgian Grand Prix was not held in either 1957 or 1959. In between, however, Spa-Francorchamps provided the setting for a dramatic race and an imperious performance by Tony Brooks in a Vanwall.

Moss led briefly in his Vanwall but retired on the first lap after muffing a gear-change, thereby leaving the way clear for a thrilling contest between Brooks and the

Ferrari of Collins. When Collins went out with mechanical trouble, no-one could catch Brooks – although he almost failed to reach the flag with his Vanwall stuck in third gear. A rapidly advancing Mike Hawthorn set a lap record at 132 mph, only to have the Ferrari blow up spectacularly as he crossed the line.

Spa-Francorchamps was the fastest road circuit in use at the time but its more menacing side became all too apparent during a depressing weekend in 1960. Events got off to a bad start when Moss crashed heavily during practice, a rear wheel parting company with his Lotus as he sped through Burnenville at 140 mph. The impact with a bank, and Moss's ejection from the car, put him in hospital with a broken nose, broken legs and a crushed vertebra.

During the Grand Prix itself, two promising young Englishmen, Alan Stacey and Chris Bristow, were killed in separate incidents. Those tragedies brought into sharper focus the loss of the brilliantly determined Scot, Archie Scott Brown, during a sports car race at Spa-Francorchamps two years before. This circuit had never made any pretensions about being easy and forgiving,

but that weekend in June 1960 made people aware of its dangers. Certainly, it did much to detract from a flag-to-flag victory for the Cooper-Climax of Jack Brabham.

A change in formula from 2.5 to 1.5 litres the following year caught most teams unprepared; most teams, that is, except Ferrari. Spa-Francorchamps was perfectly suited to the powerful V6 engines and a Ferrari led every lap, Phil Hill finally taking the chequered flag in what would be his championship year.

Strangely, for a circuit which demanded superior skills on the part of the driver, Spa did not appeal to Jim Clark. In fact, he hated the place; this, perhaps, a reflection of the circuit's bloody past and sad personal memories for the Scotsman. Yet he was to win for four years in succession; indeed, his victory in 1962 was to mark his first-ever Grand Prix win. Twelve months later he won in the pouring rain, a result which was more or less expected in a season which he dominated totally. However, Jim Clark was as surprised as anyone when he finished first at the end of the final dramatic, if rather unsatisfactory, laps in 1964.

In truth, this race had belonged to Dan

Gurney, the American's skill in the Brabham being perfectly suited to Spa as he led for 29 of the race's 32 laps. Unfortunately, his Climax engine was running rich and, when he made a late and unexpected stop for fuel, the Brabham team had none to hand! This gave Graham Hill the lead but, on the last lap, the fuel pump refused to pick up the final drops and the BRM coasted to a halt at Stavelot, not far from where Gurney would eventually run out.

Now Bruce McLaren was in the lead but, for the past few laps, he had been signalling urgently to his pit, telling them that something was wrong with the battery and the fuel pumps were being affected. Nonetheless, he struggled round on the last lap but, as he reached La Source, the engine finally went dead. Never mind, it was downhill from here to the line. As the Cooper freewheeled towards the flag, Clark, who had been delayed by a pit stop, shot past to take the flag – which had already been waved in error at two also-rans, such was the total chaos and confusion.

Clark was blissfully unaware of his success and, as he cruised round on the slowing-down lap, the Lotus also ran out fuel and stopped close by Gurney's car. As Jimmy commiserated with Dan, Clark still had no idea that he had won, until he heard it on the public address. He knew all about it in 1965, however, as he led from start to finish in atrociously wet conditions. The following year, the rain intervened once more, only this time the notoriously fickle weather had a far-reaching effect on the Belgian Grand Prix and its future at Spa-Francorchamps.

The catch-phrase of 1966 was the 'Return to Power', describing the change of formula from 1.5 to 3 litres. The Belgian Grand Prix was the second round of the championship and few teams were fully prepared for the new regulations. Nonetheless, 16 cars formed up on the grid, enough to make a race of it even though the pole-position Ferrari of John Surtees was expected to disappear into the distance.

The track was dry at the start-and-finish area, but as the drivers waited, announcements were made (in French of course) over the public address system concerning rain at Malmédy. If the drivers heard, they did not appreciate the value of such news; only Surtees, who had raced motor cycles at Spa in the past, fully understood what was in store.

Everything was in order at Les Combes, but the drivers arrived at Burnenville to be confronted by a solid wall of rain. This was before the introduction of slick tyres but, even so, the severity of the rain sent cars spinning in all directions. Jo Bonnier crashed his Cooper-Maserati, the red car ending its race balanced perilously on the edge of a bridge. Mike Spence left the road in his Lotus-BRM, Denny Hulme hit the back of Jo Siffert's Cooper-Maserati, while further down the road Bob Bondurant and Jackie Stewart spun off in their BRMs. Of these accidents, Stewart's was by far the most serious, the Scotsman trapped by the stove-in side of his car, the ruptured tank spilling fuel into the cockpit and under the hapless driver.

Stewart was eventually removed by Graham Hill and Bondurant. The race was not stopped and, at the end of the first lap,

Surtees led from Jochen Rindt, the Cooper driver having survived a terrifying series of spins, only to press on as if nothing had happened. Rindt eventually forced his way into the lead but the canny Surtees was merely biding his time. He eventually won by a comfortable margin to give Ferrari their last Grand Prix victory in Belgium for nearly ten years.

In 1967, Dan Gurney scored the sole Grand Prix win for his Eagle team, but only after Clark had run into spark plug trouble on his Lotus and the reputation of the race had almost taken another nasty knock. Running in fourth place behind Stewart's BRM, Mike Parkes had been caught out when the BRM dumped oil on the track. The Ferrari spun into the bank and flung the Englishman from the cockpit, the subsequent leg injuries ending Parkes's Formula 1 career.

Stewart led until gearbox trouble intervened, and it was the same in 1968 when it seemed he had the race sewn up in his Tyrrell-Matra. Then, a late pit stop for fuel handed victory to Bruce McLaren, the first of many for the McLaren marque.

There was no Belgian Grand Prix in 1969 and when the teams gathered at Spa-Francorchamps in June 1970, they were mourning McLaren's death at Goodwood a few days before. The race itself turned out to be a heroic battle between the March-Ford of Chris Amon and the BRM driven by Pedro Rodriguez. The BRM, normally the most unreliable of cars, held together for once and Amon never did get by but, in the heat of the chase on the last lap, he took the Masta Kink flat out. The March engineers later calculated that he had gone through there at 199 mph. It was the last time a Formula 1 car was seen on this part of the circuit. The call to have Spa axed on the grounds of safety had reached such a peak that the Belgians were forced to look for an alternative site for their Grand Prix. But where?

Politics came into play as the Flemish and Walloon territories each demanded to be satisfied. After a year without a Grand Prix, the solution was a move to a bland facility at

Nivelles, this artificial track south of Brussels then alternating with a circuit at Zolder, close by the town of Hasselt, deep in the Flemish-speaking part of the country.

Happily, there were only two Grands Prix at Nivelles and Emerson Fittipaldi won them both: in 1972 for Lotus and in 1974 for McLaren. There were few regrets when the boring and totally featureless track was dropped, leaving Zolder, for the time being at least, as the home for the Belgian Grand Prix.

Zolder was at least situated in pleasant, wooded countryside. The track was reasonably interesting although the pits and paddock were cramped and the difficult working environment was exacerbated by over-zealous officials. For the first Grand Prix in 1973 the lack of ambience was not helped by a dispute over safety modifications which had been carried out at the 11th hour at the insistence of the drivers. The track surface broke up and, for a while, it seemed the race might not take place. When it did, Jackie Stewart and François Cevert gave the Tyrrell team a one-two.

By the time the teams had returned in 1975, Stewart had retired and his obvious successor seemed to be Niki Lauda, the Austrian giving Ferrari two wins in succession at Zolder. He dominated much of the race in 1977, too, but miserably wet conditions upset many calculations and Gunnar Nilsson came through to score his one and only victory for Lotus.

The following year belonged to Mario Andretti and the Belgian Grand Prix was but one of his six victories for Lotus. Similarly, in 1979, Jody Scheckter won for Ferrari at Zolder and went on to take the championship but, like his ragged drive that day, Scheckter did not dominate the season in the manner of Andretti 12 months before. Didier Pironi led from start to finish in his Ligier in 1980 and that weekend was virtually trouble-free compared with the shambles that was about to unfold a year later.

For some time the teams had been complaining about an absurdly narrow pit lane. Matters came to a head when an Osella mechanic slipped from the signalling ledge

and fell into the path of Carlos Reutemann as the Williams driver edged his way down the pit lane. The mechanic, Giovanni Amadeo, died of his injuries.

As an ill-advised form of protest, certain drivers and team managers decided to gather at the front of the grid in the highly charged moments before the start. In the inevitable confusion which followed – and in the face of television schedules and the organisers' determination that the race should go ahead come what may – the start procedure went to pieces.

As the cars shambled onto the grid at the end of the final parade lap, Riccardo Patrese stalled his Arrows during the abnormally long wait. His chief mechanic, under the direction of the team manager, climbed the pit wall and just as he attached a line to the back of the Arrows, the race was started. Then, irony of ironies, the mechanic was struck by the second Arrows driven by Siegfried Stohr. Finally, in view of the apparent reluctance by officials to end these calamitous proceedings, it took the actions of Pironi, in the lead at the time in his Ferrari, to bring the race to a halt by pulling up on the main straight. In the end, after an otherwise excellent race, victory went to Reutemann but the sensitive Argentine was in no mood to celebrate.

John Watson won for McLaren in 1982 but he, too, was denied the joy of the moment by the lingering effects of a terrible accident during practice the previous day. Going for a quick time on his final set of qualifying tyres, Gilles Villeneuve came

across a slow car in the middle of the track. Making a snap decision, Villeneuve moved right at the precise instant the other driver did likewise in a bid to get out of the Ferrari's path. The two cars touched and the Ferrari became airborne, flinging its driver, seatbelts and all, from the cockpit. Villeneuve died of neck injuries and the loss of such a popular and hugely talented driver tainted Zolder forever.

It was fortunate, perhaps, that moves had been afoot for some time to return the Grand Prix to Spa-Francorchamps. In a first-rate piece of modernisation, the circuit had been virtually cut in half by a cleverly sculptured link which made full use of the plunging topography in the valley between Les Combes and the return leg at Blanchimont. The climb to Les Combes had been widened and straightened and the only serious blemish was the inclusion of a fiddly chicane, known unofficially as the 'bus stop', in order to slow cars through Club Corner. New pits were built just before La Source and, while the circuit may have undergone change, none of the atmosphere or the challenge had been lost. There was much rejoicing among the drivers after the first day of practice in 1983.

Andrea de Cesaris, showing surprising form, led for 18 laps in his Alfa Romeo but the nine points went to Alain Prost after another calculating drive in the Renault. It was the turn of Ferrari in 1984 as Michele Alboreto led all the way and the Italian was quickest during the one official practice period in May 1985. There was just one ses-

sion because the remainder of the race weekend was postponed when the freshly laid track surface broke up in many places. The Belgians were fortunate to find a slot in the calendar later in the year, and this time there were no problems with the track. Or, rather, there were no failures in its manufacture.

The major difficulty with the surface this time was caused by rain at the start, a period of rapid drying followed by a short, sharp shower. Ayrton Senna mastered the lot with ease in his Lotus. He finished second to Nigel Mansell the following year but, in 1987, these two were involved in a controversial clash of wheels while disputing the lead. Both drivers retired eventually, Mansell then marching down to the Lotus garage, where he attempted to throttle Senna. Prost, meanwhile, took an easy win for McLaren.

Senna made up for the disappointment when he moved to McLaren in 1988 and then won the Belgian Grand Prix for three years in succession. Each time, he started from pole and led every single lap. Each victory, he said, meant something special on a circuit like this. Much, in fact, as it had done for Juan Manuel Fangio three decades before.

The circuit may have been altered but the deep sense of satisfaction brought by success at Spa-Francorchamps remains as strong as it ever was. The track has been the making of the Belgian Grand Prix just as it has, on occasions, brought a classic motor sport event to its knees.

Serious young man. Immaculately turned out as ever, Moss waits for the start of a 500 race.

The day that Stirling Moss crashed at Goodwood, Fleet Street went into overdrive. It was Easter Monday, admittedly a traditionally slow day in hard news, but that night editors had no doubt about their lead story.

'Stirling Moss in Miracle Escape' shouted the headline in the *Daily Mirror*. It was typical of the reaction across the front pages on the morning of Tuesday 24 April 1962. It was also an indication of the high esteem in which Moss was held by the British people.

There were two aspects to this story. No-one knew precisely why Moss had crashed but, equally, there appeared to be no doubt that he would race again. True, he was unconscious and his condition was reported as 'serious'. But, as the tabloids pointed out, 'Our Stirling' was made of stern stuff.

One report spoke of an accident at Spa-Francorchamps less than two years before. Moss had broken his back and yet he had recovered sufficiently to establish a lap record and win a sports car race in Sweden seven weeks later. Why, he had even come to Goodwood a fortnight after that and walked off with the Tourist Trophy. 'Our Boy' will race again; you'll see.

He never did. Or, at least not in the front line. Moss gradually recovered from his various injuries and, 14 months after his accident, he returned quietly to Goodwood. With the minimum of fuss, and in the absence of the media, he drove a Lotus 19 sports car. The lap times were competitive but the mental effort required to produce them prompted Stirling to announce his retirement immediately. His concentration had gone; the fluency was still there but not the previously easy and impromptu method of creating it.

In fact, he had come back too soon. He was only 33 and, had he waited another year or two, he would have found that most of his faculties impaired by the accident had fully returned. On the other hand, he might never have recovered the exceptional abilities which had made him such a dominant force. But he would have been good enough to race. Whether or not being merely 'good enough' would have satisfied Moss remains unanswered.

In any case, he had made his decision and he stood by it. Either way, motor racing had lost one of the greatest talents it had ever seen. And he never would become world champion, a title he richly deserved even though the absence of his name subsequently devalued the series and brought the method of awarding the championship into question.

Perhaps Moss's greatest fault lay in the fact that he adored winning, and winning well. He would not adopt the principle of finishing first at the slowest speed. If anything, he preferred to retire having been in front, driving as quickly as he could and destroying the opposition rather than cruising cautiously and eventually accepting second best.

The winning ethic began at an early age, the money earned from success at show jumping contributing towards one of his first cars, a Frazer Nash BMW 328 two-seater sports. That was ultimately sold to make way for his first racing car, a Cooper 500, and straightaway the name S C Moss began to make an impact. He won 10 out of 14 races in 1948, his first season.

The Cooper, with its single-cylinder motor cycle engine in the back, was a nimble little device which taught Stirling a lot about late braking and consistency, the two areas in which he could eke out an advantage in a formula where the leading cars were more or less on a par.

Moss was determined to be a professional driver; he knew he had to earn starting and prize money if he wanted to survive and continue enjoying himself. He raced abroad for the first time in 1949 after driving himself and the Cooper to Lake Garda in Italy where he earned third place overall and £50 in starting money.

The Italians, amused at first by the spindly Cooper, were quickly impressed by Moss's method of handling it. So, too, was John Heath, the owner of a garage in Walton-on-Thames and a man determined to re-establish British racing prestige abroad.

Heath, having watched Moss closely throughout the season, invited him to be a part of the HWM Formula 2 team in 1950. Stirling accepted with alacrity.

He was on the go continually, criss-crossing Europe, but he soon came to realise that the very best efforts of the HWM team were hampered by limited finances and facilities. The Cooper 500 continued to bring success but, there again, Moss felt he needed to move on, to prove himself in other areas.

Sports cars were considered to be a high-profile class of racing at the time and, on the domestic scene, Jaguar were poised to set the standards with the introduction of the XK120. Jaguar did not run a works team as such but six of these strikingly beautiful cars were sold to private owners who could be relied upon to maintain the standards which Jaguar had come to expect.

Jaguar were not amused, therefore, when Tommy Wisdom, the motoring editor of the *Daily Herald*, offered his car to Stirling Moss to drive in the Tourist Trophy. Not only was this a prestigious race, but it was also to be run at Dundrod, one of the most demanding circuits of the day. And here was Wisdom handing this sought-after car to a novice.

The race, held in pouring rain, lasted for more than three hours. Moss, running non-stop, demolished the opposition and the more treacherous the conditions became, the more dominant his performance seemed to be. It was his coming of age in every respect. The following day he was 21 – and Moss rounded off the celebrations by dashing to Brands Hatch to win with the Cooper. On the Saturday, he had earned £1,400 at Dundrod (shared 50/50 with Wisdom); all in all, a fair weekend's work.

In 1951, his schedule increased in pace, Moss starting 25 races in 13 weeks during the first half of the season. He drove for HWM, interspersing trips to the Continent with races at home in sports cars and the little 500 single-seater. In all, he won 19 times that year. Then came a trough of despair.

The next season started encouragingly enough when, by taking a Sunbeam Talbot

to second place on the Monte Carlo Rally, Moss showed both his ability to diversify and an enthusiasm to try his hand at anything. A determination to race British products led to an agreement to drive the G-type ERA, but the late arrival of the car which was not, in fact, destined to be a front-runner, led to further outings with HWM.

A string of retirements, plus a crash which wrote off his Kieft 500 cc car, left Moss without a win in ten consecutive races. That may not sound much, but to a man with Stirling's insatiable desire for success, it amounted to a serious withdrawal of personal satisfaction. Just to complete the frustration, Moss had also agreed to drive the ill-starred BRM Formula 1 car. He raced it just once … in the rain, at Dundrod, of all places. Moss, for once, was quietly relieved when forced to quit, the fearsome machine overheating after four laps.

Not content with that, for 1953 Moss agreed to throw his hand in with a project to build an all-British car, the Cooper-Alta. In theory, it would be light, reasonably sophisticated and competitive. In reality, it was a good-looking car but, in Moss's words, 'a dog'. The final straw came when the flywheel disintegrated as he charged down the straight at Reims during the French Grand Prix. Bits of shrapnel gashed his leg. Moss considered himself lucky to have got off so lightly. To make matters worse, he spent the rest of the afternoon watching Mike Hawthorn become the first Englishman to win a Grand Prix since Richard Seaman in 1938.

Something had to be done. Moss's father, Alfred, who had provided unstinting support and encouragement throughout Stirling's career, went with Moss's manager, Ken Gregory, to see Mercedes-Benz. Word was out that the German firm was making a return to Formula 1 in 1954 and the Moss delegation, unbeknown to Stirling, went to enquire if the boy could have a drive. Alfred Neubauer, the authoritative team manager, provided wise council by suggesting that they should first find a competitive Formula 1 car in which Stirling could prove his

worth. Driving HWMs, Cooper-Altas and the like, said Neubauer, was hardly a useful guide.

Very well, but which car to choose? Casting patriotism aside, pragmatism – and a severely limited choice – dictated that they settle on a Maserati 250F, to be run by Stirling's own team. It would be the most important move of his career.

Moss won five national events with the 250F that year, but more significant by far was his presence on the world stage with such a useful car, one which Stirling thoroughly enjoyed driving. He finished third in the Belgian Grand Prix but missed out Reims because he had a commitment to drive for Jaguar in the 12-hour race which preceded the Grand Prix. It was a sign of the importance of sports car racing and it would also prove to be a useful move since it allowed Moss to lend his car to the works team. In return, they rebuilt the 250F and incorporated the latest modifications. Moreover, the Italian team promised to pay for a replacement engine if it failed in the next race, the British Grand Prix at Silverstone. Such was the increasing awareness of Moss's worth.

In the event, the transmission broke, but not before Moss had taken on and beaten Fangio, the Mercedes-Benz team leader. He did it again at Monza, Moss actually leading the Italian Grand Prix for 19 laps before his oil tank split. When Alfred Neubauer walked over and offered his condolences, it was clear Moss and the Maserati 250F had more than earned their keep. He signed for Mercedes-Benz on 4 December 1954.

As a bonus, Stirling would drive the 300SLR, a magnificent silver machine which, although a thinly disguised Grand Prix car, epitomised everything a sports racing car was meant to be in the mid-Fifties. Moss used one to score a legendary victory on the Mille Miglia, a hair-raising run against the clock on 1,000 miles of public roads in Italy. Moss felt he could improve his performance if he had someone inform him of what lay ahead. To this end, he chose Denis Jenkinson, a totally

unflappable journalist and a former sidecar champion, to make a series of short-hand notes during their reconnaissance runs.

Having rehearsed their double-act, Moss and Jenkinson engaged in a hitherto unseen display of mutual trust which saw the 300SLR cresting blind brows at 170 mph, Jenkinson urging the driver to keep his foot flat to the floor because the notes said he could. Moss shattered every record during a drive which remains one of the greatest performances in the sport's history.

In Grand Prix racing, Mercedes-Benz were also unstoppable. Moss did as he was told and dutifully followed in Fangio's wheel tracks, a task which Stirling did not mind in the least since he was learning at close quarters from the master himself. When it came to the British Grand Prix, however, the Mercedes-Benz drivers took turns at leading, Fangio setting a cracking pace and generally keeping Moss on his toes. In the end, it was Moss who crossed the line to win his first championship Grand Prix and, to this day, he does not know if Fangio let him. Or so he says. Fangio, in his book *My Racing Life*, is more specific. He says hints were dropped by the public relations manager of Daimler-Benz that Moss should be allowed to win at Aintree. Fangio wrote:

'It didn't matter to me that Moss won, because I was already certain of the championship when we went to Aintree. In any case, they gave me very low gear ratios for fear that I should disobey and win the race. I made a lot of headway in that last lap.'

But not quite enough, the two cars crossing the line in very close company. Not that it mattered since the record books show that Moss won and the great Argentine driver went on to become champion that year, with Moss taking the first of a regrettably high number of placings as runner-up.

It would be the same in 1956, only this time Fangio would be on board a Ferrari while Moss became team-leader at Maserati following the withdrawal of Mercedes-Benz. Moss scored excellent wins at Monaco and Monza, but perhaps the most significant result was a victory in the International Trophy at Silverstone. Maserati were not present at this non-championship meeting and Moss accepted a drive in a Vanwall. Here, at least, was everything which Stirling craved: a potential Grand Prix winner painted in British Racing Green. Moss signed to drive for Vanwall in 1957.

At first, the 1957 season did not quite run as Moss had planned. He was leading at Monaco when he went careering into sandbags and poles at the chicane, the subsequent chaos taking out two other British drivers as well.

Shortly before the French Grand Prix, Stirling went water skiing with his fiancée, Katie Molson. Not satisfied with the conventional method of skiing, Moss was trying a complicated manoeuvre when a plume of water shot up his nose. The resulting sinus infection meant Moss had to miss the race at Rouen but, happily, he was discharged from hospital in time for the British Grand Prix at Aintree.

Much was expected here and Moss did not let his public down when he claimed pole position, the sister car of Tony Brooks lining up on the outside of the front row. Between the green, however, was the red of Jean Behra's Maserati; the Frenchman could be expected to put up a fight. He did, but his initial challenge lasted barely a lap.

Moss had taken charge by the time they passed the pits for the first time and he stayed in front until lap 22, when a misfire forced a stop for swift but ineffectual repairs. He returned to the pits and Brooks was called in. Brooks was far from fit following an accident at Le Mans a few weeks before, so the plan was for him to hand over in an emergency such as this. Moss rejoined, tore through the field and won. It was a memorable and emotional victory for British drivers in a British car. And there was more to come.

Moss was victorious at Pescara in Italy and then really rubbed it in when he trounced the red cars at Monza, Vanwalls having filled the first three places on the grid. Yet it was not enough to give Moss the championship; he was destined to be runner-up once again, as Fangio took his fifth title.

In 1958 Fangio retired, leaving Moss as the undisputed master. He won four Grands Prix but, once again, he was to be denied, this time by the scoring system in play at the time. As they went to Casablanca for the final race, Mike Hawthorn had won just one Grand Prix but he was ahead on points. To take the title, Moss needed to win the race and claim fastest lap (for which there was a single point) with Hawthorn finishing no higher than third.

Moss did everything he could. He led from start to finish and claimed the fastest lap, but Hawthorn finished second, albeit a minute and a half behind. He won the championship by a single point. It made a mockery of the scoring since it was generally agreed, not least by Hawthorn himself, that Stirling Moss, week in, week out, was the man to beat.

There was another irony, too. Moss had won the Portuguese Grand Prix two races before, but it was thanks to Moss that Hawthorn had been awarded second place. Hawthorn, his Ferrari almost without brakes, had spun and stalled on the last lap. He managed to get going again but faced exclusion when officials claimed he had motored along the track in the opposite direction while restarting the Ferrari on an incline. Moss came to Hawthorn's aid at the Stewards' Inquiry by pointing out that Hawthorn was not on the track but on the footpath when the alleged infringement took place. The officials agreed and Hawthorn received his points.

Even today, Moss has no regrets about assisting his rival; indeed, he is positively taken aback by the suggestion that he should feel otherwise. He says:

'It was the correct thing, the sporting thing to do. I have absolutely no doubt about that. In the race before that at Monza, Mike was struggling to finish second and he could have been overtaken by his teammate, Phil Hill. But Phil held back so that Mike could score the points. I have no complaints about that either; it was absolutely the right thing to do. To me, that's what the sport is all about. Or, at least, what that's what it should be about. It wasn't a business then ...'

Mind you, Tony Vandervell, the owner of the Vanwall team, had his doubts about that when it was announced that a proposed change of formula for 1961 would outlaw his cars. Vandervell withdrew from racing at the beginning of 1959 and Moss chose to drive for Rob Walker's private team. His passion for being associated with anything British would cost Stirling dearly.

Walker had bought a Cooper, but since the factory would not make available one of their Jack Knight gearboxes and Stirling had great faith in the Colotti gearboxes made by GSD in Italy, Walker opted for Colotti.

Time and again Moss was to lose out because of transmission trouble. Even when he accepted an interim offer of drives in a front-engined BRM (entered by the British Racing Partnership), he frequently failed to finish. Indeed, he did not even have the satisfaction of being runner-up in the championship, despite winning for Walker in Portugal and Italy.

Slowly at first, but gathering momentum as the season progressed, the word filtered out that Moss was a 'car-breaker', an accusation which induced indignant letters from Rob Walker in the motoring press. In fact, it would only come to light in later years that Moss had been his own worst enemy by changing gear early with the Colotti gearbox in order to save the car. It so happened that the point at which he changed gear was when the Climax engine was delivering maximum torque. If he had changed gear at higher revs, he would have done less damage to the gearbox. But Moss didn't know that, for, in fact, he did not have any engineering or design knowledge worthy of the name. His painstaking efforts to save the engine were repaid with repeated mechanical failures and abuse from the press.

Walker switched to Lotus for 1960, Moss dominating the Monaco Grand Prix. Then came the accident at Spa-Francorchamps when a wheel parted company with the

Lotus during practice. Moss was out with a broken nose, broken legs and crushed vertebrae. Although he was back with a winning car seven weeks later, it was too late to make much impact on the championship.

His last full season was 1961 and during the course of it Moss was to score two superlative wins at Monaco and the Nürburg ring: a triumph of his driving ability in the fragile Lotus over the might of Ferrari.

These wins impressed Enzo Ferrari more than ever before and he redoubled his efforts to have Moss on board for 1962. Until then, Moss would have little to do with Ferrari. Stirling had been upset by a snub delivered by the Old Man, who had offered a drive in 1951, only to make the youngster look foolish by having him turn up at the race track to find that the car had been given to someone else. (In fact, this may have been connected with Ferrari having offered Moss Formula 1, Formula 2 and sports car racing. But Moss wanted to drive for Jaguar. When Ferrari said it was to be 'all or nothing', patriotic Moss in effect chose 'nothing'.)

At 32, Moss was at his peak. He was driv-

ing brilliantly, and it was clear that he needed Ferrari as much as Ferrari needed him. A meeting was arranged. Ferrari simply told Moss he could have anything he wished: Moss asked to have his car run by Rob Walker and painted in the team's colours of blue and white. Ferrari agreed. There could be no higher endorsement of Moss's talent. Unfortunately he never got to sit in the car.

The Easter Monday meeting at Goodwood was one of those traditional events which Moss would not dream of missing. Apart from the social activities, the non-championship race for Grand Prix cars, plus the supporting events, meant a day's work and a useful warm-up for the European season.

Moss was down to drive a Lotus but problems with the gear-linkage meant a pit stop. He rejoined and was about to pull back a lap on the leader, Graham Hill, when the Lotus went straight on for no apparent reason at St Mary's, a fast right-hander.

Moss made no attempt to spin the car as it bounced across the grass and headed for

an earth bank. When it dived in, nose first, the tubular frame of the chassis folded around Stirling, trapping him for 40 minutes while rescuers cut their way through the wreckage. He was removed to hospital, where he lay unconscious for four weeks and paralysed for six months.

It was never clear why he crashed at a point where he would not, under normal circumstances, have attempted to overtake another car. The obvious theories – steering failure, jammed throttle – were investigated and rejected. Stirling believes he mistook a wave from Graham Hill, as he acknowledged a flag marshal, as a signal to pass on the left, Hill then moving to the left to take his customary line for the right-hander which followed. Moss remembers nothing about the accident. Not even the exploratory drive in the sports car a year later did anything to spark his recall of the day. It is a void, a frustrating one which removed such a prodigious performer from the track.

Moss did make a return 18 years later when he drove a saloon car in the British championship. It was a mistake. Or, at

End of the road. Rescuers attempt to free Stirling from the wreckage of his Lotus at Goodwood on Easter Monday, 1962.

least, it was in the eyes of those who had witnessed his previous brilliance. It was uncomfortable to watch him struggle to come to terms with slick tyres and the trappings of a rapidly advancing technology.

In recent years, he has wisely chosen to restrict himself to historic events free from the 'win at all costs' tactics evident in so-called professional racing. Nevertheless, his determination to be the best comes through.

Moss moves with the same bustling,

urgent style, and runs his life as near-perfectly as he can. His home, down a Mayfair street in London, bristles with electronic gadgetry and efficiency. On the ground floor is a small office from which he runs a property business. His name remains in the telephone book, for he refuses to adopt the sanctimonious anonymity of some of his overblown successors. Indeed, he actively continues the promotion of a name which means almost as much outside motor sport today as it did in April 1962.

As Moss recovered from that accident, he worked on a book with the American writer Ken Purdy. Keen to understand why Moss

should be held in such affection by the British public, Purdy asked a Fleet Street editor for an explanation.

'It's because he was a knight in armour,' the editor said, 'rushing out of the castle to do battle in foreign lands, and coming back, sometimes with the prize and sometimes without it; sometimes bloody on his shield and sometimes not – but always in a hurry to go back and have another bash at the heathen.'

There can be no better summary of Stirling Crauford Moss, certainly the greatest all-round driver Britain has ever known, and the original 'Mr Motor Racing'.

The Argentine
Grand Prix

By craning his neck, Stirling Moss could get a good look at the rear tyres on his Cooper-Climax. It was, in the normal course of events, not the sort of thing a driver would do that often during a Grand Prix but, on 19 January 1958, Moss was looking back with increasing anxiety as the final laps of the Argentine Grand Prix ran their course.

He was leading but the Ferrari of Luigi Musso was closing rapidly. Moss was looking not for Musso, since his pit board kept him advised of the Italian's progress, but at the state of his rear tyres. He was running

non-stop, the only driver to do so in a race due to last for more than two hours. It had been a gamble, though, in truth, Moss had no choice.

Each wheel on the dark-blue Cooper was secured by the four nuts; the Ferraris and Maseratis had single knock-on hubs: a tyre change for Moss would have taken a ridiculous amount of time and swallowed any advantage he had earned on the track.

During practice, Moss had established that the rear-engined car handled well with a full load of fuel and that the fuel economy was good. Above all, he had discovered that the rate of tyre wear was minimal. After

The Buenos Aires Autodrome would hold more than just the Argentine Grand Prix. Taking advantage of having the Formula 1 cars in South America, there would also be non-championship races, such as the Buenos Aires Grand Prix, run in two heats on 30 January 1955. The Mercedes-Benz of Fangio and Moss (seen flanking the Ferraris of Trintignant and Gonzalez) finished first and second overall.

45

consultation with Alf Francis, the chief mechanic for this privately entered team owned by Rob Walker, Moss decided to risk running non-stop.

Luck would need to be on his side, and Moss had not had a great deal of that during the previous few days. The gearbox on the Cooper was considered to be the car's Achilles heel, and matters were not helped when the gearbox drain plug fell out during practice.

Later in the day, Stirling's wife had inadvertently poked her finger in his eye and scraped 4 mm off the cornea. Moss was in great pain and, for the duration of the practice at least, he had to wear an eye patch. A doctor advised that the injury would take at least five days to heal. The race, then, would be one to be endured in every respect.

In the midst of these trials and tribulations came the most incredible piece of good fortune, just when all seemed lost. Four laps into the race the gearbox jammed in second. Moss struggled unsuccessfully for the best part of a lap to move the gear lever and it suddenly freed just as he was about to pull into the pits.

Although Moss did not realise it, the clutch had broken. Under normal circumstances, this would not have been a major problem since a driver should have been able to continue by making clutchless changes. On the Cooper, however, a locking mechanism had been incorporated on the clutch to stop the car from jumping out of gear. When the clutch broke, the mechanism would not unlock and Moss was stuck in second gear.

Then, miraculously, a stone flew into the locking mechanism and released it. It was, for a driver dogged by mishaps which often were not of his making, the most remarkable piece of good fortune. And he would make excellent use of it.

In all, Moss had lost about 15 seconds and dropped to fifth place. He worked his way into second place despite easing the car cautiously through the corners and doing his best to avoid wheelspin in order to conserve his tyres. When the leader, Fangio, made his scheduled stop for tyres five laps

before half-distance, Moss found himself with a comfortable advantage. By another stroke of good fortune, Fangio ran into trouble and was unable to make any form of decent comeback.

Moss led the Ferrari of Luigi Musso by more than a minute and, of course, the Italians were convinced Moss was about to change tyres, a belief which had been fuelled in no small part by Alf Francis making a great play of preparing for a pit stop which only he and Moss knew would never happen. By the time the Ferrari team realised what was going on, it left Musso with little time to mount an attack. But Moss was watching his mirrors with increasing anxiety. With about 14 laps to go, he saw what he dreaded most.

A white spot appeared on the left-rear tyre and, with each succeeding lap, the spot grew longer and longer until, eventually, it became a continuous line. This was the first indication that the tyre had worn sufficiently to expose the white strip separating the tread from the carcass. Moss knew that the other tyres would soon follow.

The white line broadened and then lost its colour as the darker carcass was exposed, the edges of the worn band gradually becoming frayed as the tyre casing itself was ripped by the hot, abrasive track. And, all the while, Musso was taking seconds off the Cooper with every lap.

There was little Moss could do. Glancing nervously over his shoulder he had a clear picture of the destruction being wrought on his Continental tyres, yet he had to maintain his speed on the straights. As each lap passed safely, he braced himself for a tyre failure on the next. Towards the end, Moss was avoiding the roughest sections of the track and deliberately running on parts made slippery by oil.

On the final lap, Musso had the Cooper in sight as they rushed down the back straight. Ahead lay a couple of tight corners which Moss knew he had to take on tip-toe before he could get to see the man with the chequered flag. The Ferrari was closer now, no more than four or five car lengths.

Moss made it through the final left-

hander and, as they crossed the line, the blue car and the red car were separated by 2.7 seconds. It was, perhaps, the most tenacious, certainly the most unexpected, victory of Moss's distinguished career. He had judged it to perfection. The Argentine crowd loved every minute of it.

As 'foreign' drivers went, Moss had always been a particular favourite in Argentina. He had driven alongside Juan Manuel Fangio when they raced for Mercedes-Benz in 1955 and the Englishman was regarded as the Argentine driver's protégé. Moss had compared favourably with the great man and, more than that, he had received Fangio's nod of approval. That was good enough for the locals.

Fangio had done much to light the fire of international motor racing passion in his home country. Born in Balcarce, he was of humble stock but neither that nor his age – he was 38 when he went to Europe for the first time in 1949 – prevented Fangio from demonstrating a natural affinity with speed. He was snapped up by Alfa Romeo and, in 1951, he brought Argentina great honour by winning the world championship.

Such international acclaim for a former South American champion merely encouraged the locals as they went about their motor sporting business; they applied even more enthusiasm than usual when taking part in the type of terrifying road races on which Fangio had cut his teeth.

These *turismo de carretera* races would have sent today's safety officials into a state of apoplexy. They consisted of tuned production cars, of varying degrees of mechanical adequacy, hurtling for great distances on public roads and, as such, were extremely hazardous for competitors as well as the large crowds who chose to watch them.

International racing in Argentina grew in stature with the introduction of road races in the forest of Palermo in 1947, coupled with events at Rosario, Mar del Plata and Buenos Aires. To be known as the Temporada series, this combination of races on these and other circuits became a regular and popular fixture on the international

calendar. In 1952, Fangio returned from Europe and won them all.

There had been moves to build a permanent circuit to international standards and the impressive result was the Autodromo Municipal de la Ciudad de Buenos Aires, opened in March 1952. The circuit, located on the outskirts of the city offered 12 different variations.

On January 1953, a 2.4-mile version was chosen for the running of the first Argentine Grand Prix to count for the world championship. On paper, it should have been a splendid celebration of motor sport in Argentina. In reality it was total chaos.

Everything began smoothly. The Argentine government chartered an aircraft to bring the Ferrari and Maserati teams from Italy and, on arrival, they were greeted by Fangio and Froilan Gonzalez, the Argentine drivers being supported by a heaving mob of enthusiasts. Motor racing fever was running high and, gaining political capital from all of this, the proceedings had the full blessing of President Juan Perón.

Evita Perón had died some time before but each of the teams found it tactful to make official visits to her tomb, where wreaths were laid. Civic authorities, provincial governors, in fact, anyone who was anybody, threw receptions and parties. The populace, meanwhile, was being assaulted by constant announcements about the race from loudspeakers positioned in the streets and squares of the city. And there was much to shout about, what with the presence of the reigning World Champion, Alberto Ascari, plus the top European teams – and, of course, Juan Manuel Fangio, about to race for the first time since a fearful accident at Monza the previous September,

On race day, the entire population seemed to be carried to the Autodromo on a great wave of emotion and excitement. It was hot – and the race was not due to start until 4 p.m. As the afternoon wore on, those already crammed into the enclosures became increasingly restless as others tried to force their way in. Inevitably, the fences succumbed to both the strain and the dextrous use of wirecutters.

As the spectators spilled onto the trackside, the police tried to keep order; several skirmishes had broken out by the time President Perón arrived. When informed of what was happening, the President showed a keen grasp of reality by simply saying: 'My children, my children! Let them in!'

That was it. School was out. Mob-handed, the crowd flowed everywhere, their progress assisted by a gentleman who hooked a line to the fence, attached the other end to his truck and simply drove away. Meanwhile, there was some unpleasantness in the grandstand as those people who had paid for the privilege of being there found that a swift exit was preferable to the pain of cigarette burns inflicted by others who wished to take a seat at no expense to themselves.

By the time the drivers went to the grid, their cars were lost in a swirling sea of people. The track itself was lined by a solid wall of humanity and yet, despite all of this madness, the race itself started just a few minutes late. It would have taken a brave man to inform the populace of any major change to the advertised programme at this late stage.

Ascari took the lead but race positions quickly became academic. The crowd edged onto the track, obscuring marker boards and, eventually, the corners themselves. Some members of the public then amused themselves by waving articles of clothing in front of the cars in the manner of a bull-fighter. The inevitable was only minutes away.

A spectator ran across the track in front of Farina. Swerving to avoid him, the Italian lost control of his Ferrari and ploughed broadside into the tightly-packed mass. Nine people died and 40 were injured.

In the ensuing panic, a child dashed onto the track and was killed by another car. As officials began the hopeless task of restoring order and tending to the injured, one ambulance driver compounded the issue by driving the wrong way round the course, while another lost control and spun into the crowd to raise the death toll even further.

At one point, a mounted policeman attempted to clear a passage by overzealous use of his stock whip. For a while he succeeded but the mob then seized the man, dragged him from his horse and, according to one contemporary report, kicked him to death. The fact that the race was eventually won by Ascari was irrelevant.

Two weeks later, there was a Formule Libre event and an international sports car race at the Autodromo. In order to avoid a repetition of the scandalous scenes at the Grand Prix, the army was called in. Everything ran as smoothly as you would expect when men with machine guns are patrolling the spectator enclosures.

In any case, the crowd was much reduced, thanks to the alternative attraction of a soccer match and, perhaps, to the disappointment of having witnessed Fangio retire from the Grand Prix a fortnight before. He more than made up for that during the following years by winning his home Grand Prix four times in succession. And, arguably, there was no greater victory than his performance in 1955.

As temperatures reached 100° and the effects of racing for three hours took their toll, drivers either collapsed with heat exhaustion or staggered into the pits to hand their cars over to someone else. Even Moss, at his usual peak of fitness, had to stop at the trackside to draw breath.

Unfortunately, his cautionary behaviour was misunderstood and, before Stirling knew what was going on, he had been dragged by well-meaning officials from the searing heat of his Mercedes-Benz. The more he protested, the more convinced his rescuers became that this poor Englishman had been seriously affected by over-exposure to the South American sun. It was not until he found an English-speaking official that the confusion was cleared up.

But, throughout this blistering afternoon, Fangio motored serenely on to finish miles ahead of the next car – which had required the services of no less than five drivers to see it through to the finish.

Fangio's last appearance in the Argentine Grand Prix came in 1958, the year Moss performed his miracle with the underpowered but nimble little Cooper. Three years later and the race had disappeared from the international calendar. It remained that way for a decade, a return to the world series in 1972 being prefaced by a non-championship race, and a rare Formula 1 victory for Chris Amon, in 1971. It also marked the emergence of Carlos Reutemann, an enigmatic and highly talented local driver who, above all else, looked like a Grand Prix driver should.

Reutemann's Grand Prix debut, in front of an adoring crowd, was unbelievable. Well, almost. In fact, it was to be indicative of what would follow in a Grand Prix career which promised a great deal but, in the end, produced very little.

Carlos had finished third in that non-championship race at the wheel of an elderly McLaren. By the time the Grand Prix came round in 1972, he was a member of the Brabham team, which had now come under the ownership of Bernard Ecclestone and was about to enjoy the design brilliance of Gordon Murray.

For his first Grand Prix, Reutemann put

the white Brabham on pole position. The race, though, was dominated from start to finish by Jackie Stewart, the reigning champion engaging in what had become his customary boring ritual for the Tyrrell team. Alas, poor Reutemann: he chose the wrong tyres, was forced to make a pit stop and eventually finished seventh. But the racing fans of Argentina had found a new hero. Two years later, he really gave them something to cheer about. Well, almost.

Reutemann's Brabham was to start from the third row of the grid, but during the warm-up on race morning he had been quickest. Pete Lyons, writing for *Autosport*, summed up the scene as the cars made their way to the grid:

'The crowd's anticipation had worked up to the full riot stage. There were great shouts and chants and waving of flags and spraying of water and tossing of solid objects. Brown bodies and bright, light clothing milled through the grandstands all along the straight.

'The quieter elements of the crowd were sending out a constant haunting song about "Lolé ... Lolé ... Lolé ..." [Reutemann's nickname] and when the racing cars finally rasped into life and set out for the warm-up lap in single file and when the compact, sleek little white Brabham bearing No.7 appeared, every human-being in the grandstands sprang ecstatically to his feet. A bellow of perfect love burst from every throat and from every wildly waving fist flew long rolls of crêpe and little squares of torn paper. As Reutemann accelerated along the straight he was preceded by a wave of rising bits of paper all the way to the finish turn and beyond.

'It was a moving sight and to anyone with even a percentage of blood it had to be worth a second a lap.'

Indeed it was. On lap 3, Carlos Reutemann of Argentina took the lead. As he overtook the black-and-gold Lotus of Ronnie Peterson, the move was announced by a wall of sound, described by Lyons as 'a physical presence which beat on the head and the outsides of the ears without penetrating. It was a substance beyond anything sonic.'

There was more. Reutemann pulled away with ease. By two-thirds distance he held a 30-second lead over the McLaren of Denny Hulme. He appeared to be home and dry. And deservedly so.

Then the airbox on top of the engine cover worked loose. It was not a major drama since earlier tests had shown that the absence of the airbox only cost about 200 revs, or half a second a lap. And there were 17 laps remaining.

The airbox teetered back and forward, refusing to fall off completely. But, a few laps from home, a problem of an altogether different kind arose. A plug lead had come loose from the distributor and the strangulated sound of the engine running on seven cylinders warned of a serious drop in performance.

On the penultimate lap, Hulme took the lead. On the final lap, the Brabham ran out of fuel, Reutemann rolling to a halt beneath the silent, stunned gaze of the grandstands. As other cars rushed past the stricken Brabham, Reutemann knew he would not even gain the slim consolation of a championship point. The combination of the airbox and the spark plug had taken the edge off the fuel consumption. It was, as Lyons wrote in summary: '... a giant entry in motor racing's long list of might-have-beens.'

The Argentine Grand Prix usually marked the beginning of a new season and, frequently, produced unexpected results. In 1977 a team formed by oil millionaire Walter Wolf arrived with a new car for Jody Scheckter, a bullish South African in no doubt about his considerable natural ability. But even Scheckter did not expect to win first time out.

The British drivers John Watson and James Hunt disputed the lead initially until Watson suffered handling trouble and Hunt spun off when the rear suspension broke on his McLaren. That allowed Carlos Pace, Watson's Brabham team-mate, to take charge, but even the Brazilian found himself unable to cope with the stifling heat and humidity. Certainly, he could offer no resistance as the supremely fit Scheckter, lapping steadily, came through to collect nine points on a day when he hardly expected to score any.

There were few surprises in three out of the four years which followed, the winners, Mario Andretti, Alan Jones and Nelson Piquet, going on to become world champions in 1978, 1980 and 1981 respectively.

The Falklands War put paid to further international racing in Argentina and its absence was sorely missed. The Formula 1 teams enjoyed the city and its easy ambience even if the military presence at the race track was frequently overbearing. The threat of revolution seemed to hang in the air, yet when race day came, the highly charged atmosphere in the sweltering enclosures overcame all else. This was motor racing in the raw. Its history may have been comparatively brief but, one way and another, the Gran Premio de la República Argentina had contributed a great deal to the international motor racing scene.

Using his relaxed driving style to good effect
in the Rob Walker Formula 2 Cooper, Brooks
heads for victory at Goodwood in 1957.

TONY BROOKS

Tony Brooks conducted his career in a manner so modest it did not begin to suggest that this was one of the most naturally gifted drivers of the Fifties. Very much the team player with dignified sporting values, he epitomised the Kipling ethos: 'If you can meet with Triumph and Disaster and treat these two imposters just the same ...' During a relatively brief career he had his fair share of both.

Brooks was never world champion and yet he won at places such as Spa-Francorchamps and the Nürburgring largely because he genuinely loved to be there. He was an artist who put his principles before winning at all costs; a quiet genius, fully aware of his capabilities but, more than three decades on, still wondering what all the fuss was about. And, when you consider the absurdly low-key build-up to his first drive in a Grand Prix car, it is easy to understand why such modesty prevailed, why personal satisfaction came before financial and egotistical gain.

Charles Anthony Standish Brooks was born in Dukinfield, Cheshire, on 25 February 1932. His father, a dental surgeon, enjoyed fast cars and used them as they were intended. Lagondas, Allards and BMWs passed through the Brooks household; his mother would drive him to school in an MG.

In 1952, his father traded in an MG TC and added £300 towards the purchase of a Healey Silverstone sports two-seater so that Tony could go racing. The Healey was driven on a 600-mile round trip from Dukinfield to Goodwood, where Tony took part in a BARC Members' Meeting; he finished eighth in a scratch race and sixth in a handicap event.

His racing philosophy was formed from the very first lap. Apart from finding motor racing to be 'a most enjoyable and exhilarating experience', Brooks worked on the theory that it was better neither to force himself nor to drive fast simply for the sake of it. This sound and, for a 20-year-old, very mature policy contributed greatly towards one of the most graceful and unflustered driving styles ever seen in Grand Prix racing.

Brooks returned frequently to Goodwood, each time knocking a couple of tenths off his previous best as he worked at improving his technique. Along the way, the Brooks family fell in with another Healey Silverstone owner, Mr Hely, who offered to let Tony have a drive in his Fraser Nash Le Mans Replica. On his first serious outing with the car in May 1953, Brooks impressed everyone who saw it and he continued to drive for Hely for the remainder of the season and into 1954.

None of this was in line with the popular progression through the 500 cc single-seater category favoured by the likes of Stirling Moss and Peter Collins but, as far as Brooks was concerned, it was an important part of the learning process. The Fraser Nash needed to be kept above 4,000 rpm in order to maintain a head of steam and, in general, the heavier sports cars brought to Tony an appreciation of the true meaning of handling problems; as he said at the time, 'once a sports car starts to slide, you know all about it'.

He had done enough to arouse the interest of Aston Martin and, under the gimlet eye of team manager John Wyer, Brooks sailed through a test session to earn himself a place in the team for 1955. It was to be the start of an enormously successful and happy relationship which, indirectly, led to his first Grand Prix drive.

Brooks shared an Aston Martin with John Riseley-Prichard at Le Mans in 1955, the year of the dreadful accident when Levegh's Mercedes-Benz flew into the crowd and killed more than 80 people. As a result, Riseley-Prichard's family prevailed upon him to give up racing and he asked Brooks if he would be willing to race his Formula 2 Connaught. Since this represented a reasonably competitive single-seater, Brooks accepted. His handling of the car impressed Rodney Clarke, boss of the works Connaught team, and when Clarke found he had no-one available to drive one of his cars in the non-championship GP at Syracuse, he telephoned Brooks.

It was literally a call out of the blue. Brooks, having worked as a dental mechanic in his father's surgery, was studying hard for his exams at Manchester University and he had agreed to the drive without fully realising what he had taken on. Indeed, such was his preoccupation with his finals that he worked on his books during the flight to Sicily and occasionally wondered whether the trip was a waste of valuable time. All of which was to the good since it stifled the thought that he had never actually driven a Formula 1 car before. And there was worse to come.

Brooks missed the first day of practice due to the late arrival of the cars. Since he had never seen the circuit before, he set off in the evening on a Vespa scooter and soon discovered that this was a mean place indeed, the 3.47 miles of public roads lined by stone walls and other natural hazards. Having disciplined himself to avoid the temptation of using the grass to excess at the likes of Goodwood and Silverstone, Brooks was reasonably prepared for what lay in store. Precision, later to become a Brooks hallmark, would be everything.

Finally, he got his hands on the Connaught. He had to learn to deal with a car which was not much more powerful than the Aston Martin, but considerably more sensitive – and a lot less reliable. Since there was no back-up car and the team were desperate to earn their starting money after such a long trip, Brooks was restricted to no more than 15 laps during practice.

Even so, he went quick enough to set third-fastest time and take a place on the outside of the front row alongside the Maserati 250Fs of Musso (on pole) and Villoresi. The Italian cars were expected to dominate and that evening, Brooks still completely unaffected by the Grand Prix razzmatazz, went to church, as was his wont.

Brooks, of course, had never started a 2.5-litre Formula 1 Connaught before but he was fourth at the end of the first lap. On lap 4, he was third; on lap 8 he passed Villoresi and, on lap 16, he was in the lead. The Italians couldn't believe their eyes. Musso

retook the lead but Brooks moved in front again on lap 22 and proceeded to pull away. Not only that, he also set the fastest lap, some five seconds better than his practice time. At the finish, he was almost a minute ahead of Musso. It was a historic occasion, the first time a British car had won a Grand Prix since 1924. Brooks had been masterful without realising it. On the way home on the plane, he returned to his books …

Connaught, not surprisingly, were quick to make an offer for 1956 but Brooks turned them down in favour of running as Number Two to Mike Hawthorn at BRM. Although the BRM was not exactly competitive, Brooks and Hawthorn both felt that, with development, it could be a winner. It was very fast in a straight line, but corners were something else again: the car was simply diabolical. It was a deficiency which Brooks would prove to alarming effect in his first world championship Grand Prix, the British at Silverstone.

The BRMs had shot into the lead, Hawthorn retiring with transmission trou-
ble and Brooks stopping in vain to attend to a sticking throttle. During his visit to the pits, oil had been dropped at the very fast Abbey Curve and, as Brooks came through on his next lap, the BRM drifted wide. He lifted his foot from the throttle in a bid to have the nose of the car truck into the racing line but the BRM, its throttle sticking once more, kept going on its chosen trajectory. Once on the grass, the car went totally out of control, spinning into a bank, somersaulting and throwing Brooks from the cockpit. He was very fortunate to suffer nothing more than a chipped ankle bone.

The subsequent lay-off gave him time to consider his future. More than anything, he was afraid of sustaining an injury which might compromise his ability to perform dentistry, which remained his profession; motor racing was simply a very enjoyable, if increasingly time-consuming, hobby. A test drive in a Vanwall at Oulton Park helped him make up his mind. Whereas the BRM had been difficult to drive, the Vanwall was more forgiving and allowed
Brooks to drift the car under power. It was hardly an *easy* car to drive, but it was more predictable. At the wheel, Brooks felt relaxed again; a necessary prerequisite for his calm, authoritative style. He signed for 1957.

It was to be a memorable phase for British motor sport although, during the early races, Brooks probably did not see it that way. He was forced to retire on a number of occasions and, when he did finish second at Monaco, his left hand was raw after clutch trouble meant he had to struggle with the gearshift – not a strong point on the Vanwall at the best of times – for most of the race's 105 laps.

Gearbox trouble of a more serious kind at Le Mans that year was responsible for an accident which profoundly affected his motor racing philosophy. Brooks had taken over the Aston Martin sports car for a stint in the early hours of Sunday morning. The car was stuck in fourth gear (not a new problem for Brooks since he had managed to free the gear lever when the same trouble

53

Brooks, having taken over Moss's repaired Vanwall, chases the BRM of Les Leston through Anchor Crossing during the 1957 British Grand Prix at Aintree.

arose at a previous race) and he set about trying to repeat the cure.

He made the fundamental mistake of glancing down at the gear lever while grappling with it and, when he looked up, Tertre Rouge was approaching sooner than he thought. He narrowly failed to make the corner, the Aston Martin drifting onto a sandbank, which promptly overturned the car. Brooks was trapped underneath. There was nothing he could do as he lay in the middle of the track, listening to the sound of approaching cars, their drivers unaware of the hazard, full of fuel, waiting round the corner.

The first car, a Porsche driven by Umberto Maglioli, hit the Aston Martin – and knocked it clean off Brooks. Miraculously for Tony, no bones were broken but the abrasions were severe enough to put him in hospital and allow time to think about the meaning of life.

He was released a few days before the British Grand Prix at Aintree, where Brooks found he could manage one quick lap to claim a place on the front row but it was clear he did not have the stamina necessary to maintain that pace for 90 laps.

It was permissible at the time for any number of drivers to share one car and it was agreed that Brooks would give up his should Moss run into trouble. That is precisely what happened – much to Tony's relief – as Moss took over the Vanwall and, at the end of a legendary drive from fifth place, became the first British driver to win a world championship Grand Prix in a British car.

Aintree may have belonged to Moss that day, but in 1958, Tony Brooks truly made his mark. And he did it by winning convincingly at three classic circuits: Spa-Francorchamps, the Nürburgring and Monza. He adored them all (this was at the time when Monza was free of the chicanes which strangle the place today) and, surprisingly for a man of such a slight build, he had the physical strength to cope. A keen sportsman, Brooks had won his rugby and cricket colours at Mount St Mary's College, near Sheffield. He had represented the

school at boxing and played squash regularly while at university, all of which left him well-prepared for 24 laps of the old Spa-Francorchamps on 15 June 1958.

An interview 20 years later with Nigel Roebuck in *Autosport* reveals much about the racing philosophy employed by Brooks at the time. He said:

'Stirling made one of his lightning starts, intent on leading all the way, and I've always believed that he was out to beat me, as much as the Ferraris that day. It sounds a bit naive to say this, but I'd been to public school where one learned that "the team was the thing" and there was no way I was going to try and pass Stirling even if I might hustle him a bit. But I'm not sure he believed that and tore away, got as far as Stavelot and missed a gear! In tennis terms, it was definitely what you would call a "forced error" and after that I had no problems.'

Lest, in the present climate of petty jealousies and commercial pressures to win at all costs, the foregoing gives any impression of tension within the Vanwall team, it should be said that Moss and Brooks were the best of friends. The difference was that, to Stirling, winning was everything. It was his way of life. For Tony, it remained a bonus at the end of a pleasurable few hours at the wheel of a racing car, something that was calculated rather than wrung from a determination to go faster than anyone else at all times. And nothing gave him more personal satisfaction than to conquer Spa-Francorchamps and, two months later, the Nürburgring.

In fact, he already had experience of winning at both circuits thanks to brilliant drives for Aston Martin in sports cars in 1957. John Wyer, reflecting on his time as team manager, wrote in his autobiography:

'We had a lucky win [at Spa] with the DBR1 due again to the genius of Tony Brooks ... In the race, the oil pressure was low but Tony did everything possible to save the engine, driving just fast enough to win ...'

Such praise from Wyer did not come lightly. Even so, when Brooks went to

Monza for the 1958 Italian Grand Prix, the primary task was to help Stirling win his battle with Hawthorn for the championship. The contenders fought for the lead, Moss then retiring with a broken gearbox. Brooks's race also seemed to be run when he stopped to investigate an oil leak but he rejoined and stormed through from ninth to second. When Hawthorn ran into clutch trouble, Brooks was poised to take advantage. Mike eventually won the title and Tony finished third on the points table.

Vanwall withdrew at the end of the year and, in February 1959, under the heading 'Brooks for Ferrari?' *Autosport* had this to say about his intentions:

'Looks as though Tony Brooks will be "going foreign" for the first time in his spectacular career. He flew secretly to Italy last week, and it would seem almost definite that he went to see Ferrari.'

They were right. Brooks accepted the offer, but he did so at a time when the rear-engined Coopers were about to revolutionise Formula 1 and Ferrari were still running their front-engined Dinos. Nonetheless, Tony found the 246 a glorious car to drive and, in a sweltering French Grand Prix at Reims, he left the opposition standing, his remarkable stamina seeing him through with no trouble at all.

He won the German Grand Prix at Avus and his one regret was the cancellation of the Belgian Grand Prix since he felt the Dino would have been a match for anyone at Spa-Francorchamps, a statement which, as usual, did not do justice to the part he would have played in the proceedings. Nevertheless, when the final race of the season came round at Sebring in Florida, Brooks had hopes of winning the championship. By chance, the three contenders – Brooks, Moss and Brabham – started from the front row. Or, at least, they should have done.

A dispute over the time given to Harry Schell saw the Franco-American promoted and Brooks moved to the second row, a change which could be interpreted as having an effect on the outcome of his cham-

pionship. Brooks was now directly ahead of his team-mate Wolfgang von Trips and, on the first lap, the German inadvertently hit the rear wheel of Brooks's car.

Normally, a driver in Brooks's position would have pressed on. But, ever since the incident with the BRM at Silverstone, followed by the accident at Le Mans, Brooks had vowed never to try and compensate for any deficiencies in a car which was less than perfect. A devout Catholic, Brooks reasoned that it was irresponsible to take unnecessary risks with his life, a life which was a gift from God. If the car was damaged or broken, then too bad about the race. Accordingly, he brought the Ferrari into the pits to have it checked over.

Nothing was amiss and he continued, to finish third. Moss, meanwhile, had retired and Brabham, out of fuel, was pushing his car into fourth place. Without the pit stop, Brooks might have won the race – and with it, the championship. The Ferrari had felt okay and, by pulling in, he had gone against every instinct ever known to a racing driver. But, when all was said and done, the totting up of points mattered less than the betrayal of a genuine and deep personal belief.

At the end of the year there was some confusion. In December, Brooks bought a small garage in Weybridge, Surrey, and the commitment necessary meant he felt unable to continue with Ferrari. This came out in a statement from the Italian team as a retirement announcement. Brooks then put the matter right in *Autosport* by saying he had made no definite plans for 1960, other than to decide he could no longer drive for a team based far from home.

In fact, he was in the throes of negotiating to drive a Lotus powered by a Vanwall engine, but the deal came to nothing. He eventually accepted the offer of a contract with the Yeoman Credit team, which was running Coopers from the previous year. A remarkable place on the front row of the grid at Spa was probably the highlight of his season and, having been second in the championship in 1959, he fell to 11th after picking up a couple of minor placings.

Then he returned to BRM in the hope

Grime-free winner. Having led every lap of each heat of the German Grand Prix in 1959, a clean-faced Brooks shows the benefits of running at the front.

that the British team's proposed 1.5-litre engine would offer Ferrari a challenge as the new formula came into being. It might have done had BRM prepared themselves more thoroughly. Instead of appearing at Monaco in May, the new car was not ready until Monza in September. In the meantime, Brooks proved he had lost none of his flair by setting fastest lap during the British Grand Prix, the sopping-wet track at Aintree compensating somewhat for the deficiencies of the BRM with its dated Climax engine. When Brooks finished third in the US Grand Prix, it turned out to be his last Formula 1 race.

Despite such outstanding ability, Tony still did not see motor racing as the be-all and end-all of his life. He had married an Italian girl at the end of 1958 and, in March 1961, he opened an Austin dealership.

Present for a group photograph on the forecourt were George Abecassis, Henry Taylor, Tommy Wisdom, Stirling Moss, Reg Parnell, Innes Ireland, Raymond Mays, Colin Chapman, Bruce McLaren and Graham Hill. It is hard to imagine anyone even attempting to arrange a similar line-up of talent today …

It was clear, therefore, that Tony had his family as well as his business to consider. Both have since flourished, the expanding motor business helping support five children. But there are few ostentatious signs of the success Tony Brooks enjoyed as a Grand Prix driver; indeed, some of his friends are totally unaware of the respect and admiration he commanded on the race tracks of the world.

In December 1961, the motor sport press carried brief announcements to say that

Brooks had decided to retire at the age of 29. There had been no fanfare, no tears, no emotional talk of putting his family before his bank balance. Tony Brooks had simply enjoyed being a racing driver and there were now other matters to attend to in his life.

The modest departure of C A S Brooks was totally in keeping with his arrival on the international scene and it did nothing to diminish the stature of a gentlemanly driver with a sublime touch.

The 1961 US Grand Prix was to be the last for Tony Brooks. He went on to take third, the best-placed finisher of the drivers present in this group photograph, taken on arrival in New York. Left to right: Jim Clark, John Cooper, Bruce McLaren, Graham Hill, Jack Brabham, Tony Brooks and Colin Chapman.

The German Grand Prix

escribing the Nürburgring has never been easy. There is no circuit quite like it anywhere in the world and, no matter how generous the superlatives, they fail to portray the relentless succession of corners and the stimulating effect they had on the adrenalin. W F Bradley, a motoring journalist of the period when it was built, perhaps summed up its character best when he abandoned the usual descriptive methods and simply wrote: 'The dominating impression is that a drunken giant was allowed to reel around the Eifel mountains, and then road contractors followed in his tracks.'

Indeed, it had that endless, sometimes eerie, nomadic quality. Half-way round and drivers felt destined never to see the start-and-finish area again. That was the great attraction. It was Tony Brooks's favourite circuit. 'You don't find yourself coming up to the same corner every three miles,' he said. 'It is a place to get your teeth into, really go motor racing with maximum effort.' On 3 August 1958, he did just that.

Driving alongside Stirling Moss at Vanwall, Brooks represented the changing scene in Formula 1. Mercedes-Benz had come and gone; Maserati had withdrawn, leaving Peter Collins and Mike Hawthorn at Ferrari to fend off the persistent and increasingly successful invasion of British Racing Green as the young bloods argued

With Schloss Nürburg in the background, the field heads through North Curve at the start of the 1963 German Grand Prix.

over who should be Fangio's successor in the wake of the great man's retirement.

Moss had won at Zandvoort, Brooks at Spa-Francorchamps, Hawthorn at Reims, Collins at Silverstone. Now came the Nürburgring, and there was nowhere better to settle this argument.

In the accepted method of the day, the front row was four cars wide. And there they were: Hawthorn on pole, with Brooks alongside, then Moss, then Collins – red, green, green, red. Hawthorn had the full support of Collins in his bid to win the championship; Brooks would back Moss although, in reality, at a circuit like this, it was every man for himself. In any case, Stirling Moss was not about to wait for anyone.

At the end of the first lap, he led Hawthorn by six seconds, with Collins and Brooks trailing behind. On his second lap, Moss improved on his grid time by almost three seconds, and next time round he sliced a further six seconds off his previous best. Ferrari had no answer to such a withering display of power, and Moss led by 17 seconds as he went into lap 4. He never completed it.

News came through from Schwalbenschwanz that the Vanwall had stopped, its ignition dead. Moss climbed from the lofty cockpit and watched Hawthorn and Collins rush by in team formation. Brooks, struggling with the handling of the Vanwall on full tanks, had dropped back. He was 22 seconds behind the Ferraris as Collins took the lead on lap 5. Hawthorn took charge again on the next lap but, already, there were signs that Brooks was getting into his stride as the handling became more acceptable; the gap was down to 17 seconds.

On lap 7, Brooks gained ten seconds and, by the end of lap 8, he was right behind the red cars, Collins now leading. Brooks passed them both, but the top speed of the Ferraris was superior and he was pushed back to third on the long straight leading to the start-and-finish area. It was not difficult for Brooks to work out that he needed to get ahead on or near the beginning of a lap since the many miles of twists and turns which followed would give him a big enough advantage by the time they returned to the straight.

At the beginning of lap 10, Brooks passed Hawthorn at the exit of the South Curve, the first corner after the pits. Then, a few seconds later, he lunged inside Collins at the North Curve. Ahead lay the downhill swoops through Hatzenbach, the swift run to Flugplatz and on to the long, never-ending right-hander at Aremberg, the terrifying plunge into Fuchsröhre followed by the rise to Metzgesfeld and the devious twists of Kallenhardt.

No time to look at the superb view of the countryside beyond; ahead lay the descent through Wehrseifen to the Adenau Bridge, perhaps the most difficult section of them all. That done, the track rose steeply and curved quickly towards the right-hander at Bergwerk, barely the half-way point in this remarkable switchback ride. On through Kesselchen, the tops of pine trees flashing past on the right-hand side, and into a tight right, followed by a gently sweeping climb towards the Karussel, a bumpy concrete bowl doubling back on itself to the left and flicking the cars onto the climb towards Hohe-Acht, one of the highest parts of the circuit.

So far, the cars had covered nine miles of the lap and Tony Brooks loved every inch of it. Driving with consummate ease, he forced the pace, Collins hanging on, Hawthorn dropping back slightly. Down through Wippermann, plunging over the hump at Brünnchen, on down the dip and then steeply uphill to a climbing right and on towards Pflanzgarten. As they went through these fast curves, Collins ran wide slightly, the Ferrari then mounting the grass bank and flipping over. On witnessing this, Hawthorn lost much of his momentum, but his Ferrari would stop with clutch failure part-way round the next lap.

Brooks was now totally unchallenged and he finished eight miles ahead of the Cooper-Climax driven by Roy Salvadori, his winning average being a record 90.33 mph. It had been a brilliant drive by any standards, a victory which Brooks considered to have been one of his greatest, but the joy of the moment was wiped out entirely later than evening when news came through that Collins had succumbed to his injuries.

The simple truth was that Peter had made an error while trying to keep up, but the incident was nevertheless a terrible reminder of the perils which lay in store at the Nürburgring. It had become the ultimate test of man and machine and, over the years, it extracted its dues. Yet the principle reason for building the circuit had been to alleviate the severe unemployment in the Coblenz–Cologne area in the early-1920s.

The foundation stone was laid on 27 September 1925, the projected circuit running for 17.58 miles through forest land in the Eifel mountains. There would be two circuits: the South (or Sudschleife) at 4.8 miles and the North (Nordschleife) measuring 14.17 miles, each using the same start-and-finish area and pit and paddock complex. In total, there were more than 170 corners – not that a driver would have a moment free to count them. Perched high on a hilltop (actually a plug of volcanic rock overlooking the hamlet of Nürburg just inside the Nordschleife) sat the ruins of the Schloss Nürburg, one of the oldest castles in the Rhineland and the obvious source of the name given to the circuit. Despite lavish preparations, the Nürburgring was not ready when it came to choosing a location for the first German Grand Prix in 1926. That was held at Avus, a track which could not have been more different, the complete antithesis of the Nürburgring and everything it stood for.

The name Avus stood for Automobil Verkehrs und Übungs-Strasse, or 'Automobile traffic and test street'. The idea, mooted originally in 1907, was to provide a test track for the motor industry while at the same time, defraying the cost by doubling as a public highway. It was to be a dual carriageway running dead straight from the Grunewald district of Berlin to a railway station six miles away, the two sides linked by a hairpin at one end and a wide-radius loop at the other.

Progress was slow and building did not start until prisoners were put to work on the project during the First World War. It lay dormant for a period following the armistice and was eventually finished and opened as a toll road and race track in 1921. In the absence of a suitable circuit (the existing tracks at Nideggen and Solitude were too narrow), Avus became the obvious choice when the Automobilclub von Deutschland (AvD) applied to hold a German Grand Prix in 1926.

Almost a quarter of a million spectators are reported to have turned out to watch Rudolf Caracciola win for Mercedes, but the result was overshadowed by a number of accidents brought about by heavy rain.

Cars slid off the road in all directions, spectators and drivers being injured at regular intervals. The worst incident by far occurred when a Mercedes skidded into the timekeepers' box, demolishing it and killing the three people inside.

That put an end to racing at Avus for some time, but fortunately the Nürburgring was nearing completion. More than 3,000 workmen (some reports say as many as 25,000) had laboured for two years and the result of their endeavours was a motor racing masterpiece; the perfect place for Germany to test and show off its industrial muscle.

On 17 July 1927 it took Otto Merz almost five hours to complete the 18 laps of the combined circuits as he led a clean sweep by Mercedes-Benz in the second German Grand Prix. The following year, as in 1927, the race was for sports cars and utilised both the north and south circuits, Mercedes-Benz defending their reputation in the face of opposition from Bugatti. In 1929, however, Bugatti returned to claim the first two places, Louis Chiron averaging 66.42 mph.

The Wall Street Crash hit the German motor industry as hard as any other and there was no Grand Prix in 1930. There was a recovery of sorts during the next 12 months and the race was on again, this time using only the Nordschleife for a total of 22 laps. Rain for most of the race brought out the very best in Caracciola as he used his Mercedes-Benz to defeat Chiron (Bugatti), Achille Varzi (Bugatti) and Tazio Nuvolari (Alfa Romeo).

When Mercedes-Benz withdrew temporarily in 1932, Caracciola drove for Alfa Romeo and beat Nuvolari, albeit with a little assistance from the team manager as he deliberately delayed the little Italian during a pit stop. In 1933, the Nazis came to power and Adolf Hitler encouraged German supremacy by setting Mercedes-Benz and Auto Union one against the other. The result of the ensuing rivalry was the introduction of some of the most formidable Grand Prix cars ever seen and the Nürburgring was to be their most important showcase. The 1934 German Grand Prix turned

out to be a duel between these two teams.

Hans Stuck and Caracciola waged an intense battle, the Mercedes-Benz overtaking Stuck by running round the level road on the top of the Karussel while the Auto Union was on the banked inner section, an ironic state of affairs since Caracciola's mechanic, Wilhelm Sebastian, was reputed several years before to have discovered the method of using the ditch as a banking in order to save time through the corner. In the end, though, Caracciola's daring was all for nothing, the Mercedes-Benz retiring with engine trouble. Stuck became a national hero overnight and the Germans began to acquire a feeling of invincibility. They reckoned without the brilliance of Tazio Nuvolari the following year.

Always a loner and not a great team player, Nuvolari found himself at the wheel of a Tipo B Alfa Romeo, three years out of date and, in theory, no match for the mighty silver machines from Germany. In one of the most dramatic of all German Grands Prix, held on a damp track, Nuvolari led briefly, only to lose a disastrous amount of time when a blocked pressure pump meant his fuel had to be added by means of churns during a pit stop. Desperate to put one over on the Germans in general and the Auto Union of arch-rival Achille Varzi in particular, the little Italian leapt from his car and berated the mechanics, waving his arms with increasing frustration as two minutes ticked by.

He rejoined in sixth place and set about making the most of the Nürburgring's ability to let a driver's skill overcome the deficiencies of his car. He moved into second place and, on the last lap, took the lead from Manfred von Brauchitsch when his Mercedes-Benz destroyed a rear tyre five miles from the finish of a 311-mile race. The crowd were astonished, the Germans stunned and poor von Brauchitsch shattered as he trundled home in fifth place and pulled up some distance from his pit, the better to hide tears of utter dejection.

There was no stopping the home teams in 1936, Bernd Rosemeyer winning handsomely for Auto Union during a season in

which the brilliant young extrovert could do no wrong and Mercedes-Benz, it seemed, could do no right. All that changed in 1937, Caracciola winning the German Grand Prix for the fifth time as a young British driver, Richard Seaman, enjoyed a mixed first season with Mercedes-Benz.

It all came right at the Nürburgring the following year – or, at least, it did for Seaman if not for the spectating members of the Nazi party – when an estimated 350,000 spectators spread themselves around the Nordschleife to watch a British driver win a Grand Prix for the first time since Segrave in 1924. Seaman was helped in part by von Brauchitsch's leading Mercedes-Benz catching fire during a refuelling stop, but throughout the afternoon Seaman paced himself and made just one stop for tyres as opposed to von Brauchitsch's two. The eternally unlucky German never did win his home Grand Prix since the last race before the outbreak of war in 1939 went to Caracciola as he drove the sole-surviving Mercedes-Benz in the damp conditions in which he excelled. It was to be his last Grand Prix victory and there could have been no better circuit on which to leave his mark of excellence.

The ravages of war, meanwhile, left their mark on Germany and, indeed, on the Nürburgring itself. The passing of armies and their paraphernalia meant a resurfacing job was necessary and neither the track nor the organising clubs were ready for international action until 1950. With little money available, it was decided to run the race for Formula 2 cars and a healthy and cosmopolitan entry turned up for 16 laps around the north circuit. Alberto Ascari led all the way in his Ferrari, but he was lucky to see the finish. On the last lap, he drifted over the lip of the Karussel and the shock was enough to break half the spokes in the offside rear wheel. By the time he had completed the 226 miles, the wheel rim could almost be pulled free from the hub.

The organising club, the AvD, raised the status of the Grand Prix to Formula 1 and it was automatically included in the 1951 world championship. Ferrari arrived with

their tails up, Froilan Gonzalez having just defeated the previously all-conquering Alfa Romeos at Silverstone. Despite not having seen the Nürburgring before, Gonzalez put his Ferrari alongside the pole-position sister car of Ascari and the race developed into a battle between these two with interventions from Juan-Manuel Fangio in his Alfa Romeo. At the end of 20 laps, Fangio finished half a minute behind Ascari, with Gonzalez third.

Ascari made it three in a row in 1952, a predictable result following the universal switch by race organisers from Formula 1 to Formula 2. It might have been four for the Italian but for a wheel parting company with his Ferrari as he led the opening laps of the Grand Prix in 1953, victory eventually going to his team-mate Guiseppe Farina, with Britain's Mike Hawthorn finishing third after leading briefly.

Hawthorn continued to drive for Ferrari

in 1954 but there were clear signs that the Italian stranglehold was about to be broken following the return of Mercedes-Benz. Fangio took pole position, three seconds faster than Hawthorn, with the Maserati of Stirling Moss joining them on the outside of the front row. There was much sadness among the drivers, particularly the South Americans, when Onofre Marimon, a young compatriot of Fangio and Gonzalez, was killed during practice when his Maserati left the road just before Wehrseifen and plunged down a steep drop.

A new illuminated scoreboard, showing the position of the leaders around the circuit, told the story of a victory for Fangio after both Moss and Hawthorn had run into trouble. At one stage Karl Kling, Fangio's team-mate, had dared to ignore orders and he led the race before damaging the rear suspension on his W196. It was to be the only home win for Mercedes-Benz, because

the race was cancelled the following year as a result of the Le Mans tragedy. By 1956 Mercedes-Benz had withdrawn, their mission complete.

Into the vacuum came Ferrari and Maserati, Fangio leading all the way for the former, Moss finishing second for Maserati. During the course of the race's 22 laps, Fangio had set a new lap record at 9m 41.6s. In 1957, he slashed that to ribbons with a drive which has become legendary; one which, many years later, would make the great man shudder at the very thought of it.

Fangio, on board a Maserati 250F now, took pole position and led from the start. This was not surprising since he had elected to run with his fuel tank half full, but that plan went awry when the pit stop took an inordinately long time thanks to a mechanic dropping a wheel nut which then bounced beneath the car.

Having been half a minute to the good, Fangio returned to find he was almost 50 seconds behind the Ferraris of Mike Hawthorn and Peter Collins. For the first few laps, Fangio made little impression as he settled in with the new tyres and a full load of fuel. The Ferrari team management, noting this, urged Hawthorn and Collins to steady their pace. At the same time, Fangio was signalled 'flat out'. There were eight laps remaining; the maestro went to work.

On the next lap, he pulled back 12 seconds. Hawthorn and Collins, of course, were already into the following lap and, by the time they had completed the 14 miles, Fangio had carved yet another large chunk off the gap. Now the Ferrari team switched to full animation mode, desperately trying to alert their drivers to the impending danger. Hawthorn and Collins went motoring. But their best efforts would make no difference on a day when Fangio was redefining the peak of the Grand Prix driver's art.

On lap 17, he went round in 9m 28.5s. Then 9m 25.3s; the gap was 20 seconds. Next a lap of 9m 23.4s; the gap was 13.5 seconds. Three laps to go.

At the end of lap 20, Hawthorn and Collins blasted past the pits – with Fangio on their tail! The air of disbelief was broken only by the commentator shrieking the news that Fangio had established another new record; 9m 17.4s; an average of 91.53 mph. It was more than eight seconds faster than his pole-position time. It was also more than anyone could comprehend; quite the most remarkable performance on a circuit such as this.

Hawthorn and Collins did their best but there was to be no stopping Fangio as he forced his way through. At the end of 22 laps, he was 3.6 seconds ahead of the Ferraris. As he stepped from his car, Fangio said he never wanted to drive like that again. He never did. It was to be his last Grand Prix victory and there was none greater, not even the polished and stylish drive by Tony Brooks 12 months later as he virtually repeated Fangio's tactics by attacking the Ferraris from behind.

The greatest surprise from all of this was the news that the AvD had not enjoyed a healthy turn-out of spectators. For 1959, therefore, it was decided to return to the spectacularly boring track at Avus, made no better in 1937 by the addition of a brick-faced banked turn at the northern end and, after the war, a reduction by half of the blast along the dual carriageway due to the intrusion of the East Zone frontier.

Keen to attract tourists to the city, the Berlin authorities had agreed to indemnify the AvD against financial loss. As part of the package they agreed to supply, free of charge, a number of over-zealous policemen who would have been better off kept at home.

The mood of depression was not helped by the slack organisation. There were insufficient passes and the drivers and mechanics, already working under the strain of having the pits and paddock about a mile apart, quickly became fed up with being pushed around. On one memorable occasion Dan Gurney, in the middle of a conversation with the Ferrari team manager, refused to budge and gave his name as Adolf Hitler when threatened by an outraged police officer. The final straw came when a local dignitary was refused admission to the grandstand.

Throughout, the tense atmosphere was exacerbated by dull weather and the loss of Jean Behra who had died when his Porsche slid over the top edge of the slippery banking during a sports car race the day before. In order to avoid worries about tyre wear, the Grand Prix was divided into two 30-lap heats and Brooks, averaging 144 mph, won them both for Ferrari. As for Avus, the place was universally condemned and the Grand Prix teams never went back.

Another political decision in 1960 cost the race its championship status, the Germans keen to run Formula 2 cars in the certain knowledge that it would provide a victory for Porsche. That is precisely what they got, Jo Bonnier winning in the rain on the bleak south circuit of the Nürburgring.

It was back to normal business in 1961, however, the Grand Prix thankfully returning to Formula 1 and 15 laps of the north circuit. It was to be the scene of another classic drive, courtesy of Stirling Moss as he used all of his considerable skill and the quality of his Dunlop tyres to take an outdated and comparatively underpowered Lotus to victory over the best Ferrari could provide. And, along the way, the nine-minute barrier was broken for the first time in a race as Phil Hill gave vain chase to the privately entered Lotus. Hill eventually finished a very close third behind his Ferrari team-mate Wolfgang von Trips, the two of them having spun in unison when they unexpectedly found rain on the straight on the last lap.

In 1962 the Nürburgring was the scene of yet another superb race, but with a different cast. Ferrari were in trouble, Moss was in hospital and von Trips had been killed at Monza. On the front row were four makes of car: Porsche (Dan Gurney), BRM (Graham Hill), Lotus (Jim Clark) and Lola (John Surtees). And to add to the uncertainty it was raining.

Clark, forgetting to switch on his fuel pumps at the start, would not figure in the fight for the lead, but that did not prevent the Scot from producing a brilliant drive from the back of the field to fourth place. At the front, Gurney took charge initially but then Hill surged through, Surtees watching from third place. For 15 laps they circulated nose to tail, Hill being forced to work extremely hard for more than two and a half hours. At the end of it, mentally and physically exhausted, he had fastest lap and maximum points to show for a faultless drive, the Lola and the Porsche crossing the line a few seconds behind.

Surtees put the experience to good use the following year when, driving for Ferrari, he battled with Clark and then pulled away when the Lotus-Climax lapsed onto seven cylinders. Surtees won again for Ferrari in 1964, the year Honda curiously chose the Nürburgring to make their Grand Prix debut, and Clark once again had problems with the Lotus. The following year he had no such trouble and led every lap to score his first win at the Nürburgring in five attempts. In so doing, Clark clinched his second world championship in the best possible style.

It was a similar story in 1966 when Jack Brabham scored his fourth win in succession that year to take the title, the first time it had ever been done by a driver in a car bearing his own name. It had been raining throughout race day in 1967, but it was dry for the race itself and Denis Hulme gave the Brabham team another, though somewhat fortunate, win after Clark (Lotus) and Gurney (Eagle) had led 12 of the 15 laps before retiring.

The Eifel weather had acquired notoriety and in 1968 it reached a new level of unremitting bleakness. It rained almost non-stop through the weekend. Worse still, visibility was severely reduced in places by mist and the drivers did not know from one lap to the next where they might find rivers of water surging across the track. Nevertheless, the race went ahead, all 14 laps of it.

Jackie Stewart, hating every minute but reckoning the only answer was to get in front as soon as possible, passed two cars on the opening lap, took the lead, and was never seen again. The Tyrrell crossed the line four minutes ahead of Graham Hill's Lotus. By the time Jochen Rindt's third-place Brabham came into sight, Stewart was waiting on the rostrum.

Despite the obvious perils that day, no-one had been hurt. Indeed, that had generally been the way of things at a circuit which was waiting to trap the unwary at every corner. As a result, drivers treated the place with the respect it deserved but, in the late-Sixties, safety was the watchword. There was the beginning of unrest in 1969 when, during practice for the Formula 2 section of the Grand Prix, Gerhard Mitter was killed instantly following a steering failure. Only four cars were running at the finish of the race, Jacky Ickx demonstrating his knowledge and love of the Nürburgring by bringing his Brabham home almost a minute ahead of Stewart's Matra.

The threat of a boycott gathered strength, the drivers eventually refusing to race there until something was done about upgrading the circuit. As a result, the 1970 German Grand Prix was held at Hockenheim, a flat, banana-shaped track with a twisting section

through a stadium at one end. Originally, the circuit was a straightforward charge up and down straights which ran from the edge of the small town, into a woodland and back again. Hockenheim lies to the south of Mannheim and the growth of industry in this region led to the construction of motorways, one of which, joining Mannheim with Heilbronn, cut across the old circuit.

The Hockenheim-Ring company, in association with the local and national automobile clubs, spent £1 million on modernising and reshaping the track by using compensation money from the Autobahn department. The theory was that the motorway network would allow them to draw on the population centres of Frankfurt, Stuttgart (thus killing off the Solitude circuit), Karlsruhe, Heidelberg and Mainz. More importantly, they could dispatch the spectators with comparative ease, something which had never been the case on the narrow roads surrounding the Nürburgring (one report in 1963 stated that it took three hours to reach Altenahr, 15 miles away).

Racing resumed at Hockenheim in 1966, the truncated circuit now 4.2 miles long with the massive concrete stadium and pit/paddock area built close by the new motorway at its southern extremity. But the circuit really hit the headlines in April 1968

when Jim Clark lost his life there during a Formula 2 race. The safety drawbacks of the Nürburgring notwithstanding, it was with some reluctance that Grand Prix people made the trip to Hockenheim in August 1970. In fact, they were to be rewarded with a full house in the stadium (spectators were more or less excluded from the loop into the woods, making it an eerie place indeed) and the race proved to be a gripping contest between the Ferrari of Jacky Ickx and the Lotus of the eventual winner, Jochen Rindt.

On their return to the Nürburgring, drivers found it a more sanitised and, ironically, much faster, place with trees and hedges removed, rock faces demolished, barriers and catch fences installed, corners and bumps eased. Nonetheless, it was still the same length and much of the daunting challenge remained even though the race itself was reduced to a fiddling 12 laps. Jackie Stewart took less than 90 minutes to lead every lap in his Tyrrell. In 1972, Stewart was involved in a controversial incident as he tried, perhaps a touch unwisely, to take second place from Clay Regazzoni's Ferrari at an unlikely place on the last lap. Stewart lost out but Regazzoni made it a one-two for Ferrari, Jacky Ickx having controlled the race with ease from the first lap.

The Brabhams of Lauda and Watson sweep past a packed stadium at Hockenheim in 1978.

In 1973, however, it was Stewart's day and no mistake was made as he led home his team-mate François Cevert in majestic style for Tyrrell. It was to be Stewart's 27th and final Grand Prix win and he could not have rounded off his score at a better place. The fight to become his successor saw the rise of Niki Lauda, but the Austrian proved he had a lot to learn in 1974 when he went off while trying to snatch the lead shortly after the start. It left the way clear for his Ferrari team-mate Regazzoni to produce one of those mesmeric drives which were the product of Clay having a glorious 'on' day. Although Lauda won the championship the following year, he was out of luck at the 'Ring, a punctured front tyre costing him the lead after ten laps and allowing Carlos Reutemann, in a Brabham-Ford, to add his name to the illustrious list of winners.

Throughout this period, Lauda had been a strong critic of the Nürburgring, his main contention being that, if a driver had an accident, then the chances of receiving attention quickly were seriously reduced by the difficulties imposed by marshalling such a long circuit. He was to prove his point under near-tragic circumstances in 1976.

The race started on a wet but drying track. After the first lap most of the drivers, including Lauda, stopped to change to slicks. He rejoined in eighth place and, for some inexplicable reason, his Ferrari suddenly turned right as he came through a quick left-hander on the run towards Bergwerk. The Ferrari smashed through the ineffective catch fencing, hit the rock face and caught fire before spinning into the middle of the track, the incident being compounded by another car crashing into the wreckage. Had it not been for three drivers stopping to help a solitary marshal pull him from the inferno, Lauda would not have survived. The fact that he did has become a motor racing legend.

The race was stopped as a result, which was hard luck on James Hunt who had been one of the drivers to change tyres and was convinced he could win. At the restart, the McLaren driver carried on where he had

left off and scored one of his most impressive victories during his struggle to win the championship. But, although Lauda lived to fight another day, the accident meant the death of the Nürburgring Nordschleife as a Grand Prix circuit. It was back to Hockenheim for 1977.

Two chicanes had been added, one on each of the main straights, and they did little for the circuit's already suspect qualities. But that mattered little to Niki Lauda, on the trail of his second championship and just happy to be alive. Exactly a year after his terrible accident, and still driving for Ferrari, he walked off with the German Grand Prix; it was an emotional victory for the normally impassive Austrian.

Mario Andretti took his turn for Lotus in 1978 and, 12 months later, Alan Jones dominated in a similar fashion for Williams. Shortly before the Grand Prix in 1980, however, Hockenheim's reputation took another battering when Patrick Depailler was killed during a test session. A failure on his Alfa Romeo, just as he tackled the Ostkurve, the very fast right-hander linking the two straights at the top of the circuit, meant the result was more or less inevitable – particularly as the catch-fencing which might have saved him was rolled up behind the guardrail, waiting to be installed in time for the Grand Prix.

Whatever the whys and wherefores behind the loss of this popular little Frenchman, the Ostkurve was suddenly a dreadful place. The answer, as always on these occasions, was the eventual installation of a chicane, one that was even worse than the two already in place on the straights. The only corner worthy of the name had gone.

The race went to Jacques Laffite and Ligier, but only after the Renaults retired and the Williams of Alan Jones had suffered a puncture. Jones was in the running again in 1981 but, judging by his thunderous mood afterwards, it was clear that the reigning champion would have won but for a misfire. Nelson Piquet and Brabham gratefully accepted the gift of nine points.

The 1982 German Grand Prix ended Didier Pironi's career just as he seemed

poised to walk off with the championship. During a teeming wet practice session, Pironi had overtaken a Williams, not realising there was another car, Alain Prost's Renault, hidden in the spray. The Ferrari slammed into the Renault, became airborne, and when it landed with a terrible force on its nose, Pironi suffered appalling foot and ankle injuries. He never raced again, but, on the day, there was some consolation for the Ferrari team when Patrick Tambay scored an emotional victory.

Tambay was to experience a less savoury side of the sport the following year when his new team-mate, René Arnoux, went against a previously agreed arrangement and barged past on his way to give Ferrari their

The Grosser Preis von Europa had been held there in 1984, and for 1985 this was the site of the Grosser Preis von Deutschland, a shadow of its former self in every respect as Michele Alboreto won for Ferrari once two or three faster cars had fallen by the wayside. It was almost a relief in 1986 to return to Hockenheim, where Nelson Piquet scored a fine tactical victory for Williams-Honda by making two pit stops at precisely the right time. Piquet won again the following year, but luck entered into this win, his first of the season, after a commanding drive by Alain Prost had been brought to a premature end by a broken alternator belt four laps from home.

Prost could be forgiven for disliking Hockenheim and his feelings were not improved during the final three German Grands Prix of the decade. It rained throughout the race in 1987 and Prost was no match for the wet-weather brilliance of his new McLaren team-mate, Ayrton Senna. Twelve months later and the boot was on the other foot, Prost containing Senna during an epic battle. Then, with a handful of laps remaining, Prost's gearbox gave trouble and Senna was through. By 1990, Prost had moved on to Ferrari, neither his car nor anyone else's being a match for Senna's McLaren-Honda during the course of 45 laps.

That win was Senna's 24th, putting him on a par with Juan Manuel Fangio in the league table of statistical achievement. Comparisons are generally a fruitless exercise but it was tempting to wonder just how Senna would have rated on the old Nürburgring, a circuit which surely would have done for him what it did for Fangio's natural brilliance.

Senna has won at least as many German Grands Prix as the great Argentine driver but the significance of Ayrton's achievement would have been enhanced immeasurably by that giant of a circuit in the Eifel mountains. The German Grand Prix may have made the Nürburgring in certain aspects, but there is no doubt that the Nürburgring made the German Grand Prix a legendary race on many an occasion.

second win in succession at Hockenheim. In 1984, it was the turn of the McLaren team to dominate, Alain Prost fending off Niki Lauda as they sorted out the championship among themselves. Meanwhile, there had been activity at the Nürburgring.

With the North circuit out of favour (but still in use for national races and motor industry tests) and the South circuit long since abandoned, £18 million had been spent on the construction of a new Nürburgring. It was the model of efficiency and safety but it was totally without soul. No effort had been spared to make it clinically correct – including the moving of the natural terrain which would have given the place character – but the resulting constant-radius corners were not only boring to look at, they also prompted tedious racing. And the spectators stayed away in large numbers.

Previously, racing at the Nürburgring had been a major recreational and social event. Spectators, camping in the woods around the entire length of the old circuit, would be in holiday mood, barbecues and bouts of serious drinking running non-stop. Bockwurst and beer beneath the trees interrupted moments of passion beneath the canvas. Some of them even managed to see the cars occasionally. Now, all of that had gone. There were stands aplenty affording uninterrupted views of the new circuit, but for the most part they remained empty.

About to give the Germans what-for. Ireland in determined mood before the start of a thrilling drive at Solitude in 1961.

INNES IRELAND

Innes and Jim Clark in 1961: a relationship
which was unnecessarily strained by
circumstances at Lotus.

There is a picture, taken at Heathrow in early 1961, of Innes Ireland on his way to New Zealand. He is smartly turned out in brogues, a tweed three-piece suit and a deer-stalker. Across his shoulder is a rifle and in his hands a briefcase and a bottle of duty-free whisky. The only surprise is the briefcase.

Innes Ireland was not the business type. Indeed, he scarcely looked like a racing driver that day even though he was setting off for Australasia as the Number One with Team Lotus. His garb and paraphernalia said everything about Ireland's priorities in life; it was something to be enjoyed to the full. Racing was a bit of fun, a nice way to earn a living and, as it happened, he was about to embark on his most successful season ever.

At the end of it, he had not only won two non-championship races but also his first Grand Prix. Life could not have been better. Then, just as he seemed to have reached the crest of the wave, he was kicked out of Lotus without ceremony. Innes Ireland had many ups and downs while racing but this would be the most difficult to endure.

It was to be sadly typical of a colourful and spectacular career, one which started in the grand manner: Innes racing the same vintage 3-litre Bentley he also drove to work. The drawback with this arrangement was that he happened to be serving his apprenticeship with Rolls-Royce at the time and they did not fully approve of an employee arriving at the wheel of a rival product – particularly *that* rival.

The acquisition of the Bentley was a typical piece of Ireland good fortune. It had belonged to an old lady who lived in Kirkcudbrightshire, the Scottish county where the Ireland family settled not long after Innes was born on 12 June 1930. Innes had befriended the chauffeur and spent his days gazing wistfully at the Bentley. It says much for Ireland's great personal charm that, when the old lady died, she left him the car. Not only that but she had earlier given him a copy of Tim Birkin's book *Full Throttle*. One way or another, he had

acquired a serious taste for fast motoring.

The disquiet created by the presence of the Bentley at his place of work was eased somewhat when Ireland was called up for National Service and joined the King's Own Scottish Borderers. After receiving a commission, Innes was seconded to the Parachute Regiment and spent several months in Egypt thoroughly enjoying the comradeship. Ironically, the team spirit imbued at this stage would later contribute to his downfall in the hard-nosed and selfish world of Formula 1.

But this was some way off. In 1955, he came out of the Army and began racing the Bentley in club meetings. Acquisition of a garage business in Surrey allowed Innes to get his hands on a Riley for competiton purposes, but all along he had his heart set on a proper racing car: a Lotus Eleven. Eventually he managed to acquire one in kit form, Innes assembling it with loving care and finishing it half-way through the 1956 season.

The first test session at Goodwood was indicative of things to come. He spun off the track more than once and, on one occasion, he travelled so far into the corn that the only visible means of getting back to the track was by returning along the trail of flattened corn by which he had come. His exploits had not gone unnoticed and Innes was called before the assistant secretary of the British Automobile Racing Club, there to receive a severe dressing-down. Not that it made much difference. On his next outing at Goodwood a week later, he promptly spun off again.

Innes set himself a target of beating the works cars from Team Lotus and, throughout 1957, he did it often enough to be asked to race for the factory at home and abroad that same year. Moving away from the diet of airfield tracks, Innes was able to show his ability the following year, by using the Lotus sports car to beat a field of Ferraris at Clermont Ferrand, a proper circuit if ever there was one.

By the end of the season, more than satisfied with his progress, Innes went shooting with his brother in Scotland. While he was there, he received a call from Ecurie Ecosse

asking him to test one of their cars at Silverstone. At the time, Ecurie Ecosse was a top-flight British team, the sort of outfit a keen youngster would have given anything to drive for.

Ireland turned them down, hunting and the Highlands proving more attractive alternatives. Fortunately his brother, Allan, saw sense and persuaded Innes to change his mind, but the incident gives an adequate indication of Innes's love of life and a refusal to see the sport as the be-all and end-all.

Of course, once he sat himself in the Jaguar D-Type, he was captivated. It was a good day out and Ireland rounded it off with the team at the Saracen's Head in Towcester – and almost had them thrown out. As after-dinner entertainment, Innes made an explosive device consisting of matchheads and two cigar tubes. The resulting report terrified the landlady and scattered her highly strung poodles in all directions. She gathered them up, only to walk through the door with her coiffured brood just as the air was rent by a second salvo of bent cigar tubes and blazing match-heads. The ensuing mayhem required some mollification. And Innes still had his drive with Ecurie Ecosse as well as Team Lotus.

He raced with some distinction in elevated company in international sports car events and it occurred to Innes that he might be quick enough to make a decent showing in Fomula 1. That opportunity arose in 1959, the second season for Lotus in Grand Prix racing.

Cliff Allison had been head-hunted by Ferrari and the team drivers were Graham Hill and Pete Lovely. After the Monaco Grand Prix, however, Lovely opted to return to his business interests in Seattle; Colin Chapman decided that Ireland should fill the vacancy.

His first Grand Prix, the Dutch, brought a very encouraging fourth place, a result he repeated in the US Grand Prix later in the year. Between Formula 1 races Innes competed in sports cars and Formula 2 events, his progress notable for a marked improvement in the ability to stay on the road.

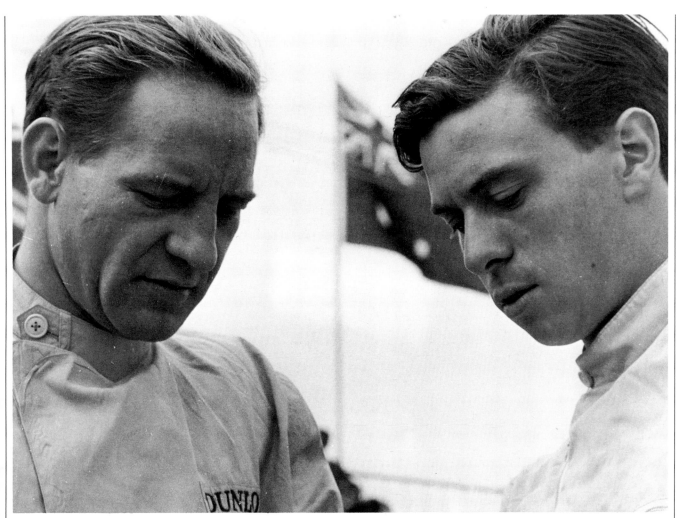

There was one major exception, however.

During a Formula 2 race at Rouen, his Lotus suffered total brake failure on the fast approach to a sharp left-hander. Ahead lay banking fashioned like a ramp. Ireland hit it head-on and took off, clearing a parked car and careering into trees on the edge of a ravine. The branches caught the Lotus and flicked it into the chasm, where it cartwheeled 150 feet to the bottom, bouncing from tree to tree as it went. Word went out that a car had left the road at a dangerous point and, assuming the worst, the organisers dispatched an ambulance. When it arrived, the medical crew peered over the edge, failed to see the distant wreckage and drove off. Miraculously, Ireland was not only alive but also able to climb to the top of the ravine and summon assistance.

The reliability of the Lotus – any Lotus – was questionable in those days and Ireland had his fair share of exasperating moments. During the French Grand Prix, the right-front suspension broke. In Portugal, as he walked to his car on the grid, Innes noticed a split in the main chassis tube which carried the front suspension. It did little for his

confidence to watch the mechanics weld the fracture moments before he was about to start a 209-mile race.

In general, Ireland was pleased with his driving and a successful integration into the world of Formula 1. As a junior, he felt it best not to complain excessively about the worrying number of mechanical failures. At least the team was making progress and he was more than happy to accept the role of Number One driver when Hill left to join BRM in 1960.

It was to be a traumatic and difficult year even though it started on a high note, Innes winning at Oulton Park and Goodwood. In fact, that was part of the trouble. Innes had at his disposal the first rear-engined Lotus, the 18. It handled much better than the Cooper raced by Moss. When Innes beat Stirling twice in succession, the press went beserk, hailing Ireland as the wonder boy and failing to see the facts behind the story.

Innes was distinctly embarrassed since he considered Moss to be in a different league; nonetheless, for a young driver approaching 30, the publicity was useful. However, once the Grand Prix season

proper got into its stride, Ireland found he had more serious problems to deal with. It all came to a head at Spa-Francorchamps.

The mechanical failures on his cars had begun to cause more than passing concern and, when a driver of Moss's calibre then crashed his Lotus, Ireland was certain something had broken. Sure enough, a rear hub failure was diagnosed and, when the three works cars were examined, the similar hubs on two of them were found to be in a sorry state. Then another Lotus, Innes's former car now driven by Michael Taylor, crashed with steering failure. It did little for anyone's confidence.

All of that was overshadowed by events in the race. Chris Bristow was killed when he lost control of his Cooper and, not long after, Alan Stacey went missing in the works Lotus. Ireland had retired and, knowing his team-mate had not intended to take any chances in his first race at Spa-Francorchamps, felt sure that Stacey had either broken down or suffered a minor accident. When he saw an ambulance arrive in the paddock, Innes went to investigate. He was totally unprepared to discover that his close friend was dead. It had been a freak accident, a bird hitting Stacey full in the face. Poor Innes was inconsolable.

Le Mans was next and, ironically, Michael Taylor had been down to share a Lotus Elite with Ireland. After Taylor's crash, Alan Stacey had agreed to take over. So now there was a third co-driver, Jonathan Sieff. When the young Englishman suffered a terrible accident during night practice, and Innes saw the horrifying extent of his injuries when he visited the hospital, the combination of circumstances over the previous few weeks became unbearable.

The team understood perfectly when he chose to withdraw and, unable to sleep that night, Innes threw his belongings into a borrowed car and drove back to his home in Wales. His mind was reeling, yet he knew that he would never give up racing. All he needed was room to breathe, and a reunion with his family and friends on the Welsh coast did the trick.

His spirits were lifted by one or two good performances before the inevitable mechanical failures took their toll. Even so, he finished his first season fourth in the championship, just one point behind Moss. By the time he was ready to set off from Heathrow for that Australasian tour at the beginning of 1961, he was thinking mainly of the promise which lay ahead: the hunting, the parties and the racing ... probably in that order.

But there was to be an additional bonus on this trip. Innes was introduced to the pleasures of flying. Not one to do things by half-measures, Ireland moved out of his Sydney hotel and lived at the airfield for 16 days. At the end of an intense period of flying and cramming, he won his licence. Now he was about to be let loose on the skies as well.

On his return, he bought himself a Miles Messenger (in typical Innes style, it belonged to a finance company, although he was unaware of that). He managed to amaze a spectating Colin Chapman – himself no angel when it came to aeronautical manoeuvres – by landing sideways and in the

wrong direction at Snetterton and then disappearing through a hedge. Innes taxied through the hole he had just made and calmly parked as though this was his normal method of arrival. Indeed, in those pioneering days of Ireland's airborne travels, it undoubtedly was.

The aircraft's purpose was to provide Innes with a more convenient means of reaching the European races. Ironically, he had to make the return journey from the first race at Monaco by commercial airliner since the Messenger could not accommodate the owner with his leg fully encased in plaster. He had crashed during practice and, as ever, it had been a spectacular affair.

Lotus had fitted one car with a ZF gearbox which had a reverse shift pattern to normal. This took some getting used to and, in truth, Monaco was not the ideal place to try it out. Innes having also used the car with the standard gearbox, eventually felt he had the hang of the ZF; going for a quick lap, he snicked the lever from third to fourth – and found second. The instant he realised what he had done, the rear wheels locked and that was that. This occurred in the tunnel (much shorter then than it is now) and Ireland emerged on his own, bouncing down the track, the Lotus cavorting after him in several pieces after flinging itself at the wall.

Apart from bruising and nasty gashes, the main injury was a torn artery in his left leg. After five weeks and many hectic nights in St Thomas's Hospital with his motor racing mates, plus an unannounced visit by a photographer from the *Daily Express's* William Hickey column, Ireland was back at the wheel, none the worse for wear.

To prove it, he won a non-championship race at Zeltweg in Austria and followed that with a brilliant victory at Solitude, a wonderful road course in the foothills outside Stuttgart. This, of course, was on the doorstep of Porsche System Engineering and a vast crowd turned up to see the local firm wipe the floor with the opposition. The pressure was on Jo Bonnier and Dan Gurney to perform, and the only thorn in their side turned out to be I. Ireland. This trio broke away from the rest and a mighty bat-

tle ensued. During the course of it, Innes worked out that if he could lead into the final series of fast curves, the Porsches would be unable to overtake.

At the start of the last lap they rushed by, nose-to-tail, the Lotus sandwiched between the two German cars, prompting Chapman to turn to his mechanics and utter the classic remark: "Well, we'll either win this race or we shall never see Ireland again."

It was close to the truth. Innes tried to make his move at the end of the back straight but Bonnier would have none of it. Undaunted, Ireland was forced to do most of his braking on the grass and took the lead as they went into the final curves. He won by a tenth of a second and, just for good measure, paid Bonnier back by leaving the minimum of room as the Swede made a vain attempt to draw alongside at the flag. The dour Bonnier was not best pleased.

Ireland's mood was far from heavy and the celebration raged into the night. It would have continued longer had the hotel manager not seen the danger signs and closed the bar prematurely. On their way to his room to consume a bottle of wine, Ireland and a friend fell into the lift and, by dint of pressing all the buttons, emerged on the top floor – which was still under construction and open to the night air.

When the manager unwisely attempted to remove them, an altercation took place which finished when Ireland and his mate departed, letting off fire crackers as they went. Unfortunately, this story gained something in the telling, the news agencies reporting that the British driver had been firing a pistol from the hotel roof. It was enough to have him banned from the German Grand Prix two weeks later.

Although the organisers relented, Innes probably wished they had stood their ground. About 15 minutes into the race, his car caught fire. Comprehensively. Once Ireland had evacuated the cockpit and extinguished his blazing overalls, he returned to watch helplessly as the Lotus was burned to a cinder.

As a result, Ireland had a new car for the Italian Grand Prix, which he sportingly

offered to Moss, since Stirling and the Rob Walker team were in with a chance of the championship and yet Moss's car was patently slower than Ireland's latest example. Stirling accepted but to no avail; a hub bearing collapsed and it was no consolation to learn that his original car had also fallen apart in Ireland's hands. Nonetheless, this exemplified Innes's attitude, a sporting code which was rapidly and regrettably being abandoned. Indeed, he was appalled when Lotus's trade sponsor Esso complained of assistance being rendered to a team supported by BP.

Reliability remained a far-off goal, a fact of which Innes was reminded during practice for the US Grand Prix when a steering failure sent him into the undergrowth. But the repaired car held together long enough to give Innes his first – and Team Lotus's first – Grand Prix win. Everyone was delighted and full of hope for 1962. It seemed they had finally turned the corner.

Innes flew back to Europe and amused himself by visiting the London Motor Show at Earl's Court. While he was there he learned, through a third party, that something was amiss and he really ought to talk to Chapman. Looking ill-at-ease, Chapman informed Ireland that his services would no longer be required. No reason was given.

Devoid of the power of speech, Innes walked away and drove back to Wales to cogitate. There had been no warning whatsoever. It was a complete shock.

Ireland had put up with a lot. During three seasons, he had suffered the continual uncertainty of cars which might fail under him; he had endured broken suspension, wheels falling off, brake and steering failures; and now, just as the pay-off seemed imminent, he had been thrown out on his ear.

He felt great bitterness towards Chapman and not a little animosity towards Jim Clark, the new light in Colin's eyes and obviously a man of the future; a man who, Ireland would agree, was more dedicated than he. But why had Chapman not had the guts to say so? That was what irked Ireland. Matters were made worse when he travelled to the Lotus headquarters to finalise arrangements for an agreed trip to South Africa only to find that Chapman had somehow forgotten to tell Ireland he would not be required for that either.

Ireland's sagging morale was given a boost when he received an offer from the British Racing Partnership to drive for their UDT-sponsored team. On the rebound, as it were, he agreed. The next day, he had a call from BRM asking him to join Graham

Hill for 1962. Clearly this was a better offer, but, since he had given his verbal agreement to BRP, Ireland felt duty-bound to honour it. Such commendable ethics would be laughed out of the paddock today. Indeed, in the Nineties not even a signed contract is beyond being breached.

At least the deal with BRP allowed Innes to compete as well in one or two wonderful Ferrari GT cars, but for Formula 1 it was back to the Lotus chassis and a step behind the works cars to boot. True to form, his first Grand Prix for BRP in Holland ended in a large accident when the brakes mysteriously locked, while in Monaco he was bundled onto a wall at the first corner. When he got going again, the fumes from leaking fuel in the cockpit almost asphyxiated him.

In the midst of all this there occurred something most strange. Out of the blue Ireland received a call from Ferrari. Would he care to drive one of their cars in the International Trophy? What a question. Innes went to the factory, was royally received, measured for the cockpit, had lunch with Enzo and flew home. The car, with a squad of mechanics, duly arrived at Silverstone where Ireland, struggling with a handling problem, nevertheless finished fourth. He was asked to report on the car, which he did. And that was the end of the matter. It

was suggested that this, in fact, was the Ferrari ear-marked for Stirling Moss until he rowed himself out of racing at Goodwood the previous Easter. But no-one, least of all Innes, really knew.

On the Grand Prix front a succession of failures contributed to a solitary championship point at the end of the year. While racing for the Rosebud sports car team in the United States, he was arrested once or twice for speeding and he had a hand in the bet which said a car's headlights would not work under water. The hirer of the rental car promptly drove it into the hotel swimming pool – where it sank to the bottom, the headlights blazing.

Hertz's motto said that it would collect its cars from anywhere, but was not amused at first. Then the company saw the promotional value of the incident and the car was removed in a thunder of publicity. The following year, Ireland returned to the hotel in Monterey to find that the management had placed a 'No Parking' sign at the bottom of the pool ...

He continued with BRP in 1963, winning a non-championship race at Goodwood in a BRM-engined Lotus 24. BRP eventually produced their own chassis, but various problems forced him frequently to revert to the Lotus chassis. He almost won a non-championship race at Zeltweg with this car until in the final laps the engine went off song. At the prize-giving that night, Ireland received a 'Hard Luck' trophy: a broken bolt embossed on a metal plate. In many ways it summed up his fortunes, not just in Austria, but around the world, and, anyway, Innes had the consolation that racing was still *fun*.

Going back to his hotel that night, Ireland discovered someone, presumably a colleague, larking about and following closely as they drove along. Assuming this person knew where he was staying, Ireland speeded up and then swung without much warning into the narrow entrance of his hotel. The pursuing driver did not know about this arrangement. The noise of the subsequent collision woke the neighbourhood, Ireland's VW careering into a parked

E-Type which, in turn, was shoved into a Porsche. The E-Type was brand new, with only 800 kilometres on the clock. Innes Ireland was certainly never a man to do things by halves.

Indeed, at the end of the year, he had a massive accident at Seattle, the Rosebud Racing Lotus flying off the road and colliding with a Mercedes-Benz which someone had rather thoughtlessly left parked by the side of the track. Considering the force of the impact, he was fortunate to get away with nothing more than a dislocated hip. In fact, it was so severely dislocated that the doctors could not understand why his legs had not been shattered. Ireland also had to suffer bravely because he had discovered he was allergic to pain-killers.

He was fit and ready for the start of the 1964 season. A win at Snetterton – the first victory for the BRP-BRM – augured well, but then disaster seemed to heap upon disaster. A peculiar handling problem on this latest BRP sent him into a spin at Abbey Curve at Silverstone and the brand-new car was wrecked against the bank. Then he moved on to Monte Carlo, wrote off a borrowed Renault on the road outside Nice airport and crashed the team's Lotus at the chicane when a rear brake locked. In the space of a few days, Ireland had written off two-thirds of the team's equipment and the thought depressed him mightily.

The rest of the season was plagued by BRM engines which were, in Innes's opinion, not up to scratch, and a continuation of the handling problem which was not cured until later in the year. Two fifth places were his best results and Ireland was not unduly surprised when a failure to break into the closed-shop agreement made between the leading constructors and the race organisers helped BRP make their decision to call it a day.

Ireland felt he had had enough anyway and decided to retire. However, a call from Tim Parnell persuaded him to spend 1965 at the wheel of one of his Lotus-BRMs. While the year was not particularly successful, Innes found it enjoyable and filled out much of his spare time successfully cam-

paigning sports and GT cars. In 1966, he competed in just two Grands Prix, driving a 2-litre BRM for Bernard White in the USA and Mexico. Then, finally, he hung up the familiar white helmet with the chequered band.

Surprisingly, Ireland turned to journalism and became sports editor at *Autocar*. Surprisingly, because he seemed the last person capable of conforming to the strict discipline required. That reservation, to the frequent distress of his Editor, turned out to be justified, but his writing was superb.

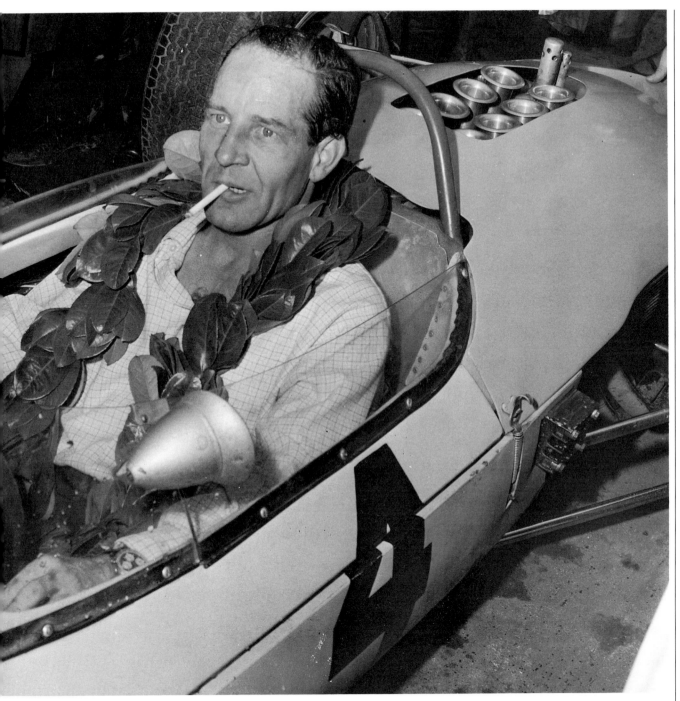

There was none finer than his obituary of Jim Clark.

Ireland had been covering a race at Brands Hatch that day and, on hearing the news, he went straight home and more or less poured out his soul in print. Not only did he pay genuine and fulsome tribute to a fellow Scot, he also made amends for the animosity which had so regrettably arisen between the two drivers following Innes's unfortunate departure from Lotus. He had made his peace in the most moving manner.

From writing he turned to fishing, running a trawler out of Kirkcudbright harbour until that project fell on hard times. Then it was back to writing and an authoritative post as Grand Prix reporter with *Road & Track* in America.

Although he is too much of a gentleman to say so, it is clear that the money-grabbing methods of the modern Grand Prix star leave him cold. He raced purely for enjoyment. Certainly, he also raced to excess and many of the problems he encountered were of his own making. But a high number were

due to mechanical failures which simply would not be tolerated today.

For Ireland the competition and the camaraderie were the thing. The team came first. Unfortunately, the team let him down at a time when the emphasis was beginning to switch to the individual and material gain. The truth is that Innes Ireland's personality and style belonged to the previous decade, but that did not prevent him from leading life, as he found it, to the limit. Very few Grand Prix winners can make such a wholesome claim.

The US Grand Prix

The Vanderbilt Cup at the Roosevelt Raceway tempted the Europeans back in 1937 for the self-proclaimed 'World's Richest Race'. Nuvolari (Alfa Romeo), Rosemeyer (Auto Union) and Caracciola (Mercedes-Benz) prepare for the start, Rosemeyer winning after a thrilling struggle between the two German teams.

Mechanical failures were not new to Innes Ireland but a snapped steering arm at Watkins Glen in 1961 certainly got his attention. He was doing at least 145 mph at the time and preparing himself for the fast right-hander at the end of the main straight. He never made the corner, the Lotus ploughing into the undergrowth, Ireland emerging with nothing more than a collection of bruises and another dinner party tale.

The car, though, was not so healthy; again, not an unusual state of affairs at this time for the beleaguered Lotus mechanics. They managed, as Ireland put it so matter-of-factly, 'to iron out most of the kinks overnight'. One problem which they could not cure, however, was a dent in the petrol tank. Not only were they unable to fix it, they left the tank in the car for the race. Such were the limitations in 1961 of spare parts and the standard of preparation. Ireland, meanwhile, was just happy to be fit enough to take part in the United States Grand Prix, one of the richest races on the calendar.

He knew he could do well, what with

Jack Brabham running a Coventry-Climax V8 which was still in the early stages of development and Ferrari, having wrapped up the championship, withdrawing their entry for Phil Hill. The main competition would come from Stirling Moss (who chose not to race the Climax V8 in favour of the trusty four-cylinder in his Rob Walker Lotus), the BRMs of Graham Hill and Tony Brooks, Bruce McLaren's Cooper-Climax and the Lotus of Ireland's team-mate Jim Clark.

The race developed into a scrap between Moss and Brabham, but after 58 laps they were both out with engine-related problems. That left Ireland with a fairly comfortable lead as he headed towards his first Grand Prix win. It would also be the first victory in a championship race for Team Lotus.

Then, to his horror, Innes noticed the fuel pressure sinking rapidly. The dent in the fuel tank meant the capacity had been reduced by a gallon or so. Here was Ireland on the brink of a cherished ambition – and about to run out of fuel. He eased off but the pit signals were warning him of an impressive charge by Roy Salvadori in a Cooper. Luckily for Ireland, Salvadori's Climax blew up. Now it was simply a matter of luck.

The Lotus kept going. With the pressure gauge reading zero, Ireland had no idea where the fuel was coming from. But the Climax continued its flat drone and he was still running when the lavender-suited figure of Tex Hopkins leapt into the air with the chequered flag.

Lotus were thrilled – which was more than could be said for Ireland 16 days later when he learned that he had been fired – and the people of Watkins Glen in New York State were equally delighted with the success of their first Grand Prix.

Formula 1 was new to the region – indeed, to North America as a whole since this was but the third running of the US Grand Prix. Historians were able to point out, though, that a country which was perceived to be solely the land of Indianapolis and oval racing could justifiably claim to have one of the oldest national Grands Prix in the world.

It is true. The French had run the first-ever Grand Prix a few months before in 1906, but after such a grand beginning, the American race lost its way. A chequered and inconsistent history has weakened any claim that the US Grand Prix is among the classics. Yet, in its time, there have been both superb and controversial races, starting with the very first Grand Prix in 1906.

W. K. Vanderbilt, a wealthy enthusiast, had founded his own series. Known as the Vanderbilt Cup, the races were run on a 28-mile course on Long Island, near New York City. By and large, the racing was close, but the organisation left much to be desired. Unruly spectators were allowed to wander at will and there appeared to be equally scant regard for the safety of competitors. In one instance, a Mercedes narrowly missed a train as the two attempted to make use of the open Oyster Bay level crossing at the same moment.

The Europeans were not impressed and they abandoned American road racing. In an effort to tempt them back, a 'Grand Prize' was created in Savannah, Georgia. According to contemporary accounts, this was a magnificent circuit: smooth roads, a variety of bends, adequate medical facilities and beautiful scenery. There was also the startling sight of convict labour working hard to finish the roads in time for the first race in 1910.

The Americans succeeded in attracting entries from Fiat, Benz, Renault and Itala, driven by the great names of the day: de Palma, Nazzaro, Wagner, Hemery and Szisz. Run over 24 laps of the 17.3-mile circuit, this was an epic race. It took almost six hours but, in the end, the Benz of David Bruce-Brown won from the similar car of Victor Hemery by 1.42 *seconds*. There had been incidents aplenty, but nothing serious enough to damage the reputation of the 'American Grand Prize'.

Bruce-Brown won more easily in 1911, but this talented American was to lose his life while testing for the Grand Prize in 1912. A tyre burst on his massive Fiat and both Bruce-Brown and his mechanic were killed. This cast a pall over the race – won by Bragg's Fiat – and it coincidentally marked the beginning of a decline in road racing in the United States.

The Indianapolis Motor Speedway had been opened in 1911 and, with the subsequent popularity of oval racing, the Grand Prize was moved to less attractive and less successful venues on the West Coast. The intervention of the First World War banished all competition for a time, and road racing, although held on a local basis, never truly recovered on an international scale despite attempts to revive the Vanderbilt Cup in 1936.

The Roosevelt Raceway was laid out at Mineola on Long Island, but it was found to be as inadequate as the organisation. A winning margin of no less than 11 minutes for the Alfa Romeo of Tazio Nuvolari did not help, yet such had been the high level of hospitality that the Europeans were tempted back in 1937. Bernd Rosemeyer won for Auto Union. The impressive improvements were not enough, however, and the Vanderbilt Cup faded as an international event. It was not until the 1950s that the Europeans returned, thanks largely to the efforts of Alec Ulmann, a racing enthusiast involved in the aviation business.

In his capacity as manager for the Briggs Cunningham team, Ulmann had visited Le Mans in 1950 and immediately saw the need for a world-class endurance race in the United States. It so happened that he was charged with finding space for surplus war-time aircraft and his search took him to Hendrick Field, previously a base for B-17 bombers near Sebring in Florida. One look at the pair of two-mile runways and attendant buildings convinced Ulmann this would be the ideal place for a long-distance sports car race.

With commendable speed he had a local event organised for later in the year. The race suffered from the usual teething problems and semi-ridiculous scenes, such as the moment of confusion during the Le Mans-type start. Competitors were positioned opposite their cars, but one driver, John Bentley, was making final adjustments and failed to notice the race was about to start. Realising his error, he sprinted towards his position just as the starter dropped the flag and Bentley thus met his

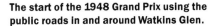
The start of the 1948 Grand Prix using the public roads in and around Watkins Glen.

rivals running in the opposite direction.

In 1952 the prizes were presented from the tailboard of a lorry which had been backed into the paddock, but the Sebring 12 Hours gained serious credibility the following year when the Aston Martin team entered and thus opened the door for further participation by the European teams. Ulmann was intent primarily on establishing his race as a round of the World Sportscar Championship, but he liked the idea of promoting a World Championship Grand Prix so much that he confirmed his intentions at the prize-giving for the 1959 12-hour race. He mentioned October of the same year as the date granted by the CSI, the world governing body of motor sports. He had less than seven months to prepare.

The news of a Grand Prix of the United States was greeted with enthusiasm in Florida, but certainly not in Europe. The CSI had ignored a rule stating that a race organiser must first run a non-championship Grand Prix to prove himself; Sebring had been granted an exemption on the grounds of its sports car activities. There was much tutting in the British journals. Criticism was also levelled at the state of the airfield track with its bumpy runways. Moreover, the addition of a US Grand Prix to the calendar highlighted another contentious issue: the inclusion of the Indianapolis 500 in the world championship.

No-one fully understood why the Indy 500 had been a part of the series since its inception in 1950. The event carried great prestige but it bore no relation whatsoever to Grand Prix racing and the appearance of names such as Lee Wallard and Bob Sweikert on a one-off basis merely served to confuse the statistics. The practice would stop after the 1960 Indy 500.

But in 1959 two races in North America counted towards the title. As luck would have it, the Sebring event, being the final round, would settle the championship.

It was a three-way fight between Stirling Moss (Rob Walker Cooper-Climax), Tony Brooks (Ferrari) and Jack Brabham (works Cooper-Climax). Moss had covered the 5.2 miles faster than anyone else – indeed, 20

seconds quicker than the lap record which he had established some months before at the wheel of an Aston Martin. More than that, Moss was 44 seconds faster than the slowest man on the grid, Rodger Ward, the Indianapolis winner bravely attempting to run a USAC Midget dirt car.

The main interest concerned the opposite end of the grid, all three championship contenders finding a place on the front row. But what should have been a happy coincidence for the organisers turned ugly shortly before the start when Harry Schell, credited with 11th-fastest time in his BRM, felt he should have been third. The Franco-American discovered that the officials had indeed recorded a solitary lap some six seconds faster than the time given, but, disbelieving the evidence of their watches, the time-keepers had refused to recognise such an amazing performance. Gregor Grant, reporting for *Autosport*, describes what happened next.

'There was plenty of excitement when Schell found himself relegated to row four. He protested vociferously that he had done 3m 5.2 secs and he was going to get his rightful place on the front row. After much bickering, the time keepers admitted their error. Harry pushed his car jubilantly alongside Brabham's, and Brooks was moved back.

'The fun then started again and as the girls of the Sebring band and the majorettes tried to get into line, they were swept aside by an angry bunch of gesticulating Italians, with Tavoni [the team manager] almost doing his nut. Arguments raged to and fro with Alec Ulmann and others doing their best to restore order. It looked exactly like a free-fight in a Glasgow dockside pub – and even noisier. Then the majorettes started up the band and the girls stamped their feet. As if by magic, the jostling and shoving ceased, although Tavoni and Co. shuffled off with black looks for Harry Schell, and both Moss and Brabham were trying unsuccessfully to keep their faces straight.'

Schell was pleased for reasons which went beyond the obvious. He later admitted to

The aviating Tex Hopkins flags home
Fittipaldi's winning Lotus at Watkins
Glen in 1970.

Innes Ireland that he had found a short-cut on the far side of the track. By using a service road, he could cut a mile or more from the circuit length and, with careful timing, he could rejoin and cross the line with the super-fast time which was just about plausible. Had he not hung about but carried on, his lap time would have been so outrageous that the organisers would have smelled a rat. As it was, a time a fraction slower than Stirling Moss stretched the bounds of credibility. But he got away with it.

This amusing farrago had its serious side since the championship was at stake and, significantly, the switching of places was to affect the outcome of Brooks's race. On the opening lap he was struck from behind by his team-mate, Wolfgang von Trips, and the subsequent pit stop cost Brooks valuable time. Shortly afterwards Moss disappeared with broken transmission, leaving Brabham untroubled at the front and *en route* to the title.

Then, on the last lap, Brabham ran out of fuel, leaving his young team-mate, Bruce McLaren, to score his first Grand Prix victory. Jack, meanwhile, pushed his car across the line to finish fourth and take his first championship.

It had been as dramatic a race as Sebring could have wished for, but afterwards there were many complaints about the quality of the circuit and aspects of the organisation. The latter came in for particular criticism from the likeable Gregor Grant, although some of this may have been provoked by the organiser's gaff in failing to invite the *Autosport* editor, an accomplished socialite, to the eve-of-race press party. In any event, it was the first and only time the US Grand Prix visited Sebring.

There was much relief when, 12 months later, the Formula 1 teams arrived at Riverside and found it an altogether more suitable venue. Situated on the edge of the desert, some 50 miles east of Los Angeles, the 3.27-mile track had been completed in 1957. A long straight, also used for drag racing, formed the mainstay of a variety of layouts. While Riverside possessed more smog and dust than luxurious ambience,

it proved to be a challenging GP circuit.

The presence of Grand Prix stars, however, was not enough to lure the Californians to the final race of the 2.5-litre era. The organisers had hoped for a repeat of the 80,000 turn-out for a sports car race the previous month, but only a third of that number came to watch Jack Brabham take the lead at the start of 75 laps. After four of them, the Cooper was in the pits with an engine fire, leaving Stirling Moss to win easily in the Rob Walker Lotus-Climax.

Innes Ireland finished second, an excellent result which earned the Lotus driver $5,000, by far and away his biggest payday of the season even though he was contractually obliged to give a percentage of it to the team. Furthermore, Innes had also agreed to Chapman's request that, for this race, all three Lotus drivers – Ireland, Surtees and Clark – should share any prize money regardless of their finishing positions, this being Chapman's way of preventing his drivers from racing each other to the detriment of the sometimes frail machinery. Ireland was miffed at having to hand over his hard-earned cash, particularly as Surtees had spun and Clark had instantly rammed his team-mate.

Innes being Innes, he put all of that to the back of his mind at an end-of-season party thrown by Lance Reventlow, Woolworth heir and owner of the Scarab team, which was celebrating a rare finish, in 10th place, for Chuck Daigh in the race.

Reventlow had a swimming pool which was half in and half out of his Beverly Hills home and, during the course of the soirée, guests indoors were treated to the sight of Ireland emerging from the water clad only in his underpants. He was soon joined by other revellers who did not bother to reach the same state of undress. On the question of finance, there was no doubt about the prize money at Watkins Glen 12 months later when Ireland scored his first Grand Prix win. The question of his future contract, of course, was another matter entirely.

Watkins Glen, in fact, became the race's happy home for 19 years. Located at the

southern end of Lake Seneca in the Finger Lake region, the small town knew all about motor sport. The first post-war US road race had been held there, using 6.6 miles of streets and public highways. A devious course it was too, reports speaking of the mountain descent which involved a plunging, never-ending right-hander which brought you sharply into a 90-degree left close by the drug-store in the town.

Popular it may have been, but the race ran into trouble when, two years in succession, cars left the road and caused fatalities. Future races were out of the question, but by this time members of the Chamber of Commerce had become racing enthusiasts and they could see the benefits of having visitors in the area. The Wakins Glen Grand Prix Corporation was formed and charged with finding a new venue. A 4.6-mile course, some distance from the town, was used in 1953 but this was seen as nothing more than a stop-gap measure.

When it became clear that the US Grand Prix was looking for a base, following financial problems at Sebring and the reluctance of the Californians at Riverside to accept the controlling influence of Ulmann and other 'Easterners', the people of Watkins Glen went to work.

In 1956 a 2.3-mile track had been constructed as a community project in the rolling countryside above the town. Since the site was only 200 miles north-west of Manhattan, it was reasoned that there were adequate population centres to draw from if the race could be seen as a success. And the friendly locals went out of their way to ensure it was just that.

The Formula 1 teams gladly returned in 1962, Jim Clark and Graham Hill providing a spirited battle throughout most of the 100 laps, victory going to Clark's Lotus by 9.2 seconds. The weather had not been brilliant but that had always been the risk of an October date in upstate New York. In any case, the promoters were pleased and further money was invested for 1963.

The mechanics were delighted to find a technical centre, in the form of a large prefabricated shed which housed all the teams

(with the exception of Ferrari who chose, as ever, to go elsewhere). The Ford Motor Company, seeing the promotional value of the 1963 Grand Prix, placed Thunderbirds and Galaxies at the disposal of the teams and arranged to launch the Mustang II at the circuit.

Watkins Glen was rapidly becoming a popular venue and there was much to satisfy Gregor Grant, the *Autosport* editor noting with pleasure that New York State champagne had been the staple refreshment at one particular reception. Another, at the house of promoter Cameron Argetsinger, won Grant's approval because admission by ticket had held the gate-crashers at bay. On such important issues do races rise and fall from grace.

The crowd liked it too: 60,000 spectators, many from across the Canadian border to the north, had watched Graham Hill lead home a one-two for BRM. And, at the end of it, in another rare and clever piece of thinking, the organisers thoughtfully distributed a lap chart, personally signed by the chief time-keeper, to members of the press. There was no doubt, then, that there would be a further Grand Prix in 1964.

A win for Graham Hill's BRM, with John Surtees finishing second for Ferrari, put the championship in a delicately poised position for the final round which followed three weeks later in Mexico City. There had been a high number of retirements, Innes Ireland opening the list when the gear lever on his BRP-BRM snapped off at the roots. Innes was not best pleased when he discovered that it was the same lever which had broken some time before and had simply been welded together again, supposedly as a temporary measure.

A dose of 'flu ruined Ireland's race at Watkins Glen in 1965 and he retired his Parnell-entered Lotus-BRM after a handful of laps. Graham Hill won for the third year in succession, prompting Louis Stanley and BRM to hold a grand victory dinner in the Glen Motor Inn down by Lake Seneca that night. Naturally, Gregor Grant was present and devoted a paragraph of his report to naming the guests. Well, the important ones anyway.

Sadly, the 1966 race was to be Innes Ireland's penultimate Grand Prix and he lost sixth place when the battery went flat on his privately entered BRM with just over ten laps to go. The result, a win for Jim Clark, was something of a surprise since Lotus had

elected to race their car with the complicated and potentially unreliable BRM H-16 engine. Indeed, a similar engine had blown up during practice, necessitating an overnight change by the Lotus mechanics in the 'Kendall Technical Center'. And when Clark rolled onto the front row of the grid alongside Jack Brabham, there was so much oil dripping from the BRM engine that the mechanics felt sure the Lotus would be forcibly removed before the race had even started. There seemed little chance of Clark lasting the distance, never mind winning. Jack Brabham (Brabham-Repco) and Lorenzo Bandini (Ferrari) took turns at leading until engine failures struck them both, after which Clark was free to score his only win of the season.

By 1967, of course, Clark had at his disposal the Lotus 49 with the Ford-Cosworth DFV. Such had been the superiority of this combination that Ford, anxious for a good showing in the United States and keen not to have Clark and his team-mate Graham Hill race each other to destruction, asked for tactics to come into play. On the toss of a coin it was agreed that Hill should win with Clark following into second place.

Everything appeared to be going to plan until Hill had clutch trouble and Clark, under pressure from Amon's Ferrari, had to overtake. When Amon retired, Clark was unsure what to do since he had a massive lead over Hill's hobbled car. Then, with a few laps remaining, a bolt dropped out of the rear suspension on Clark's car and, for a terrible moment, it seemed that neither Lotus might finish. But Clark, with his right-rear wheel canted at a drunken angle, got to see the aviating Tex Hopkins in his now traditional lavender suit.

Jackie Stewart led from start to finish in his Matra-Ford in 1968 but the meeting, for the locals at least, was made memorable by Mario Andretti placing his Lotus on pole position for the American's first Grand Prix. Andretti retired with clutch trouble, but, one way or another, Lotus were to have a major say at Watkins Glen in the following two years.

Jochen Rindt won his first Grand Prix at 'the Glen' in the 1969 race, which also saw Graham Hill suffer a nasty accident in Rob Walker's privately entered Lotus. In 1970 victory went to Emerson Fittipaldi in only his fourth Grand Prix. This was a poignant result for Lotus since it meant that Rindt, who had been killed at Monza a month before, became the first posthumous world champion. As 24-year-old Fittipaldi stood on the rostrum, a small black banner was raised from somewhere deep in the crowd with the simple legend 'Jochen Lives'.

The Grand Prix was now an accepted part of the North American social calendar, so much so that the organisers were able to claim the largest crowd in the race's history (although no figures were actually given) turned out in 1971. Happily, the circuit could cope because a new loop had been added to increase the length from 2.3 to 3.37 miles. The pits and paddock had been moved to a new site before what had previously been the final corner and the circuit was lined with pale-blue armco for most of its length.

During the course of the building work, and thanks to years of neglect, a swamp had developed in the depths of one of the public enclosures. Known locally as 'the Bog', this area became a cult centre where strangers feared to tread, even in daylight. At night, every long-haired spook in the county seemed to appear from the undergrowth and the hysteria would build in proportion to the consumption of substances with no brand names. Come race morning and the Bog would have devoured at least one car. As the years went by, the denizens became bored with that and tried to set fire to a Greyhound bus. Some, it is rumoured, even managed to see a racing car in action during the course of the weekend.

Had they bothered in 1971, the revellers would have witnessed the $50,000 first prize going to a Tyrrell driver – but not to Jackie Stewart. The Scotsman had won six races and he looked like making it seven when he took pole. Then tyre trouble cut his pace and he waved through his team-mate, François Cevert. Stewart did his best to protect the young Frenchman, but once Jacky Ickx had stormed into second place, Cevert was on his own. He drove faultlessly, the pressure only being relieved when the distributor broke on Ickx's Ferrari. Cevert, his dark eyes flashing, was exultant as the beaming figure of Ken Tyrrell raising his protégé's arm in triumph.

Cevert was back on the rostrum in 1972, but this time Stewart's car had behaved perfectly and the Frenchman dutifully finished second. During the season which followed, Cevert matured and developed to such an extent that he was, on occasions, faster than his team leader. By the time the 1973 US Grand Prix came round, Stewart had decided to retire and it was clear that Cevert was more than ready to fill the Scotsman's shoes. Watkins Glen would be Jackie's 100th and final Grand Prix; all very neat and tidy. Too neat, in fact.

During practice on Saturday, Cevert had been the quicker of the two and he went out for one more lap. Going through the fast esses, the Tyrrell left the road and crashed into the barrier with great violence. It was a horrific accident and Cevert was killed instantly. The Tyrrell team, in deep shock, withdrew from the meeting.

Spirits were lifted by a thrilling contest the following day as Ronnie Peterson led all the way, the Lotus driver chased across the line by the impudent March-Ford of James Hunt. Carlos Reutemann finished third, outpaced by this battle, but the Brabham driver had it all his own way when he took pole in 1974 and led every lap.

Niki Lauda dominated the race for Ferrari the following year, but in 1976 the Austrian returned to the Glen embroiled in his furious battle for the championship with James Hunt. Driving brilliantly, Hunt waited for the six-wheeled Tyrrell of Jody Scheckter to drop from the lead before moving forward to give McLaren their first

Grand Prix victory in the United States.

Hunt won again in 1977 and Mario Andretti was fully expected to take the honours at home 12 months later. After all, 1978 had been Mario's year, but, at Watkins Glen, the Lotus was beaten by the combination of Carlos Reutemann, Ferrari and Michelin tyres.

Ferrari won again in 1979, but this had little to do with tyre superiority. In a straight fight between Gilles Villeneuve and the Williams of Alan Jones on a wet/dry track, Ferrari's slick pit work won the day, while a fumbled stop cost Jones any chance when a wheel flew off his car not long after he had left the pits. Jones more than made

up for that 12 months later when he arrived in Watkins Glen as the newly crowned 1980 world champion and then breezed through the race to give Williams maximum points once more.

By now, much had changed in the world of Formula 1 and Watkins Glen, for all its genuine warmth and endeavour, had not kept pace. The Kendall Technical Center, once the Ultimate in working conditions for the teams, was no longer adequate and neither were the pits. The circuit itself was deemed to be too bumpy, while the spectator areas developed into a glutinous mess at the merest hint of rain. There was not enough money in the kitty, nor perhaps the

local enthusiasm, to put in hand the necessary work. Besides, a circuit such as this was no longer flavour of the month for the increasingly pampered members of Grand Prix society.

Since 1976 Watkins Glen had been forced to share the American billing with Long Beach in California. Known as the USA Grand Prix West, this street race had been inspired by Christopher Pook, an expatriate Englishman with a keen understanding of the needs of Grand Prix racing in the Seventies. More than that, his race was scheduled for the spring, the agreeable climate of the West Coast being considerably more acceptable than the inevitable cold and misery

associated with Watkins Glen in October.

The first world championship Grand Prix at Long Beach, won at a canter for Ferrari by a beaming Clay Regazzoni, was an outstanding success. That was in 1976, and from then on Pook's race went from strength to strength, so much so that he was able to rail against the financial demands of FOCA in 1984, switch to CART racing and *still* pull in a crowd in excess of 80,000.

The circuit had changed over the years to suit the redevelopment of the city but, even so, the Grand Prix teams would miss the visits to Long Beach. There had been easy wins for Villeneuve, Nelson Piquet (his first Grand Prix victory) and Jones; pole positions for Riccardo Patrese and Andrea de Cesaris; a memorable and commanding victory to mark the year of Niki Lauda's return to Formula 1 in 1982; and an amazing drive from the back of the field by John Watson in the final year.

The appreciation of Long Beach had been heightened by visits in 1981 and 1982 to a car park masquerading as a race track in Las Vegas. Laid out behind a major hotel and casino complex, this race, the final round of the championship in each case, had nothing to offer but novelty value. And that quickly wore off.

It seemed wholly inappropriate that the Caesar's Palace Grand Prix should be the one to settle the championship. The circuit, a featureless jumble of tarmac and concrete, provided nothing but a test of stamina. When Jones drove a stunning race in 1981 to win for Williams, Piquet, the new world champion, had to be lifted from his Brabham. Michele Alboreto gave Tyrrell a welcome victory the following year and, by finishing fifth, Keke Rosberg laid claim to his one and only title. The anticipated crowds had declined the opportunity to fry in the searing heat at great financial expense to themselves; the offer of a race through the streets of Detroit was quickly taken up in 1983.

Seemingly a bit of a joke at first, this venue quickly established a popularity with the local motor industry, even if the drivers and teams were less than enamoured with the working conditions. The circuit, running along the riverfront and through the fringe of downtown Detroit, was slow and stilted – and bumpy, too, according to the flood of complaints from the drivers. But from day one the atmosphere was electric as the people of Michigan, and from Canada on the far side of the river, embroiled themselves in 'partying' as only they know how.

The smoked-glass ziggurat of the Renaissance Center, dominating the circuit, provided hotel accommodation as well as the press room and it was from here that news went out of another win for Alboreto and Tyrrell in 1983. There was high drama within seconds of the start the following year as Nigel Mansell tried to force his way through the middle of the front row, the resulting carnage causing the race to be stopped and restarted. Piquet, a victim of Mansell's excesses, still managed to win for Brabham and BMW.

It was Keke Rosberg's turn in 1985, the Williams-Honda driver having to give best to Ayrton Senna in the early stages. Senna learned his lessons well and found the perfect combination to win for Lotus-Renault in 1986. It was to be the first of a hat-trick for the Brazilian as he mastered the special qualities required to complete 63 laps of a simple but physically demanding circuit. Then, just as the race seemed to be getting into its stride, the perennial problem of money raised its head and the organisers felt they could not find the necessary cash to carry out the modifications demanded.

Meanwhile, in 1984, there had been an interesting diversion to Dallas where the dramas associated with that particular Grand Prix would not have been out of place in the popular television soap opera of the same name. The track, arranged in the grounds of Fair Park, was as interesting and challenging as any temporary circuit can be. Unfortunately, the surface proved to be no match for either the oppressive heat or the punishment meted out by the cars and their fat tyres.

On race morning there were serious doubts that the Grand Prix would take place for contractors were still putting the finishing touches to repairs to the asphalt. It was so bad it was a joke, and Jacques Laffite arrived wearing his pyjamas for the warm-up at the absurd hour of 7.0 a.m.

The race did go ahead but it quickly turned into a lottery as the racing line became fringed with crumbling tarmac. Cars crashed in all directions but these were the perfect conditions for a tenacious drive by Rosberg. As the Williams crossed the line to the approval of the rich and famous in their air-conditioned boxes, Mansell was pushing his crippled Lotus towards the finish. Then, with a flourish in keeping with the soap opera, he collapsed in a heap. The locals thought he was wonderful.

Despite the problems, it had been a promising venue and it was with regret that Formula 1 was unable to return, largely because one of the promoters had created havoc with the cash box.

So, with Detroit out of favour at the end of 1988, where to next? Why Phoenix, Arizona. In the middle of June. The locals were sensible enough not to venture from their homes as the drivers tried to accustom themselves to the humidity and a rather bland circuit. Senna led for McLaren but team-mate Prost was ready to take charge when the Brazilian ran into mechanical trouble.

In 1990 the Grand Prix was run at a more climatically acceptable date in March and this time Senna went the full distance, albeit after a splendid but brief struggle with the Tyrrell-Ford of Jean Alesi. Senna won again in 1991, a commanding drive which never seemed in doubt from the moment practice had started.

Indeed, one of the few highlights had been the unexpected appearance on the track of a man on crutches. He was apprehended and taken back to the institution from which he had been released that morning. The Grand Prix of the United States had come a long way since the scenes of disorder at Long Island in 1906, yet, in some respects, it had not changed in the least. It was still transient, homely and occasionally unruly.

Mr Motor Racing.

The United States Automobile Club considers the Indianapolis 500 to be the centre of the universe. Nothing else matters. The 2.5-mile oval and the running of the classic close to Memorial Day each year epitomises everything that is noble and good about the sport of automobile racing. That's the way the good folk of USAC see it, and, by and large, they are right. Their race is one of the world's great sporting occasions. It's just that they like to tell you about it at frequent intervals.

In 1966, Graham Hill went there for the first time. It did not take long for a leading official to ask the Englishman what he thought about it all. It was clear that the man expected one answer and was preparing to preen himself in the reflected glory.

Hill told him he didn't like it. He said he didn't like it because there were neither partitions nor doors on the toilet cubicles. He said the loo was the one place where he liked to be in private – and he thought the open-plan practice was 'embarrassing, indecent and undignified.' The official was, well, caught short.

It is a measure of Hill's standing (perhaps, sitting is a more appropriate word here) that partitions had been fitted to every cubicle in the paddock by 6.30 the following morning. Graham Hill was, after all, a former World Champion.

But Hill's direct reply to a bland question was also indicative of the straightforward and utterly determined manner which had brought him success in the first place. He didn't mince his words, and certainly not when directing his efforts to winning a motor race. The 1966 Indianapolis was a case in point.

Someone rashly told Hill that drivers never won at Indianapolis on their first visit. It merely strengthened Hill's resolution to do his best but, two seconds into the race, it seemed such a claim might have some merit. A multiple accident wiped out 11 cars; Hill's was one of the last to get through unharmed.

After the restart, Hill gradually moved forward and eventually found himself a dis-

tant second to Jackie Stewart. When Stewart's oil pressure failed with eight laps to go, Hill won the Indy 500 first time out.

Now started the pomp and ceremony on a scale which only the Americans can dream up. It was then a tradition for the winner to drink from a large glass of milk. This Hill did but, shortly afterwards, an official anxiously explained that, because of the restart, there was some confusion with the lap-scoring; Hill might not be the winner after all. Quick as a flash, Graham replied 'No way, mate. I drank the milk ...'

Thirteen years earlier, Hill had also been handed a beverage when he least expected it. Motoring down Cricklewood Lane in north London, Hill's Morris 8 was accosted by a laundry van emerging unexpectedly from a side-turning. The Morris overturned and Hill was trapped until help arrived to right the car. Out of the blue, came a hand bearing a cup of tea. It was, Hill recalled, as if they had been brewing up on the pavement in anticipation of the accident.

The car was written off and, in the subsequent court case Hill, to his great surprise, was found partly to blame and ordered to pay his costs. It left him with a jaundiced view of the British judicial system. It also left him penniless. But, as in many cases of apparent calamity in his life, Hill managed to see the funny side.

The Morris 8, built in 1934, had been so unreliable that he always carried a bicycle in the back. As a result of the collision, the mangled bike ended up on the side of the road and Hill found it difficult to stop his rescuers from searching for an injured cyclist. The more he protested, the more convinced they became that he was trying to cover up some desperate crime.

That Morris, in fact, had a lot to answer for since it had opened what would become a spectacular association between Norman Graham Hill and the motor car. Unlike many of his motor sport contemporaries, however, Hill had little interest in cars, largely because his family never possessed one.

Hill bought the Morris 8 shortly before

his 24th birthday. He paid £110, climbed on board and headed for home across London. He had never driven a car before. Not only did he make it but he also passed his driving test a few weeks later without the benefit of a single lesson. His introduction to motor sport would also be a sudden affair.

The first race he ever saw was the one he was in. A chance encounter with a motoring magazine had introduced Hill to the idea of paying five shillings (25p) to complete a lap of Brands Hatch. Hill bought a £1's worth of circuits and, from that moment on, he thought of nothing but getting himself back into a racing car – preferably without having to pay.

The solution was to offer his services to a racing drivers' school and, in lieu of payment as a mechanic, Hill was allowed to take part in a race at Brands Hatch. He finished second after taking the lead and then losing it because, not having seen a race before, he didn't quite know what to expect.

He knew, however, that a constant shortage of capital would defeat what had become his sole objective. Indeed, money was in such short supply one weekend that he found himself spectating at Brands Hatch with no means of getting home. A passing conversation with an entrant and his team got Hill a lift back to London. It would turn out to be the most fortuitous move of Hill's career: he had just met Colin Chapman.

The Lotus empire, at the time no more than a shed behind a pub, was in its formative days and Hill quickly assessed the potential. He went to work for Lotus in the hope that he could scrounge a drive in a customer's car but, in the end, he reached an accommodation with Chapman himself. As in all things connected with Lotus, the arrangement was very much in Chapman's favour.

He lent Hill the bits to build the car – a Lotus Eleven sports car – and Chapman retained ownership while Hill prepared and raced it. Not surprisingly, all prize and starting monies went Chapman. But at least

Early days with the 1959 Lotus 16 Grand Prix car.

Hill was now racing on a regular basis as the 1956 British club racing season got underway.

Being a personable sort of chap, Hill quickly established relationships with other drivers and entrants and it was not long before he was being offered drives and, in some cases, being paid as much as £100 (including bonuses from the likes of Esso if he won) for the privilege of doing what he liked most. Indeed, matters reached the point where Chapman thought it best to have Hill drive for Lotus rather than the opposition, and Graham duly signed for Team Lotus in the latter half of 1957.

In 1958 Lotus planned to go Grand Prix racing for the first time and thus Hill, without having a particular burning desire in this direction, suddenly became a Formula 1 driver. And his first race would be the Monaco Grand Prix, an event which would later become his personal property. That seemed an unlikely proposition at the time, as Graham and his wife Bette drove there in a recently acquired Austin A35 – hardly the 'big time'.

The race was not much better. Hill found himself in fourth place even though he had started the cigar-shaped car from the back of the grid and had not passed a soul all day. There were 30 laps to go; he thought Grand Prix racing was a doddle. Then a back wheel fell off. And, when he climbed from the car, he promptly fell over with heat exhaustion.

Proof that Formula 1 was not a push-over came at Spa Francorchamps, scene of the Belgian Grand Prix. Hill frightened himself silly on his first acquaintance with this truly daunting road circuit and he pulled into the pits in the genuine belief that he had exceeded his limits. However, it was typical of the man that a brief period of thought and personal assessment should nurture the same steely determination which would eventually carry him to the very top. He climbed back into the car and simply came to terms with his surroundings. By the end, it had ceased to worry him at all.

The Lotus was generally unreliable although Hill did manage to coast across the line – out of fuel – at Monza and score his first championship points by finishing fifth. By the end of the following year, though, Hill had had enough. He accepted an offer from BRM and began a frequently brilliant partnership which was to last for seven years.

At first Hill feared he had made a big mistake. Lotus, with their first rear-engined car, began to do rather well whereas BRM, under a rather autocratic system of management, tested Hill's patience on occasions. When the points were totted up at the end of 1960, Lotus were second in the Constructors' Championship whereas BRM had scored a mere quarter of the Lotus total.

But, along the way, Hill had enjoyed one of his best races. He had put the BRM on the front row at Silverstone – and then stalled at the start. He produced an epic comeback drive to take the lead of his home Grand Prix but, with five laps to go, failing brakes sent Hill off the road while under pressure from Brabham's Cooper-Climax. Hill received a standing ovation as he walked back to the pits, typical of the warm relationship which Hill had developed with the crowds wherever he went.

BRM were ill-prepared for the change of formula from 2.5 to 1.5 litres in 1961. The new chassis was ready in May but BRM did not finish work on their V8 until September. The engine caused so many problems that it was withdrawn from the Italian Grand Prix, the penultimate race of the season. During the winter, serious work was carried out but, as the start of the 1962 racing programme in Europe drew nearer, Hill became concerned because there had been virtually no development work on the chassis. Hill need not have worried. He was about to embark on a memorable season.

He won his first Formula 1 race at Goodwood on Easter Monday, although Graham's joy that day was tempered with concern for Stirling Moss, unconscious after the crash which would end his brilliant career.

Moss's subsequent absence opened discussion over the identity of his successor and it so happened that the ensuing period was to mark the rise of Hill and the man with whom he would have many a memorable battle: Jim Clark.

The two Britons produced a nail-biting contest during a very wet *Daily Express* meeting at Silverstone, Clark nursing his Lotus along while Hill made up ground rapidly to cross the line alongside, and sideways, to win by a whisker.

Invariably, Clark would be on a pole position and the winning seemed to be split between the two, Hill scoring his first Grand Prix victory in Holland. That win had been comparatively straightforward, unlike a dogged performance at the Nürburgring where he suffered a terrifying accident during practice and then went on to win in the back-up car.

By the time the teams had finished with the penultimate race of the season at Watkins Glen in the United States, Hill and Clark had won six of the eight Grands Prix between them. For the championship decider, they would have to wait until the South African Grand Prix at the end of December.

From the moment practice began it was clear that Clark's Lotus had an advantage and, even though Hill was ahead on points, a win for Clark would give the Scotsman the title. That seemed to be the way of it until a tuppeny-halfpenny bolt worked loose on the Lotus and Clark was out. Graham Hill automatically became world champion. It may have been fortuitous, but no-one begrudged the Londoner after such a determined slog to the forefront of his profession.

It was a bit of an uphill struggle in 1963, too. While the BRM remained virtually unaltered, Clark had the superlative Lotus 25 at his disposal and he won almost everywhere. The one exception was Monaco – Clark's race until the gearbox broke – and that was to initiate Hill's remarkable run of success there.

Hill's win in the principality in 1964 launched his bid for the title. For a while it seemed the championship would be the property of either Clark or Hill, but a late run by John Surtees in the Ferrari opened the contest into a three-cornered fight, a win for Hill at Watkins Glen strengthening his particular chances as they went to the final round in Mexico.

In simple terms, Hill needed to finish no higher than third to win the championship, regardless of how Surtees or Clark got on, and he seemed set for his second title as he did just that. Then along came Surtees's team-mate, Lorenzo Bandini, and, with a fairly desperate lunge, succeeded in knocking Hill off the road as the Italian took third place. The collision with the barrier had damaged the exhaust on the BRM, so when Hill rejoined after a pit stop, it was more in hope than anything else.

In the end, Clark retired when in a winning position and Bandini, obeying the frantic gestures of the Ferrari team, slowed to allow Surtees through to second place and enough points to secure the title.

Hill, meanwhile, was not entirely sure of how he stood but, as he returned to the pits, the disconsolate expressions in the BRM camp told him all he needed to know. The disappointment was acute. You would think, therefore, that recriminations would flow. Well, you would, given today's standards. But this was 1964. Hill wrote:

'Bandini certainly earned his money for Ferrari that day, apart from the rather desperate effort at the hairpin. A lot of people suggested at the time that it was deliberate, but I certainly didn't think so. I wouldn't believe that of Bandini; it was obvious to me that he was making a desperate manoeuvre to get by and he just overcooked it. Well, that was that and my tough luck.'

Never mind; *L'Equipe*, the French daily sporting newspaper, voted Hill the Driver of the Year, but in 1965 Clark was to clean up once more. Hill produced his usual party piece with a particularly brilliant display at Monaco, the BRM of that year (and the season before) being, in Hill's opinion, one of the nicest cars the firm from Lincolnshire had ever built.

BRM continued to make good use of it in the early part of the 1966 season even though the formula had changed yet again, from 1.5 litres to 3 litres. For this, BRM

eventually raced a 16-cylinder engine which was ultimately defeated by its own complexity. By now, Hill was ready to move on.

The change he had in mind took everyone by surprise. He gave up his position as undisputed Number One to return to Lotus, a team which effectively belonged to Jim Clark. More than that, however, Hill was placing himself in direct comparison with his old adversary.

In fact, comparison was rendered immaterial because Lotus were to produce the 49, a car in which any driver would have been happy to finish second to Clark. Hill, though, had his say when he put the Lotus on pole first time out at Zandvoort and proceeded to lead until engine trouble intervened. He claimed two more pole positions but never actually won a Grand Prix in 1967. Clark, meanwhile, won four.

It took a driver of considerable courage and confidence to accept the offer of driving alongside Clark but Hill's strength of character was to be put to a massive test the following year.

In April 1968, Clark was killed in a Formula 2 race in Germany. The effect on the Lotus team can be imagined but, two weeks later, Hill put his grief behind him and won the Spanish Grand Prix. Not long after, Mike Spence was killed at the wheel of a Lotus at Indianapolis and Hill stepped forward once more to lift the shattered team by scoring yet another imperious victory at Monaco. And he hadn't finished yet.

Hill found himself in another three-way fight for a title to be settled, once again, in Mexico City. This time, Hill simply had to win the race, to 'beat those other buggers fair and square'.

Grand Prix technology had fostered the use of aerodynamic aids on the cars: nose wings at the front, high-mounted devices on spindly stalks at the rear. For Mexico, Chapman introduced a system whereby the driver, by pushing a pedal, could flatten the rear wing for maximum speed on the straight and return it to an angle for increased downforce while cornering. When it worked, it worked well.

On the third lap, Hill pressed the pedal – and it went light. One of the rubber control bands mounted just below the wing was flapping in the breeze; he faced the prospect of relying on the one remaining band for the rest of the race. Without it, the wing would not work while cornering and the car would be unmanageable. It held. And Hill won. In view of such a harrowing season, there could not have been a more popular champion. Hill was at his peak.

In constant demand, he used his Piper Aztec (bought from his Indianapolis winnings in 1966) to fly the length and breadth of the country, making public appearances, opening garages, committing himself to miles and miles of testing for Lotus and Firestone tyres. He was awarded the OBE, appeared regularly on television panel games and came second to Olympic Gold Medallist David Hemery in the BBC *Sportsview* Personality of the Year competition. The nation took him to its heart as 'Mr Motor Racing'.

It must be said that he was also a bit of a sod. The public persona of natural charm and sparkling wit did not always match the gruff and occasionally uncivil character known by those who worked close to Hill. He did not suffer fools gladly and all of this was the side-effect of a total determination to be successful. Unfortunately, Hill was about to enter a period where his rate of success would be on the decline.

The perfect motor racing ambassador. Hill shows the royal visitors around his Lotus at Brands Hatch in 1968.

Victory at Jaráma in 1968 gave Lotus a tremendous fillip in the aftermath of Clark's death.

He won for a fifth time at Monaco, a slightly fortunate result and one that would turn out to be his last world championship victory. His new team-mate, Jochen Rindt, claimed five pole positions and finished fourth in the 1969 championship. Hill, the defending champion, finished seventh. But, much worse than that, he suffered an appalling accident during the American Grand Prix at Watkins Glen.

Lying fifth and unhappy with the handling of his car, Hill had spun on oil. As he got out to push the Lotus down an incline, Hill noticed that the rear tyres were long since past their best. He jumped back on board, restarted the engine and signalled to the pits that he would be in next time round for fresh tyres. He never made it.

The right-rear tyre collapsed and threw the car into a spin, the Lotus crashing into a bank before overturning. Hill had not been able to fasten his seat-belts again and he was flung from the cockpit. He suffered a fractured right knee and dislocated the left one, tearing all the ligaments. And, even in these moments of adversity, Hill found time to joke. He asked the surgeon if, while he was about it, he could see his way clear to straighten the left leg, which had been bandy ever since a motor cycle accident 21 years before. 'It will make life easier for my tailor,' said Hill.

Graham received a hero's welcome when he was finally flown back to London. Those who thought this might be an appropriate moment to retire reckoned, of course, without Hill's cold resolve not to be beaten. Driving Rob Walker's privately entered Lotus, Hill finished a gritty sixth in his comeback race in South Africa. He completed the full season, picking up points here and there but suffering the indignity of starting from the back row of the grid at the British Grand Prix.

Again, though, he fought a major battle within himself and returned in 1971, this time with the Brabham team. And, again, he pulled success from the seemingly impossible, winning the International Trophy at Silverstone and a Formula 2 race at Thruxton. The following year, he went

one better by sharing the winning Matra at Le Mans to claim a Triple Crown – the World Championship, Indianapolis and Le Mans – which no one has managed before or since.

At the end of 1972, Hill was dropped by Brabham. He was 43. The time seemed right to retire. But Hill did not see it that way. 'I continued motor racing because I enjoyed it physically and mentally,' he wrote. 'I enjoyed the stimulus, the physical sensation, the controlling of a racing car at high speed and the whole business of trying to do it better than someone else.'

Hill was now running his own team, first with cars built by Shadow and then with Lolas from Huntingdon. It would have

been a major struggle just to go racing with a totally new outfit but Hill was taking on the additional responsibility of driving the car as well. As an inevitable consequence, results were thin on the ground, even when the team expanded to two cars.

A variety of drivers worked for Hill but the most significant was Tony Brise, a cocky youngster who had his first outing with the Embassy-Hill team at the Belgian Grand Prix in 1975.

Hill took to the Englishman immediately and was highly impressed by his potential. Lying in the bath after the first day of practice, Graham decided he really ought to be supporting his driver rather than trying to do everything himself. It was a decision

everyone fervently hoped Hill would reach sooner rather than later. A few weeks before he had failed to qualify for the Monaco Grand Prix – 'Graham's Grand Prix' – and it had been desperately sad to see a former champion of such quality trying to defeat the inescapable effects of the calendar.

The formal announcement was made at the British Grand Prix. There was no better place for it. The crowd lined the edge of the track and cheered him all the way as he completed a lap of honour, the 'old boy' admitting to having a lump in the throat for most of the journey.

Now he could concentrate fully on his team. A promising one it was too. A new car was built for the 1976 season and tests were

carried out at the Paul Ricard circuit in November. Hill was due to fly home from the south of France the next morning but, in the event, they finished early and it was decided to make a run for it that evening. On board were Graham, Tony Brise and four members of the team.

Approaching Elstree aerodrome in freezing fog, the twin-engined aeroplane crashed on Arkley golfcourse. Everyone perished in the fire which followed. Radio and television programmes were interrupted that night to give the news. Nobody was prepared for this. Irony was heaped on irony. After 176 Grands Prix, for Graham to die like this seemed an absurd waste.

The accident brought forth tributes from

all over the world. Everyone had a funny story to tell but the sense of loss went beyond merely looking to the past. Graham Hill would have been one of the sport's great political ambassadors, a man who would have applied his considerable charm to good effect – and the occasional cutting remark when appropriate.

He had worked hard for everything he had accomplished on the track and yet he was held in great affection by people who neither knew nor cared about racing. That was the mark of his endeavours and achievements just as surely as two world championships and 14 Grand Prix victories – not to mention the installation of those lavatory partitions at Indianapolis.

The Monaco Grand Prix

In the mid-1960s, Bob Anderson was one of those doughty privateers who clung to Grand Prix racing by his finger-tips and loved every minute of it. As a former motor cycle racer, hardship was no stranger and he lived a hand-to-mouth existence as the Formula 1 circus criss-crossed Europe each summer.

As the major-league teams invested increasingly in smart transporters, Anderson would arrive with his immaculate Brabham perched on the back of a high-mileage Volkswagen pick-up. Not exactly what you would expect to see rolling into the prim and proper streets of the Principauté de Monaco on a sunny afternoon in May.

Usually, the Volkswagen's tax disc was

out of date. But that was a small detail. So long as his entry for the Grand Prix had been accepted (each team dealt with various race organisers on an individual basis and its place in the programme was usually based on previous form and the whim of a local official), Anderson knew he had the chance of earning enough money to take him to the next race.

In any case, he had been making a bit of a name for himself ever since he had taken delivery of a brand-new Brabham-Climax just after the start of the 1964 season. He had claimed a couple of third places in non-championship races – of which there were a considerable number in these less regimented times. He had also given a good account of himself on his first visit to

Moll, the surprise winner in 1934, blasts his Alfa Romeo into the Tir aux Pigeons tunnel. Note the back of the railway station above. This section is now completely enclosed by the new tunnel under the Loews Hotel and the conference centre.

Monaco that year. There was no reason, then, for the Automobile Club de Monaco to refuse his entry in 1965, which, in some ways, was just as well since Bob Anderson was inadvertently to lay the foundations for a truly superb drive by Graham Hill.

There was no question, of course, about Graham Hill's right to going racing through the streets of the principality. He was the Number One driver with the BRM team – then a force to be reckoned with – and he had been up to the royal palace to take tea with the Rainiers after winning their race during the previous two years.

A hat-trick was asking rather a lot, given the natural hazards lying in store over 100 laps of this devious track, but Hill was the favourite, particularly when he placed the BRM on pole. In many ways, the Monaco Grand Prix was tailor-made for Hill. It required judgement, stamina, total concentration and a refusal to be beaten. He would need all of those attributes in 1965.

For the first 20 laps or so, Hill appeared to have everything under easy control. He had made a clean start and, followed by his new team-mate, Jackie Stewart, the BRMs had pulled effortlessly away from the rest of the field. As quarter-distance approached, the dark-green cars were 14 seconds clear of Lorenzo Bandini and John Surtees in the red Ferraris, and there was little sign of an immediate challenge since the Italian cars were being kept busy by Jack Brabham in his Brabham-Climax.

As for Anderson, he was having a spirited run in the mid-field as he closed on the second works Brabham of Denny Hulme. But on lap 25 Anderson's car became stuck in first gear, a victim of the fierce mechanical pounding dealt by the bumps, undulations and wicked cambers of the public thoroughfares.

Anderson was on his way towards the harbour-front but, first, he had to negotiate a chicane. As he approached almost at a crawl, Hill blasted out of the tunnel and swept through the long right-hander at 120 mph. As he crested the rise before dropping towards the chicane, Hill suddenly saw Anderson's stricken Brabham. There had been no warning flags of any kind.

Hill's split-second assessment told him that Anderson would probably arrive in the narrow confines of the chicane just as the BRM, travelling much faster than the Brabham, needed to occupy the same piece of road.

Hill stood on the brakes and aimed for the chicane. As he was about to reach the point of no return, Hill's initial judgement proved correct; he was now certain that he would not make it through without crashing into the Brabham. Releasing the brakes for an instance, Hill flicked the steering straight, aimed for the escape road and slammed his foot back on the brake pedal. The ensuing trail of smoke and rubber bore witness to the effort required to bring the car to a halt some distance into the waiting cul-de-sac.

There was no alternative but for Hill to climb from the BRM, push it back towards the track (expressly forbidden today), climb on board and restart the engine (now impossible given the absence of an onboard starter and the need to refasten the seat harness). He rejoined in fifth place, having lost at least 30 seconds. He was, as he later wrote, 'pretty narked and cheesed-off about all of this'. That is probably a fairly mild interpretation of his mood at the time.

The danger, of course, would be to allow his sense of frustration to deliver him into a kerb or a wall. Mistakes at Monaco are easily made and, in most cases, heavily punished. For Jackie Stewart, however, a spin on oil dropped at Ste Dévote corner resulted in no mechanical harm, although that was of little consolation since he had just thrown away a comfortable lead and the chance of his first Grand Prix victory.

The mood in the BRM pit verged between disbelief and exasperation as their command of this race appeared to be wiped out in the space of five laps. But anyone thinking the British team was done for the day reckoned without Hill.

Chin jutting, moustache bristling, the very embodiment of everything British, Hill got down to work. Smashing the lap record, he caught and passed Stewart to take fourth and set off after the Ferrari drivers who, in the midst of this excitement, had been overtaken by Brabham. Jack's lead did not last long, however, and he retired with engine trouble on lap 42.

Bandini led Surtees and any thoughts of continuing their in-house battle were quickly cancelled by pit signals informing them of Hill's progress. Surtees closed on the Italian with a lap of 1m 34.1s but Hill then covered the 1.97 miles in 1m 33.9s. On lap 50, he knocked another six-tenths of a second off that and, as the leading trio reached half-distance, they were covered by less than two seconds.

On lap 53, Hill passed Surtees and then began to probe Bandini's defences. It took 11 laps before Hill overtook the Ferrari on the plunge from Casino Square to Mirabeau – precisely the same spot where he had overtaken Surtees. Bandini responded and, together, the BRM and the Ferrari reduced the lap record even further. Surtees then matched their times in an enthralling contest of nerve. As the race entered the final 20 laps, Surtees moved ahead of Bandini; now the *really* serious business of the day was about to start.

The gap was rarely more than three seconds and not even a spectacular diversion, as the Lotus of Paul Hawkins crashed into the harbour, would disrupt the intensity of this battle. Finally Hill eased away and, on the penultimate lap, Surtees suffered the unspeakable frustration of having his car run out of fuel. He was eventually classified fourth and Hill, after two and a half hours of tightly controlled aggression, finished almost a minute ahead of Bandini and Stewart.

That night, Hill took the traditional winner's route. After the formal prize giving in the Hôtel de Paris, Graham and his wife Bette walked down the hill to the Tip Top bar. It was hardly a salubrious place, but that did not matter: this was, and still is, the watering hole for the British racing crowd.

Graham bought drinks for the BRM mechanics; race fans, poseurs and well-wishers closed in to see and be seen; the crowd spilled onto the street which, earlier that day, had been part of the circuit. In such conducive surroundings, it was hardly surprising that the celebrations stretched effortlessly into the early hours. It was, Hill would later recall, one of the best races he had ever run. And he did it in one of the most charismatic settings ever chosen for a motor race.

The first Monaco Grand Prix, in fact, had been run in 1929, the year Hill was born. The reason for the staging of the race had little or nothing to do with romantic idealism. It was largely a commercial decision, a promotional ethic which, some would say, has gathered force, detrimentally, in recent years.

In 1929 Monte Carlo was an élitist habitat; a warm winter place for those with little to do. But the fiscal fabric of the principality could not survive on that alone, particularly during the off-season. The introduction of a race through the streets was seen as a way to attract the kind of visitors who would leave a goodly portion of their ready cash in the casino and other establishments in the town. It would also serve to increase Monaco's stature and independence in the eyes of the world.

The Monte Carlo Rally had already been created for similar reasons but the Grand Prix possessed that additional cachet of glamour and drama. The circuit, rising steeply from sea level at Ste Dévote to the narrow gap between the Hôtel de Paris and the casino, then plunged downhill to the splendid Hôtel Métropole, swung right, negotiated a sharp hairpin in front of Monaco station, dropped steeply once more before joining a short straight under a railway arch and levelling off on the sea-front. The right-hander at Virage du Portier began the return leg.

With the Mediterranean on the left and a sheer rock face on the right, the track curved through the Tir aux Pigeons tunnel which, before the massive rebuilding programme which changed this area almost beyond recognition in later years, was just long enough to ensure that the exit could not be seen from the entrance.

Then followed a brief downhill run towards the chicane leading onto the quayside. At Tabac, a fast left-hand bend (by a tobacconist's kiosk) took the cars to the promenade and a quick dash to the final corner, a very tight hairpin bend named after the nearby gasworks; it was hardly a romantic appellation but that seemed to matter little given the splendour of the palace on the imposing rock above.

The circuit totally disrupted life in the principality but the local community, by and large, welcomed the race. It was the single most important event on the Monaco social calendar and the responsibility for the first Grand Prix lay with Antony Noghès, founder and president of the Automobile Club de Monaco.

Noghès had to overcome stiffer opposition from outside the principality than within. No-one believed it was possible to hold a motor race – a Grand Prix no less – in a confined space which did not possess, as *The Autocar* put it, '… a single open road of any length, but has only ledges on the face of a cliff … This affair should be the nearest approach to a Roman chariot race that has been seen of recent years.'

Regardless of the doubts expressed far and wide, the ACM was delighted to receive an entry of reasonable quality prepared to do battle on 14 April. Bugattis accounted for precisely half of the 16 starters but a 7.1-litre SSK Mercedes-Benz, driven by the renowned Rudolf Caracciola, attracted considerable interest, not least because of the machine's apparent unsuitability for such a cramped circuit.

That did not seem to bother Caracciola as he engaged in a tense battle for the lead with a green Bugatti driven by William Grover, an expatriate Englishman known simply as 'Williams'. Critics were at first dumfounded that the race should work so well and then they became engrossed as Caracciola took the lead on lap 30, only to have Williams snatch it back five laps later. The pit stops were to prove decisive, a particularly tardy stop by Caracciola costing him more than a lap. Williams, with his peaked cap worn back to front, won easily. The race, with only two minor casualties, was adjudged an outstanding success.

There was further interest, particularly for the locals, when Monégasque driver Louis Chiron led most of the way in 1930. Mechanical trouble in the closing stages left him unable to respond to a spirited challenge from another Bugatti driven by René Dreyfus, the Frenchman earning his first Grand Prix victory.

Chiron made up for his disappointment by winning the following year, but any hope of repeating the performance in 1932 was literally turned on its head when he rolled his Bugatti at the chicane. Chiron, although leading, had been coming under intense pressure from the Alfa Romeo of Tazio Nuvolari, and Chiron clipped a sandbag while attempting to squeeze past a spinning back-marker. He was unhurt, and the win for Nuvolari was another landmark in the portfolio of one of the greatest drivers of all time.

There was, however, one rival intent on proving he was a match for the so-called Great Little Man. His name was Achille Varzi and, although ice-cold, enigmatic and quite different to Nuvolari, he had the talent to back his claim. The two Italians had been rivals since their early days in motor cycle racing and that intense but friendly conflict was to manifest itself in the most spectacular manner at Monaco in 1933. It would turn out to be a breathtaking contest as they fought for 97 of the 100 laps.

Varzi led from the start, but Nuvolari was ahead by lap four, Varzi's Bugatti taking charge again four laps later. This set the standard, Nuvolari leading after ten laps, Varzi after 20, Nuvolari after 40, Varzi after 50. These facts alone take no account of the furious pace and the place-changing that went on in between: Nuvolari in front on lap 60, where he stayed until the Bugatti took the lead on lap 81. Two laps later and Nuvolari's Alfa Romeo was leading again. It was anyone's race.

Going into the final lap, they were neck and neck – after almost three and a half hours. Both drivers pushed their machines to the limit, and it was the Alfa Romeo which failed, a broken piston bringing Nuvolari to a halt. He had led for 66 laps but his arch-rival had been ahead when it mattered most.

Inevitably, the Grand Prix in 1934 was mild by comparison, the French-Algerian Guy Moll taking the lead when his Alfa Romeo team-mate, Chiron, lost certain success after making an error on the 98th lap. In 1935, victory for Luigi Fagioli's Mercedes-Benz was a sign of the times, both politically and in terms of the impending

domination of the German teams. The following year, the silver cars were present in even greater strength as Auto Union joined their rivals.

Caracciola, driving brilliantly in the rain, won for Mercedes-Benz, this victory being a personal triumph after a lengthy period spent recovering from serious thigh injuries, the result of a crash during practice at Monaco in 1933.

He would have won in 1937, too, had the Mercedes-Benz team management had their way. In fact, the German led a major portion of the race but, by dint of a faster pit stop, his haughty team-mate, Manfred von Brauchitsch, took the lead and refused to give it up despite increasingly frantic signals from the pits.

This in-house dispute saw Caracciola shatter the lap record as he closed in and eventually, with no assistance from his so-called team-mate, took the lead again. However, another pit stop put paid to his chances and he finished second. But Caracciola had made his mark in more ways than one; his lap record at 66.79 mph would stand for 18 years.

Much of that, of course, had to do with the advent of the Second World War and the absence of Grand Prix racing in the principality until 16 May 1948. The comparatively poor quality of the field also contributed to Caracciola's record remaining intact.

The fastest lap, at 62.67 mph, was claimed by Giuseppe 'Nino' Farina, the Maserati driver winning more or less as he pleased from the ever-popular Chiron in a Talbot. But these were difficult times and the financial strains imposed on the principality, which stood the inevitable losses, prompted the decision not to hold the Grand Prix in 1949.

The following year was different, for 1950 saw the introduction of the World Championship and, in the eyes of the Monégasques, it seemed only right and proper that their race should be part of it. The Monaco Grand Prix was marked down for 21 May and an exciting race was in prospect as the Ferrari team threatened to offer some sort of challenge to the imperious progress of Alfa Romeo.

Alfa Romeo had been absent for a year but they had picked up where they had left off, a single car for the highly promising Juan Manuel Fangio having won at San Remo. The full works team then totally destroyed the opposition at the opening round of the championship at Silverstone.

There were three cars at Monaco for the 'three Fs' – Farina, Fangio and Fagioli. Of the three, Farina had it in his mind that he should win this inaugural championship. His weekend got off to a bad start when Fangio was quickest during practice, and there was worse to follow.

Farina led through Ste Dévote but Fangio was in front by the time they reached Casino Square. The pair of Alfa Romeos pulled away from the rest and, as they tackled the harbour-front for the first time, Fangio discovered that wind-whipped spray had dampened the quayside at Tabac. Farina, following closely, did not see it.

The Italian spun, the rear of his car striking the wall on the inside of the corner before coming to a halt, broadside, on the opposite side of the track and just out of the sight of those following. One or two cars managed to get through without incident but, for the majority, there was no escaping some kind of contact in the mounting chaos as damaged cars blocked the track. Almost half of the 19 starters were wiped out in as many seconds. Remarkably, there was no fire, even though methanol was pouring

onto the track from ruptured fuel tanks.

Fangio, meanwhile, was oblivious to all of this. As he negotiated the chicane for the second time and headed towards Tabac, he sensed something was amiss even though the track ahead seemed to be clear. Somehow, the mood seemed to be different and, after a few seconds, Fangio discovered what it was.

Instead of being confronted by a sea of faces, Fangio noticed that the spectators were not looking his way, even though he was leading the race. Something around the corner at Tabac was holding their attention. He backed off and was able to pull up when suddenly confronted by the mayhem. Picking his way through, Fangio was able to continue towards an untroubled victory. In fact, he would become the first driver to win the Monaco Grand Prix by a clear lap.

The organisers, meanwhile, were continuing to balance on a shaky financial footing. There was no Grand Prix in 1951, and in 1952 they chose to run sports cars in lieu of the Formula 2 cars which made up Grand Prix racing at the time. Indeed, it was not until 1955 that the Monaco Grand Prix regained its status and began its present unbroken run.

Apart from the removal of tramlines in 1934 and the frequent repositioning of the chicane, the circuit and its layout had remained unaltered. In 1955, however, the organisers took it upon themselves to move the start/finish line from its position on Boulevard Albert 1er to the opposite carriageway on the quay of the same name. Thus, the 20 starters faced the prospect of a rush to a virtual standstill as they negotiated the Gasworks Hairpin.

The predicted bumping and barging took place, but nothing to match the incidents which would follow in later years. The Mercedes-Benz of Fangio and Stirling Moss emerged unscathed and took control of the race after a brief intervention by the Lancia of Eugenio Castellotti. Moss followed the Old Master who, by now, had won two of an eventual five world championships, and the Englishman was ideally placed to take the lead when Fangio stopped at half-distance with transmission failure.

Moss's first world championship victory seemed to be assured until lap 81, when his engine broke. That should have allowed the Lancia of Ascari to take the lead, but he promptly misjudged the chicane and shot straight into the harbour. Ascari swam to safety and, in the midst of the commotion, the Ferrari of a surprised but delighted Maurice Trintignant took a lead he would not lose.

Moss made up for his disappointment by scoring a beautifully judged victory for Maserati in 1956, the year the number of starters was reduced to 16. As happened to a number of winners at Monaco, he had an undistinguished race the following year even though he appeared to be in a position to give the Vanwall team their first victory.

Moss led from the start but, on the fourth lap, he slid straight on at the chicane towards the escape road – except that the escape road was blocked off by a substantial barrier consisting of sand-bags and telegraph poles.

Debris flew in all directions and Peter Collins, following closely in his Ferrari, crashed on the quayside as he tried to take avoiding action. Fangio, as you might imagine, motored through the middle of it all but Tony Brooks, slowing to a crawl in his Vanwall in order to ride over a pole, was hit from behind by Mike Hawthorn, the Ferrari then careering into the abandoned car of Collins. At a stroke, three British drivers were out and with them went the hope of a battle between Vanwall, Ferrari and Maserati. Fangio won easily for the latter.

The British, however, left their mark in a more positive manner – positive for some, at any rate – in 1958 as green cars began to overwhelm the red of Ferrari and the odd privately entered Maserati. The front row of the grid consisted of Brooks on pole in a Vanwall, with the BRM of Jean Behra and the rear-engined Cooper-Climax of Jack Brabham alongside. Coopers filled row two: a green one for Roy Salvadori and a blue one for Trintignant (Rob Walker's privately entered example). Behind were a pair of Vanwalls, for Moss and Stuart Lewis-Evans, and Hawthorn's Ferrari. Two cars from the back was a Lotus driven by Norman Graham Hill.

Hill was destined to retire, along with two-thirds of the field, leaving Trintignant to add a significant paragraph to the Monaco history books as he scored a Grand Prix win for a rear-engined car. By 1959, the writing was on the wall for the 'traditional' car with its engine ahead of the driver. Moss's Cooper led most of the way until transmission trouble intervened to allow Brabham to win his first Grand Prix and complete the demonstration of the Cooper's suitability to this circuit. By May 1960 most of the leading runners had begun to follow Cooper's philosophy.

At the fore, of course, was Lotus boss Colin Chapman who was quick to realise the potential of the rear-engine trend. The result was the Lotus 18, a box-like car which was light if fragile. Rob Walker took delivery of one for Moss to drive and the Englishman elected to race it at Monaco. He duly won, giving the Lotus marque the first of many victories. It was, in fact, Stirling's 13th win in a *grande épreuve*, but none would perhaps mean as much as his totally brilliant performance at Monaco the following year.

The advent of the 1.5-litre formula came in 1961. And the British couldn't quite believe that it had actually happened. The announcement in 1959 of the impending change from the popular 2.5-litre formula provoked a great deal of spluttering in Britain. Indignation was still rife as 1960 reached its end but, unlike most of the teams, Ferrari were quietly getting on with producing a car and engine in readiness for the new season. The result was the 'sharknose', a beautiful car which made it clear that Ferrari had got nicely into the swing of this rear-engined business. Monaco was the first championship race and Ferrari, with cars for Richie Ginther, Phil Hill and Wolfgang von Trips, were favourites. But they reckoned without Moss.

Rob Walker had to stick with the Lotus 18, now looking even less attractive with the advent of the slimmer and sleeker Lotus 21s run by the works team for Jim Clark and Innes Ireland. Lotus, in fact, had been ordered by Esso, their sponsor, not to sell a

Lotus 21 to the BP-sponsored Walker/Moss team. Anyway, Moss put the dark-blue car on pole, with Ginther and Clark alongside.

Ginther was half a second faster than his team-mates, a reflection of the American's familiarity with the Ferrari thanks to a winter spent developing the new car. And, because of his sterling work, he had been given the latest wide-angle V6 engine; Hill and von Trips had to make do with the older 65-degree units. Either way, the Ferrari engines were reckoned to have as much as 30 bhp more than the four-cylinder Coventry Climax in Moss's Lotus. But at Monaco power alone is not the answer.

Moss was well-prepared. On race day, he had the cockpit side-panels removed, the better to keep him cool during two and three-quarter hours of racing. And they got down to serious business straightaway.

Moss had claimed pole position with a time of 1m 39.1s. On lap 10, he went round in 1m 40.2s while chasing Ginther's leading Ferrari. Ginther replied with a lap of 1m 40.1s. And there were more than 80 laps to go.

Moss took the lead on lap 14, Ginther dropping to third behind the Porsche of Jo Bonnier, and then to fourth when he allowed Phil Hill, the Ferrari team leader, to move ahead at Station Hairpin. When Bonnier eventually fell from contention, it was down to a straight fight between Moss and the best that Ferrari could provide.

As half-distance approached, Ginther closed up on Hill, the team leader turning in a lap of 1m 39.1s to reduce the gap to eight seconds. Moss responded by dipping into the 38's. Gradually, though, the Ferraris whittled away Moss's advantage but, by the time Hill was within five seconds of the Lotus, the Ferrari's brakes were past their best. And Ginther was showing signs of wanting to take up the chase. On lap 75, Ginther moved into second place – and immediately went round in 1m 37.7s to equal Moss's best time set some laps before. Now the battle was on in earnest.

Moss replied with 1m 37.6s. Ginther posted a 1m 36.9s on lap 79, then a 1m 36.3s on lap 84. Moss equalled it on the next lap.

And that seemed to be the pattern. Despite Ginther's supreme efforts, Moss was controlling the race with apparent ease. In the end, they were 3.6 seconds apart, their joint fastest lap being an astonishing *three* seconds quicker than Ginther had managed during practice. It had been a superb chase, a measure of both men.

That lap record took a hammering as the 1.5-litre formula got into its development stride in 1962, Jim Clark recording 1m 35.5s, a tenth slower than his pole position time, before losing second place when the Lotus retired with engine and transmission trouble. That left Graham Hill with a comfortable lead but the BRM faltered with about ten laps to go, Bruce McLaren then taking his first Grand Prix victory in Europe for Cooper.

The race had started in a chaotic fashion as three cars were eliminated during the scramble round the Gasworks Hairpin. For 1963, the organisers finally saw sense and moved the start line back to its former position, where it has remained to this day. And, once again, Clark was on pole and apparently in command of the race when his gearbox broke, leaving Graham Hill and Ginther to a one–two for BRM. They repeated this exceptional result in 1964, but not before Clark and the Brabham of Dan Gurney had taken turns at the front.

Hill added another historical statistic by scoring his hat-trick after that memorable drive in 1965, a year that saw the start of changes to the grand old face of Monaco.

With the advent of a new railway tunnel and the relocation of the station, the splendid building which had given the hairpin its name was knocked down and the track removed. In its place, eventually, would come the Loews, a monument to glitz and typical of faceless luxury hotels the world over. As the building work proceeded, so did the construction of a conference centre on the seaboard side of the hotel, resulting in the replacement of the Tir aux Pigeons tunnel with one much longer. But in 1965, and for several years to follow, the site of the demolished station provided the perfect location for a grandstand.

There were changes, too, in the international formula. In 1966, the 1.5-litre gave way to engines twice that size although, ironically, because the Monaco Grand Prix was the first race of the season, the state of unreadiness on the part of most teams meant the race was won by Jackie Stewart in a 2-litre BRM V8. In any case, this car was perfectly suited to the circuit and Stewart led in a similar model the following year until transmission failure handed victory to Denny Hulme. But that particular race would be remembered for something other than the New Zealander's first Grand Prix win.

Hulme was driving a Brabham, a relatively straightforward car which, that day, allowed Hulme to exercise a flamboyant, power-sliding style which was totally out of keeping with the man. The Brabham was easy to drive and 100 laps presented little problem for the tough Kiwi. Not so the Ferrari with which Lorenzo Bandini gave chase. Bandini was team leader, an Italian driving for *the* Italian team. He had finished second at Monaco in 1965 and 1966. Now he felt it was time to win.

As the race reached the 80-lap mark, Bandini was tiring. Attempting to sweep through the chicane for the 82nd time, Bandini made an error and crashed, the Ferrari overturning and bursting into flames. The inferno, with Bandini trapped inside, pitifully exposed the hopelessly inadequate fire-fighting and rescue facilities. By the time the car was righted and Bandini lifted free, he had suffered appalling burns. He died three days later and the shame of the tragedy focused attention on the ever-present hazard of fire and the need to deal with it effectively.

It was a stain on Monaco's otherwise impressive safety record. Until then, only three drivers had been seriously injured in accidents involving Grand Prix cars, although, over the years, there had been three fatalities in other classes. Now, at a stroke, the circuit was branded as a killer by the rapacious press.

Responding to the need to contain the rising speeds, the organisers tightened the chicane and moved it further down the harbour-front for the 1968 race. Ironically, it would catch out Johnny Servoz-Gavin, a Frenchman with outstanding flair, as he led the race briefly in his Tyrrell. In the end, it came down to experience, Graham Hill giving Lotus a morale-boosting win despite a late and dramatic charge by the BRM of Richard Attwood.

In 1969, Hill won for the fifth and final time, providing yet another demonstration of how to apply caution as he waited for the likes of Jackie Stewart to fall by the wayside with mechanical trouble. It was the same for Stewart the following year, the Scotsman being forced to relinquish the lead when his March failed. But his departure would clear the way for one of the most astonishing finishes ever seen at this or, indeed, any other cicuit.

As the final ten of the race's 80 laps unfolded, it seemed that Jack Brabham, 11 seconds ahead of Jochen Rindt's Lotus, was set for a straightforward victory. The Austrian had driven an average sort of race; once he had worked his way into third place,

then found himself second on the retirement of Chris Amon's March, Rindt appeared to gain a new lease of life.

Suddenly, the red-and-gold Lotus was being hurled around the circuit in the most spectacular fashion. And, into the bargain, Brabham was badly delayed by a backmarker. As the leaders went into their final lap, a mere 1.3 seconds separated the cars. Rindt destroyed the lap record but, despite this extrovert performance, Brabham appeared unbeatable as they headed towards the Gasworks Hairpin.

Then, unbelievably, Brabham made an error, locked his brakes and slid straight into the straw bales. An astonished Rindt nipped through and the man with the chequered flag failed to wave it, such was his surprise over the final result.

There was a similar story, but with a more predictable ending, the following year when a superb charge by the March of Ronnie Peterson failed to upset Stewart's concentration in the winning Tyrrell. In 1972, however, Stewart was all at sea, the combination of an ulcer and teeming rain produc-

ing a dismal performance as the Scotsman spun more than once. The appalling conditions, however, were perfectly suited to Jean-Pierre Beltoise and BRM, the little Frenchman having his day of days as he left the field for dead. He never won another Grand Prix at Monaco – or anywhere else.

The 1972 race had been the last to be run on the traditional circuit layout. By May the following year, an alteration was in place which would bypass the Gasworks Hairpin and, in so doing, deprive the circuit of its one useful overtaking spot.

Instead of mounting the short ramp onto the promenade at Tabac for the final, curving blast behind the pits, the cars were now directed along the water's edge and into chicanes either side of a swimming pool. And, as if that was not bad enough, drivers then faced a fatuously tight hairpin which circumvented La Rascasse restaurant and led towards the final corner which, of course, was no better than the rest.

On the plus side, the now vacant piece of promenade could be used for the pits, thus relieving team personnel of the perils of working by the side of the main straight. On the other hand, the addition of a pit lane allowed even more room for the Monaco poseurs to roam with impunity.

Stewart mastered the new layout better than most, the Tyrrell driver taking pole position and leading for 71 of the 78 laps. By now the Monaco Grand Prix no longer opened the season, following the return to the championship calendar of races in South America and South Africa. Indeed, by 1974, Monaco constituted round six and the race looked to be going the way of the Ferrari team until Niki Lauda and Clay Regazzoni ran into trouble, leaving Ronnie Peterson to score maximum points for Lotus.

Lauda put matters right in 1975 by taking pole once more and leading all but one of the 75 laps, the sort of performance which was to become the norm for the Austrian. He did it again the following year but failed to complete his hat-trick in 1977, the Ferrari being no match for Jody Scheckter's Wolf-Ford despite a hard-charging drive by Lauda. Having switched to Brabham for 1978, Lauda figured once more as he produced a mesmeric comeback drive after stopping to replace a tyre. In the end, though, he was unable to deny Patrick Depailler a most popular victory – and the last win for Tyrrell for a considerable time.

The Frenchman set the fastest lap the following year as he climbed back to fifth place after being shovelled out of the way by another competitor at the Station Hairpin, now renamed Loews Hairpin in deference to the glass-and-concrete box which had

taken over this prime position. It was unlikely, however, that Depailler would have been able to do anything about Scheckter, the Ferrari driver leading all the way and repulsing a heroic late charge by Regazzoni's Williams.

The British Williams team earned their first victory at Monaco in 1980 when a typically stylish performance gave Carlos Reutemann the result which had eluded him in the past. Indeed, Williams seemed set to score maximum points again 12 months later.

Alan Jones came to Monaco as reigning World Champion, and his long-standing love/hate relationship with Nelson Piquet manifested itself when Jones pressured the Brazilian into a mistake. Now he was comfortably ahead of Gilles Villeneuve but a misfire on the Williams, and a pit stop to top up with fuel in the belief that this was the problem, cost Jones the race. The win for Villeneuve, with the cumbersome Ferrari turbo, ran against every prediction. But it was nothing when compared with the chaos at the end of the Grand Prix in 1982.

With the race seemingly in his pocket, Alain Prost spun off in the closing stages on a track made slick by a light shower. That handed the lead to the Brabham of Riccardo Patrese but he, too, spun and then stalled. Pironi now took charge, only to have his Ferrari grind to a halt with electrical trouble. At the same time Andrea de Cesaris's Alfa Romeo ran out of fuel and Derek Daly clobbered the back of his Williams against a barrier just as the novices were poised to take the lead. All of which put Patrese, who had managed to restart, back in the lead. But he didn't realise that he had won his first Grand Prix until he returned to the pits.

Luck played a small part in 1983 when Keke Rosberg gambled correctly and started his Williams on slick tyres on the assumption that the damp track would dry. It was the opposite in 1984 when torrential rain brought the race to a premature end, officials causing controversy by showing the flag just as Prost's McLaren was on the point of being caught by the Toleman-Hart

of Ayrton Senna who, in turn, was being reeled in by the Tyrrell of Stefan Bellof.

There was no dispute about Prost's win the following year and he made it three in a row for McLaren in 1986. During this period, however, Senna had always been in contention and he finally triumphed for Lotus in 1987, though only after Nigel Mansell's Williams had stopped with turbo trouble after leading for 29 laps.

Senna finally seemed to have the measure of the place but, in 1988, the devious nature of the circuit and the need for total concentration was painfully demonstrated when Senna threw away a comfortable lead by hitting the barrier at Portier. McLaren, however, had the consolation of watching Prost move through to win yet again.

The incident shook Senna just as much as the suspension of his car and it took all his mental strength to come back and truly conquer Monaco by leading every lap in 1989. He did it again the next year and although the duration of the Grand Prix had gradually been reduced to under 1 hour 30 minutes, the unique challenge and the elation of winning there remained.

Monaco's place on the international calendar has been questioned frequently in recent years. The development of the cars has long-since outstripped the usefulness of the track itself; the races, by and large, are processional, the drivers totally frustrated by the absence of overtaking places. The cramped environment has not permitted the expansion found at other tracks and yet, because of that, much of the circuit is just as it was when 'Williams' confounded all predictions in 1929 by winning the race which many critics said would never happen.

Monaco is undeniably steeped in legend and pageantry. It is a breathtaking place. And nowhere else makes the spectator more aware of the drama and bridled forces within a Formula 1 car. As a race, it is often short of quality. As a spectacle, it has no equal. But, assuming the race had never been held before, if you suggested running a Grand Prix at this circuit today, your proposal would be laughed right out of court – much as it was in 1929, in fact.

Wrestling with the Honda at Zandvoort in 1967, Surtees leads the Lotus-BRM of Chris Irwin and Bob Anderson's privately entered Brabham-Climax. After running in the mid-field, Surtees retired with sticking throttle slides.

JOHN SURTEES

When John Surtees bought his first car, a Jowett Jupiter, he was thrilled. Life would be different from now on – but not for the reasons you might imagine for a lad of 18.

Acquiring a car meant he could carry motor cycle parts back to his lodgings and work on them at night. Girls, he admitted some ten years later in a rather solemn autobiography, played but a small part in his life. As he wrote in the formal style of the time: 'I could not then spend the time demanded by a regular friendship of that nature.' Quite.

Everything had its place. The aim – the sole aim – of John's life was to win races. But in the proper manner. Not for him the inherited victory, the cruise-and-collect mentality, the reliance on luck. Which is why, when he won the 1964 world championship for Ferrari in Mexico, he was far from satisfied.

Never mind the fact that he had just become the first – and, to date, only – man to win world championships on both motor cycles and cars. The point was that the Ferrari V8 had not performed satisfactorily on the day. The fuel injection had not been as competitive as he would have liked and the title fell into his hands only after Jim Clark's Lotus failed.

That sort of thing troubled a perfectionist such as Norman John Surtees. It was made worse when gushing hangers-on said he had deserved to win. There was no satisfaction in that. For Surtees, the success he savoured most came from making something work after being told that he faced an impossible task.

Such total dedication brought him seven world championships on motor cycles and six Grand Prix wins with cars, but, along the way, this incurable and at times infuriating stubbornness earned him more enemies than friends. Not that he would have been surprised, since a brutal honesty, to which he subjected himself as well as anyone who crossed his path, had made John realise at an early age that being a loner and working to be the best were necessary bedfellows.

His father, a motor cycle dealer and racer, had instilled independence while, at the same time, keeping a discreet and watchful eye as John prepared his first bike, a Tiger 70, for competition. John had left school at the age of 15 to work for his dad but, after a couple of years, it was decided that a broadening of his engineering knowledge was necessary. John began a five-year apprenticeship at the Vincent motor cycle factory and it was during those years that he rose to the top in racing.

Surtees won for the first time in 1951, and by 1954 he was capable enough to win 50 of the 60 races entered in one season. The dedication involved took some beating, yet John's basic honesty never allowed him to take advantage of his employer's generous attitude. It became a point of honour for John to start on time on a Monday morning, even if it meant sleeping in the back of the van while his mother drove from some distant race meeting to the Vincent factory at Stevenage.

When the pace of his racing increased, thanks to a contract with MV-Agusta in 1956, Surtees left Vincent and concentrated on being a full-time professional. He stayed with the Italian team for five seasons, claiming double world championships in three successive years.

At the end of 1958, the year of his first double, Surtees attended a sports lunch and found himself at a table with Mike Hawthorn (celebrating his world championship on four wheels) and Tony Vandervell. Discussion turned to the merits of both sports and whether or not a master of one discipline could necessarily deal with the other. Vandervell ended the conversation by offering Surtees a test run in a Vanwall; John showed willing but thought no more about it.

In any case, he was too busy in 1959 winning the double once more, as well as the Junior and Senior TTs on the Isle of Man. In October, however, he received an offer to try an Aston Martin sports car at Goodwood. Surtees thoroughly enjoyed the experience and was taken aback when offered a contract on the spot. He declined

for the moment and soon had Vandervell on the telephone demanding to know why, if he was that interested in cars, he was not driving a Vanwall.

This suited Surtees since he was curious to try a Grand Prix car. He completed 170 laps at Goodwood, his best time being under the lap record for the car, a performance which prompted Vandervell to make an offer for 1960 too. Surtees was in a quandry now since he was committed to MV-Agusta for another season and yet the tests had strengthened his desire to switch eventually to cars. He was nervous, too, about joining a works team when he lacked experience. Always the pragmatist, Surtees wanted to be judged on his future performances as a car driver and not on his past achievements as a bike racer. So he chose, instead, to buy a Formula 2 Cooper.

This presented another problem. He did not have the necessary licence and, to get one, the RAC required that he take part in a club race. But with what? While at the Cooper factory John had met Ken Tyrrell, and the shrewd entrant offered a solution by asking Surtees to drive in the Tyrrell Formula Junior Cooper-Austin. John accepted.

His first race at Goodwood was nothing short of sensational. In a wheel-to-wheel battle with Jim Clark and Trevor Taylor, Surtees eventually split the Lotus pair and left observers in no doubt about his natural ability. He was granted a full FIA licence without further ado. Two weeks later he made an equally impressive Formula 2 debut by finishing second to the Lotus of Innes Ireland at Oulton Park.

It was enough to prompt Colin Chapman to offer Surtees a Formula 1 drive, a move which did not sit well with Ireland, particularly when Surtees missed a gear and stuffed the nose of his Lotus into the bank during a test drive. At the following race meeting at Silverstone, Ireland made it clear that such behaviour was not the ticket – and then went out and rearranged the front of his car against oil drums lining Woodcote Corner. Innes, being by nature a gentleman, did not hesitate to apologise to Surtees for such a rude welcome to the team.

The winning smile: John Surtees enjoying
what he could do best. Unfortunately, he also
chose to involve himself in several other
facets of racing.

John's first Grand Prix at Monaco ended in retirement with mechanical failure and, by now, the motor cycle season was in full swing. In a remarkable few weeks, Surtees won the Senior TT for the fourth time, claimed the Belgian motor cycle Grand Prix and then rushed to Silverstone, where he finished second. It was only his second Grand Prix on four wheels. There was more to come.

For his third Formula 1 Grand Prix, Surtees put the Lotus on pole position. Indeed, he would have won the Portuguese race had he not made an elementary mistake, become stuck on the tram lines which were a part of the Oporto circuit, and rammed a kerb with the nose of his car.

In some ways, it summarised an approach to motor racing which occasionally appeared to verge on the desperate. Surtees was driven by this desire to prove that he was as good in cars as he had been on motor cycles – but he had to do it in double-quick time. Showing enormous courage, he set new standards in sheer determination and perhaps did things which, on reflection, would make him wince.

Nonetheless, it had been an impressive first season and Chapman was quick to offer him a contract for 1961. This agitated Ireland somewhat since he felt that he had already lost out on one or two of Chapman's promises. Rather than cause a scene and be accused of receiving favours simply because he was a motor cycle champion, Surtees declined the offer and decided instead to drive a Cooper for the private Yeoman Credit team.

Free of motor cycle racing commitments, Surtees chose a bad year in which to concentrate fully on Formula 1. Ferrari dominated the 1961 season, and although Surtees won a non-championship race at Goodwood, the best he could do in the title race was finish fifth in Belgium and Germany. Along the way, though, he had gathered useful experience without being under the pressure associated with a leading team.

At the end of the season, he received an offer from Ferrari; this, surely, was the answer to his prayers? No, not quite. Surtees,

being Surtees, he felt the time was not yet right. If he was going to drive a Ferrari, then he wanted to be capable of making full use of it.

In fact, it was a sound move in more ways than one because Ferrari were to suffer the most appalling season in 1962. Surtees, for his part, stayed with Yeoman Credit (soon to become the Bowmaker Racing Team) but switched from Cooper to Lola. The move suited him since he was able to use his engineering background and collaborate with Eric Broadley, the Lola designer.

It was a promising venture, but one that ultimately was defeated by a lack of development time and, in turn, confidence-sapping mechanical failures. Surtees still finished the season fourth in the championship. When the team folded, Surtees finally felt he was ready when Enzo Ferrari called for a second time (that, in itself, being a measure of the Englishman's standing).

Surtees was exactly right for the team at this time: Ferrari needed his relentless dedication and the ability to pursue technical perfection. Enzo Ferrari had cleared the decks and 1963 proved to be a year of successful rebuilding, so much so that Surtees took his first Grand Prix win at the Nürburgring. A year later, a second victory for Surtees in the German Grand Prix would prove to be a major turning point.

His hopes had been pinned on Ferrari's V8 engine for 1964 but, as the season got under way, Surtees found that Formula 1 was taking a back seat to Ferrari's efforts to win Le Mans. With that accomplished in June, the factory effort switched back to Grand Prix racing and the win at the Nürburgring was the start of a late rally. A further victory at Monza put Surtees in contention for the title and led to that historic, if slightly fortunate, result in Mexico City on the last lap of the last race of the season.

Cautious as ever, Surtees forecast that he would have difficulty in retaining the title in 1965. It was an accurate prediction, but not quite for the reasons he had imagined.

Surtees did not confine himself to Formula 1 and he raced world championship sports cars for Ferrari with some success.

Early in the year, he also formed his own sports car equipe, Team Surtees, and became involved with Lola in the dollar-rich CanAm series. But in October, during practice for a race at Mosport in Canada, a hub carrier failed and pitched the big car over a guard rail. Pinned under the wreckage and soaked in fuel, Surtees suffered leg, hip and back injuries. Dr McGoey from the local hospital said that Surtees was lucky not to have suffered paralysis and he described his patient as 'a stiff-upper-lip Englishman who is determined to make a rapid recovery'. In fact, Surtees was lucky to be alive.

John was released from St Thomas's Hospital in London in January 1966 and he immediately set about working on a return to fitness. Fortunately the season was not due to start until Monaco late in May and Enzo Ferrari had maintained his faith. Not so the Italian press, and word was out that John would not be strong enough to cope with the latest 3-litre Grand Prix cars. He answered that by completing a Grand Prix distance and breaking the lap record at

as he surged into the lead. Surtees won the final round in Mexico, which was some consolation even though he felt the championship could have been his but for the stupidity of the polemics associated with everyday life at Ferrari.

There had been none of that at Cooper. Instead, John felt he was handling all of the development himself, and the offer to help Honda make a return to Grand Prix racing in 1967 appealed to him more. He had, however, underestimated the drawbacks of working with a major manufacturer on the far side of the world. Development was painfully slow and the car was big, heavy and temperamental. He worked night and day, yet it was a thankless task. Finally, he took the decision to miss the Canadian Grand Prix and, with Lola, to build a new chassis.

Within five weeks, they had the car ready for Monza, where he won after a memorable last-corner battle with Jack Brabham. The Italians, who still held 'Il Grande John' close to their hearts, loved it. So, for that matter, did the man himself. After all, they said it couldn't be done. This was just the sort of victory he relished. Unfortunately, it was to be his last.

More hard work was needed in 1968, and the season's early promise translated into only 12 championship points and, at the year's end, Honda called it a day. Surtees was deeply disappointed since he could see the firm's potential but other outside forces were compelling the Honda management to spend their money elsewhere.

Now Surtees moved into positively the worst phase of his Formula 1 career; he joined BRM. In an interview some time later, he said of 1969:

'Without a doubt, my worst year in racing. I'd rather not discuss it, frankly. That was just paying penance. It was hell.'

When asked what was wrong with the team, Surtees exploded:

'What do you do when you've got woodrot? You cut it out. I started to cut it out but I certainly didn't finish it. I couldn't have

Modena, effectively Ferrari's test track, and then winning a non-championship race.

The Grand Prix season started well when John led at Monaco before the new V12 failed. Then he took a brilliant win in the rain at Spa-Francorchamps but, in truth, all of this was actually creating trouble within team and especially with the team manager, Eugenio Dragoni.

Dragoni favoured the Number Two, Lorenzo Bandini, and did his best to set one driver against the other. Surtees, who got on very well with his Italian team-mate, could see through the politics, but matters came to a head at Le Mans when, by a controversial choice of driver pairings, Dragoni implied that Surtees would not be fit enough to cope. That was more than John could take. He walked out on the spot.

He found a ready berth at Cooper as they laboured with their Maserati-powered car, Surtees putting it on the front row (between the Ferraris of Bandini and Michael Parkes!) for the next race at Reims. Unfortunately, a coupling to the fuel pump broke

A late surge in 1964 brought Surtees and Ferrari the championship.

done. At the end of that year, my health, physical and mental, was at a very low level. I had come to the end of my road and seriously considered getting out of motor racing altogether.'

After a period of convalescence, he decided to build his own Formula 1 cars. He had already manufactured successful Formula 5000 cars and his first Grand Prix machine appeared at the 1970 British Grand Prix. It was on the pace straightaway and John used it to win the non-championship Gold Cup at Oulton Park later in the year. There were to be no Grand Prix wins, however, even though one or two of his later cars had excellent potential. In the end, the task of designing, driving and running the team took the inevitable toll.

Indeed, a refusal to delegate was perhaps his most serious failing. Surtees would agree that he should not really do everything himself, but argued that he could not afford to employ the necessary staff. And yet employees were rendered incapable of making the most straightforward decisions.

On one occasion Bill Gavin, preparing an article for *Speedworld International* magazine in 1968, visited Surtees only to find that John was bogged down in discussions on a wide variety of minutiae. For instance, John wanted to decide where to put the oil catch tank on his CanAm car, the tank's capacity and the material it should be made of; whether or not the suspension should be chromed or phosphated and which firm should be trusted with the work; how a suspension pick-up point should be designed and whether a bolt should be inserted from the top or the bottom. And that was just the CanAm car.

He also threw himself into the management of the Honda project, the negotiation of all contracts, the fixing of entries for the races and the arrangement of travel, the provision of premises, the preparation of the cars, the running of a separate design consultancy. Meanwhile, someone would be hovering, waiting for him to sign a cheque and agree the petty cash. Small wonder he often found it necessary to work from 8.00 a.m. until midnight, lunch consisting of a bacon-and-tomato sandwich warmed on a wall heater.

On top of that, he would scour the motoring press, checking every detail and firing off a long letter to the editor to correct any perceived injustices. It was all part of his forthright nature, something which his employees had to endure as they tried to meet his standards of perfection and avoid the inevitable criticism should they fail.

110

A period he would rather not talk about.
Surtees tackles Montjuich Park with the
BRM V12 in 1969. Note the flimsy protection
for the crowd.

Yet he could be a likeable man; friendly, honest and unsophisticated, with a winning smile. His enthusiasm was infectious, but John had to struggle to maintain it as he tried to run his Grand Prix team in an era when sporting values were being ousted by commercial pressures.

Having fought his way, strictly on merit, to the top, Surtees found it difficult to accept that drivers who patently were not ready for Formula 1 could simply buy their way in. On one occasion he told a driver with a bag of gold that he really ought to have a season in Formula 2 or Formula 5000 first, only for the youngster to turn up not long after in another, less scrupulous, Grand Prix team.

Sponsors were hard to find, and running a serious team on less than a full budget was anathema to him. On top of that, a recurrence of problems from the Mosport injuries meant spending time in hospital which could have been utilised chasing the necessary backing. The false hopes born of promises which ultimately would be broken did nothing to allay either his growing distaste for Grand Prix racing or the strained financial situation. At the end of 1978, he closed the team.

Yet throughout his career he had maintained a shrewd approach to money, a by-product of a streetwise motor cycle racer of the Fifties. He had invested wisely and, once free from racing, Surtees turned to property ownership and development. He spent five years renovating the manor house in which he now lives, with his second wife and family, on a 35-acre spread near Edenbridge in Kent.

A very contented man, he dabbles with his impressive collection of racing machinery, the bikes generating more affection than the cars. In some ways, that sums up his career. The pity is that such a messy end to his association with cars tends to smother the reputation of a very fine driver indeed. Had John Surtees stuck to that task alone, his record in Formula 1 might have come close to matching his remarkable achievements on two wheels. His talent, largely wasted, was that impressive.

The Mexican Grand Prix

John Surtees won the Mexican Grand Prix in 1966, but the race he lost by 69 seconds two years before brought him considerably more acclaim. Second place in Mexico City on 25 October 1964 was good enough to give Surtees his one and only world championship on four wheels and, while that is memorable in itself, he is not likely to forget the drama which surrounded this final race of the season. With Graham Hill and Jim Clark also in the running, the championship passed between all three during the last two laps, but when the music stopped John Surtees and a delirious Ferrari team were left holding the title.

The Mexican Grand Prix had been a fairly recent addition to the championship calendar. Fast motoring was not necessarily the reserve of the wealthy, as the local drivers, their dilapidated machinery permitting, frequently tried to prove; Mexico had already earned a somewhat questionable reputation within international motor sport.

The Carrera Panamericana road races, running from town to town and teetering from potential crisis to potential crisis, had been a spectacular part of the scene. On a smaller scale, European magazines sometimes carried reports in the late-Fifties of circuit races at Puebla and at Avandaro, a 2.4-mile track 100 miles to the west of Mexico City.

The government of the day was totally against motor sport but that changed in the early-Sixties when Adolfo Lopez Mateos, the new President, turned out to be something of an *aficionado*. He encouraged the Comité Directivo del Gran Premio de

Ginther's Honda leads Rindt, Brabham and, the eventual winner, Surtees, in 1966.

Mexico to set about securing a major international race and, to see them on their way, permission was granted to construct a track from the roads within Magdalena Mixhuca, a municipal park in the suburbs of the city.

There was racing there in January 1961. According to the locals, it was an 'international' event, although that may seem of marginal importance when it is revealed that the winning car was a Sunbeam Rapier. More significantly, it was driven by Ricardo Rodriguez, the 18-year-old beating another Rapier – driven by his brother, Pedro, aged 20. They finished 15 seconds apart and lapped the third-placed man who was driving what was vaguely described in *Autosport* as 'a French car'.

The result was not surprising since Ricardo was reckoned to be the more gifted and unrestrained of the two. The brothers, apart from possessing enormous ability, had the support of their father, a wealthy businessman and land speculator. Nothing was too much trouble for his boys and Ricardo could not wait to try his hand at Grand Prix racing.

In 1962 he joined Ferrari during a lean year for Maranello, but his presence in Formula 1 had a lot to do with the setting up of a non-championship Mexican Grand Prix in November 1962. Things were so bad at Ferrari, however, that it was decided not to enter; a major blow for young Ricardo. No matter, he was then in a position to accept a drive in a Lotus entered by Rob Walker, joining the distinguished company of Jim Clark, Jack Brabham, John Surtees and Bruce McLaren.

First reactions to the 3.1-mile track were mixed. The circuit was flat, there was a long straight and, on the back section, an interesting series of curves which increased in speed. None of the foregoing presented any major problems but there were serious doubts over a very slow hairpin at the end of the straight and a banked 180-degree turn at the beginning of it.

The latter was so bumpy that many drivers considered it to be too dangerous. Jack Brabham said: 'You think to yourself, "This is ridiculous to be going round here so slowly. I'll speed up next time." But the next time, and every time, you don't because when you try to speed up, you steer and nothing happens; or, at least, not until the wheels come down for an occasional pitter-pat on the surface. There's no way you can take it flat.'

That rule did not apply to Ricardo Rodriguez. Aged 20, and very much the national hero, he was said to be taking the banking without lifting. As the first practice session unfolded, Clark looked like having secured provisional pole position when Rodriguez went out once more. On the banking, he lost control, hit the guard rail at the top and was thrown from the car. He died of his injuries in front of his parents,

brother, wife and an adoring public. It was the most terrible start to Mexico's first official connection with Grand Prix racing.

On race day, the President arrived and met the drivers. Absent from their number was Moises Solana, the local Formula Junior hero having withdrawn his services because, he claimed, the Cooper-BRM, in which he had been entered by the Bowmaker Team, was not fast enough to enable him to win the race – if you please.

For an utterly chaotic few minutes, it seemed there might not be a race at all. At one stage there were three gentlemen attempting to start the Grand Prix and they could not agree on what to do when Clark's Lotus, on pole position, suddenly stalled. As the mechanics went to work, the start was delayed. Then the trouble really began.

Reporting for *Motor Racing* magazine, Frank Falkner painted the most wonderful picture of the disarray which ensued on the grid. Falkner wrote:

'Still, the Lotus wouldn't go. Eventually it did, after two push starts.

'Are we all ready now? No, indeed, for Surtees' car is on fire – gently, but on fire. So is [Walt] Hansgen's four-cylinder Lotus, and not so gently! Fire extinguishers, mechanics and officials everywhere, and the three starting gentlemen are bouncing hard. One is standing on Jim Clark's wheels, and signalling to the grid to be ready. The second one signals to all that there are 30 seconds to go. The third one, who has the flag, immediately drops it and the motor race is on.

'Messrs. Brabham and Clark shoot off. The starter using Jim as a platform leaps into the air, bounces off the front end of the Lotus and is missed by a hair by [Roger] Penske. Brabham nearly clouts the second "assistant" and only the starter with the flag is safe.'

Clark pulled out his expected lead but, on lap 9, the officials decided a push-start was not allowed and black-flagged the Lotus, Clark duly coming into the pits. That left McLaren and Brabham to fight for the lead but, since this was a non-championship

race, Lotus pulled in the third-place car of Trevor Taylor. The Yorkshireman jumped out, Clark slid into the cockpit and was away without the Lotus having lost a place. McLaren dropped out with impending engine failure and Clark, really motoring now, caught and passed Brabham to win the first Mexican Grand Prix. Lotus were delighted since this particular Climax V8 was on its last legs, having done the US Grand Prix *and* 143 laps of the Indianapolis Motor Speedway in preparation for their assault of the Brickyard in 1963.

That was to be quite a year for Jim Clark. He claimed his first world championship and then came to Mexico, where he won his sixth Grand Prix of the season. This time, the race had been granted championship status, and this time there was no confusion at the start – and no need to have Clark black-flagged.

That dubious honour went to John Surtees after the Ferrari mechanics had push-started his car following a pit stop. There was a fair amount of excitement in the Italian pit when the official relayed the news to team manager Mauro Forghieri. Not that Surtees had been in a position to challenge for the lead since Clark had taken pole position and then gone on to demolish the opposition, setting fastest lap for good measure.

The Mexican Grand Prix became an established part of the calendar, and a welcome one at that, the fussy members of the establishment going so far as to say it was the best organised race of the season. That would soon change. Meanwhile, the teams, more accustomed to being billeted in various garages and odd temporary structures on or near the circuits, luxuriated in the permanent pit buildings at the autodrome, now named in memory of Ricardo Rodriguez. The organisers had also taken note of comments regarding the 180-degree corner and it had been rebuilt, making it smoother and faster.

This race, the last of the season, assumed an even greater importance when Graham Hill won the penultimate round in the United States and Surtees finished second, thus ensuring that they joined Clark in the battle for the championship in Mexico.

To take the title for the second year in succession, Clark needed to win, with Hill lower than third and Surtees lower than second. Surtees had to finish either first or second (with Hill outside the top two), while Graham was the favourite simply because he would automatically become the 1964 world champion if the other two did not finish well.

Clark, true to form, took pole. Surtees was on the outside of the second row, his team-mate, Lorenzo Bandini, alongside. And, as was the custom with Ferrari, nothing was straightforward. Bandini was faster because he had used a flat-12 engine, Surtees relying on a V8. With the freedom to choose, Surtees decided to stay with the V8 for the race in the interests of reliability, Bandini saying he would do everything in his power to help his revered team leader. It was a genuine gesture but it caused a problem or two in the race.

As an aside, the Ferraris were painted blue and white, ostensibly the national racing colours of the USA and the North American Racing Team but in reality a snub by Enzo Ferrari against the governing body of the sport and the Italian national club for their refusal to admit Ferrari's LM coupé as a GT car in sports car racing. By comparison, life was fairly quiet at BRM, with Hill qualifying on the outside of the third row.

Clark tore into the lead, followed by Dan Gurney (Brabham) and Bandini, and the Scot seemed to be in a very strong position right from the start since Hill and Surtees were already in trouble. Graham's goggles had somehow slipped and he was still fiddling with them when the flag fell. Surtees, meanwhile, had a misfire caused by a vapour lock.

Hill was into his stride almost immediately, moving swiftly from tenth place to third – just where he needed to be to win the championship – in the space of 12 laps, by which time Surtees was sixth. Bandini had been demoted to fourth but he was not about to let Hill get away, and two or

three times the very quick flat-12 Ferrari took a run at the BRM as it braked for the hairpin

Hill would have none of it, but Lorenzo was keen to make a good impression – which is precisely what he did against the side of the BRM as the race neared half-distance. Hill spun backwards into the barrier, seriously damaging the exhausts. He made for the pits where the mechanics set about removing the offending parts with crow bars, Hill's chances now looking slim, particularly as Clark was cruising easily in the lead.

As the final laps beckoned, Clark idly wondered who was dropping oil on the track. Taking care to avoid a treacherous patch on the racing line, he was horrified to notice next time round that the trail of oil now followed his new line. He was the culprit. A low-pressure rubber hose had burst. Soon there was no oil left to be spilled. All Clark could do was keep going and pray.

Starting the 65th lap, he slowly crossed the line, both hands in the air pleading with fate to see him through the final three miles. It was not to be. The V8 seized solid not long after. The Lotus team, so close to winning the championship, were utterly distraught.

Now Hill could win the title because Surtees was only third, not far behind Bandini. But if John could finish second, the six points would give him the championship. It took a millisecond for this to dawn on Forghieri and his crew. Instant pandemonium erupted as they ran hither and thither and leapt up and down, desperately urging Bandini to reduce speed, stop if necessary – *anything* but finish second. Lorenzo got the message, backed right off and Surtees swept into second place and the championship.

Everywhere, emotions were confused: elation at such a thrilling finish to the race; delight for Surtees to have won titles on four wheels as well as two; commiseration for Clark as he sat silently with Colin Chapman; great sympathy for Hill as he gamely struggled home in 11th place; and, last but not least, belated congratulations for Dan Gurney, the overshadowed winner who led the one lap which counted most.

Clark made up for the disappointment the following year by wrapping up the championship at the Nürburgring in August, almost three months before the final round in Mexico City. This was to a be historic occasion for reasons other than bidding farewell to the 1.5-litre era.

The race was led from start to finish by the works Honda of Richie Ginther, this marking the first win by the American driver and a non-European manufacturer. It also signalled the opening victory by Goodyear in an association which would see the American tyre giant notch up more than 250 Grand Prix wins during the next three decades. And still the Mexican race remained the most popular on the calendar. Frank Falkner:

'The organisers really look after the visitors and the event has become better each year. They have achieved that most difficult of all states – efficient yet mature and gentle firmness. The lock-up pits are the best anywhere and, finally, the Mexicans are just nice people. Faults? Yes, the park is a sort of waifs and strays dogs' camp, and they

and Denny Hulme came to Mexico to settle the championship. Hulme, now with McLaren, was seen as the outsider; Stewart was expected to win; but the sentimental money was with Hill, now carrying the Lotus team as they struggled on, still in shock over the death of Clark earlier in the year.

There was a diversion during practice as the Rob Walker Lotus of Jo Siffert took pole, with Amon's Ferrari alongside, but neither would be around long enough to interfere with the title fight. And neither, come to that, would Hulme, the New Zealander spinning off (a broken shock absorber) while running in formation with the other two.

Now it was the Lotus and the Tyrrell-Matra: a straight fight. Low fuel pressure accounted for Stewart, but even though Hill appeared to have it made, Graham knew otherwise as his hopes literally hung on a rubber band.

This was the period of absurdly high wings and, Chapman being Chapman, he had decided to take it a stage further by incorporating a device which would flatten the rear wing at speed, or raise it for increased downforce while cornering. The entire operation depended on rubber bands at the point where the wing was mounted on two spindly uprights. One of the bands broke early in the race. But the other hung on to give Mexico another well-deserved winner.

In 1969, Denny Hulme had one of those days when everything went right. Having failed to score a single championship point since the previous June, Hulme came to Mexico City and looked a winner all the way. Not even a poor start would deny him and he sliced through the field to lead and then fend off an attack from an on-form Jacky Ickx, the orange McLaren leading the green Brabham across the line by 2.56 seconds. This had been the seventh world championship Mexican Grand Prix and, while everyone still liked the place, the organisation was becoming lax and the track itself rather frayed round the edges. The honeymoon was over. The separation

occasionally pop out onto the course, causing heart block to several drivers each year.'

In fact, that very problem would occur during practice for the Grand Prix in 1966. A dog ran into the path of the privately entered BRM driven by Innes Ireland, damaging the nose cone, bending a steering arm and cracking a brake disc. It was a sign of the impoverished standards at the back of the grid that the entrant, Bernard White, had arrived in Mexico with very few tools and virtually no spares. Ireland had no option but to race with the cracked disc. It survived the 28 laps Ireland was in the race, the gearbox giving up instead.

Once again, this was the last race of the season and it brought a broad smile to the face of John Surtees as he put his cumbersome Cooper-Maserati on pole and then led for 61 of the 64 laps – some justice for John after he had left Ferrari mid-season. It was also the only victory for Cooper that year and marked one of the final high-points of a marque which was about to go into even more serious decline.

Twelve months later, for instance, a

shortage of engines meant there was just one works Cooper present, driven by Pedro Rodriguez, who finished two laps behind in sixth place. This race provided another opportunity for Jim Clark to display his brilliance, particularly after he had been caught out by the starter choosing to move the flag sideways as a signal to set the race in motion. Clark had been on pole position (his sixth of the season) but momentary hesitation dropped him to third. After four laps, he was in the lead, never to be seen again by the competition, except when all but second-place man Jack Brabham were being lapped.

Indeed, the stunning exhibition by Clark (and also by Chris Amon, who held second place until his Ferrari ran out of fuel) overshadowed the finale of the championship. Denny Hulme slipped quietly into the role by finishing fourth and earning enough points to prevent his boss, Brabham, from continuing in office for a second year. A far cry, this, from the thrill of the chase three years before.

There was everything to play for in 1968, however, as Jackie Stewart, Graham Hill

Chaos of the highest order brought the Mexican Grand Prix to its knees in 1970 and ensured its absence from the calendar for 16 years. Ickx leads Stewart.

would come during a disastrous weekend in October 1970.

Initially the signs were good, Jackie Stewart commenting that the organisers had willingly made the requested safety alterations. All was in order until the day of the race. With about 30 minutes to go before the start, Stewart walked into the pit lane and peered down the straight. He was horrified by what he saw.

Spectators were wandering across the circuit, the flimsy fencing having given way under the pressure of numbers; the crowd was now settling on the edge of the track itself. Victory for Pedro Rodriguez in the Belgian Grand Prix earlier in the year had heightened the already keen sense of anticipation but, unlike the mob at Monza, these people seemed to possess little regard for self-preservation. They were either blissfully unaware of the danger or simply couldn't care less and wanted to share the element of risk with the drivers.

When Stewart and Rodriguez toured the circuit in the course car and made impassioned pleas, they were greeted with beaming faces and warm applause, the fans delighted to have such a close sight of their heroes. In any case, shrugged the spectators, they would move back to the fence if they could but the people there would not let them back in. What did Señor Stewart suggest?

There was little the officials could do. The army had been barred from the circuit because their heavy-handed methods were bound to incite a riot, and the police officers present were equipped with nothing more powerful than whistles. Their best efforts to get the crowd to move back were greeted with laughter and a hail of bottles. Now the track was covered in broken glass.

The drivers did not want to race and the organisers' response was to reassure them that there was adequate insurance; if a driver killed a handful of spectators it would not matter since the driver would be covered.

In the face of this perverse logic, the drivers realised they were fighting a hopeless battle. 'Anyway,' argued the organisers, 'if you don't race there will be a riot' – the inference being that the mob would wreck the place and trample the teams under foot as they went. To compound the absurdity, it was suggested that the drivers should race at reduced speed to prevent the risk of a car leaving the road. Common sense had clearly deserted the officials and the teams reluctantly accepted that they had no alternative but to perform at great risk to all concerned.

The Ferrari of Clay Regazzoni was on pole, with Stewart's Tyrrell-Ford alongside. Within seconds, the field was travelling at 170 mph with the crowd, in places, being no more than five feet away. Jacky Ickx, closing his mind to the hazards, pushed past Stewart and Regazzoni to take the lead and not long after, Stewart had a brief respite when he stopped to attend to a loose steering column. For once, Stewart was sorry to find his mechanics could effect a speedy repair and he rejoined, fearing disaster any second.

On lap 33, a large dog sprang from the crowd and ran in front of Stewart's car. The impact wrecked the front of the Tyrrell and almost sent Stewart into the spectators sitting on the opposite verge. He was livid. After campaigning for improved safety around the world, to have his life, and that of many others, threatened under these circumstances was too much to bear. When he arrived back at the pits, Stewart gave the officials a piece of his mind. And still the race went on.

Victory went to Ickx and Ferrari. By sheer good fortune, no-one had been killed but there was no doubt in anyone's mind that the Mexican Grand Prix would be wiped from the international calendar forthwith. From being the best and most popular race in the series, it had degenerated into the most shambolic affair imaginable.

Besides, the novelty value had long since worn off and the teams were becoming weary of the need to monitor closely what they ate and to avoid, at all costs, the local drinking water. There were few regrets that the visit on 25 October 1970 would be the last for the foreseeable future. And the final blow to the Mexicans came nine months later when Pedro Rodriguez lost his life in a sports car race in Germany.

The circuit continued to be used for local events and although there was never another Mexican driver in the same class as the Rodriguez brothers, there was a continuing desire to have the Grand Prix reinstated. That aim matched Bernie Ecclestone's wish to promote Formula 1 on a truly worldwide basis, so he was keen to listen when approached by a consortium of

Williams-Honda if he won in Mexico. The Englishman did his chances no good at all by failing to find first gear on the line, although in the event tyre wear dictated the outcome as Gerhard Berger ran non-stop to victory in his Pirelli-shod Benetton-BMW.

Berger strongly criticised the track when he returned in 1987. He said he liked the circuit layout but declared the bumps positively dangerous, particularly on the approach to the banked 180-degree Peralta turn leading onto the pit straight. That did not prevent the Austrian from placing his Ferrari on the front row alongside Mansell's pole-position Williams-Honda. The race was run in two parts after Derek Warwick had crashed heavily at the exit of the banked turn, and a one-two for the Williams team meant the championship would be between Mansell and his team-mate Nelson Piquet.

The following year, the race was switched to May to tie in with the Canadian and US Grands Prix, Prost taking a commanding win for McLaren-Honda. In 1989, however, the Frenchman was roundly beaten by his team-mate as Ayrton Senna made the correct tyre choice and led every lap. Twelve months later, the pendulum was to swing dramatically the other way.

Prost had moved to Ferrari and, when he could do no better than 13th place on the grid, it seemed he had little hope of success. Senna led as he pleased for 60 laps but a slow puncture brought unexpected retirement for the McLaren and rewarded a stealthy drive by Prost. Indeed, the end result was a one-two finish for Ferrari as Mansell pulled off the most outrageously audacious move on the penultimate lap by running round the outside of Berger's McLaren – on the banked Peralta corner.

Mansell's manoeuvre was the talk of the paddock afterwards and the Mexicans loved it. It was, they imagined, precisely the sort of move either Ricardo or Pedro Rodriguez would have pulled off on one of the few challenging corners remaining in Grand Prix racing. The Mexican Grand Prix may have had its ups and downs but it had certainly contrived to make its mark on the sport in more ways than one.

local businessmen in the mid-1980s. A massive, US$10 million programme of improvements had been put in hand and Ecclestone was given assurances that there would not be a repeat of the fiasco in 1970. It was agreed that the Grand Prix would return after an absence of 16 years.

The Mexicans were as good as their word. The autodrome had been renamed 'Hermanos Rodriguez' in honour of Pedro as well as Ricardo, the two tight hairpins had been removed, a new pit complex built

to the latest standards and, of greatest importance, the circuit had been lined with two layers of fencing, the inner being topped with barbed wire. Not that it was necessary since the high prices endemic to international sport reduced the attendance to 50,000, a quarter of the number which brought the race to its knees in 1970.

This time, the race was the penultimate rather than the final round of the championship but, even so, there was the possibility that the title could go to Nigel Mansell and

Clark and the Lotus 25 cleaned up in 1963.
Jimmy on his way to victory at Reims.

The pair of Hinchman overalls Jim Clark wore when he won Indianapolis in 1965 hang by the door. They remind you of his small build, but elsewhere in the room the trophies and mementoes tell you that Clark stood much taller than 5ft 6in in the eyes of the motor racing world. Everything about the Jim Clark Room sums up the man and his achievements. It is compact and unobtrusive, totally devoid of pretension, crammed full of success.

Given over by the Environmental Services Department in their headquarters at the end of Newtown Street in Duns, the room is a memorial to a local racing driver who happened to be one of the greatest the world has ever seen. That's the way James Clark was perceived by the proud folk in the Border region. To them, he was a farmer first and a Grand Prix driver second.

But for motor racing fans scattered across the world, the sport has never been quite the same since 7 April 1968, the day Clark was killed in a Formula 2 race at Hockenheim. It marked the end of a brilliant career and confirmed the reality that motor racing is a dangerous game. Until that moment, Jim Clark had seemed indestructible, such had been the easy manner of his driving and a natural ability to make success the end result. When Clark died, many of his colleagues suddenly became aware of their own mortality.

More than that, though, they suffered the loss of a modest, likeable man; a reluctant hero who loved the sensation of speed and control in a car but, once away from the cockpit, felt ill-at-ease amid the hype and hassle of the Grand Prix paddock. His natural habitat was the fields and farms at Chirnside. Motor racing was something which, in Clark's early years at least, became a satisfying pastime rather than a consuming passion.

Jim Clark was born on 4 March 1936 in Kilmany in Fife. Six years later his parents moved to the Borders, settling at Edington Mains, a farm just outside the village of Chirnside. When he left school, Jim went to work on the farm, but in his spare time he established something of a reputation for fast and exciting motoring as he dashed around the countryside in his Sunbeam Talbot saloon.

Clark was friendly with Ian Scott Watson, a local farmer who raced and rallied with determination and a smattering of success. Jim would accompany him on many an occasion, enjoying the spirit of the competition but showing no outward signs of desperately wishing to usurp his friend.

On 3 June 1956 Clark entered his first event, a sprint meeting at Stobbs Camp. Driving the Sunbeam, he won his class against relatively lightweight opposition. A week later, he accompanied Scott Watson to a bleak and exposed circuit at Crimmond, to the north of Aberdeen.

Scott Watson was driving a three-cylinder, two-stroke DKW saloon, the sort of car which, you would imagine, would quickly reach its maximum and require little in the way of skill. Scott Watson asked Clark if he would like to have a go. Clark refused at first, then agreed. Borrowing Scott Watson's helmet and gloves, Clark set off and, on his first flying lap, took the DKW round Crimmond three seconds faster than it had ever gone before.

Scott Watson, no mean driver himself, was stunned. Those who had accompanied Jimmy on the roads had always been impressed by his natural control. Now here was proof of it. Scott Watson insisted that Clark race the car. He finished eighth – but events that day were to have a far-reaching effect and the world of Grand Prix racing would later be thankful for it.

Clark drove mainly in the sprints and trials in 1957 but, at the end of the year, Scott Watson bought a Porsche 1600 Super. He handed the sports road car over to Jimmy and Clark showed his skill by winning a handicap event at Charterhall.

Jim Clark and Graham Hill: friendly rivals,
later to become team-mates.

It was clear to Scott Watson and his mates that they had among their number a driver of quite outstanding ability. The problem was that Ecurie Ecosse (in effect the Scottish national team thanks to their success at Le Mans) attracted the limelight and the trade support. Scott Watson and Jock McBain, another leading light in local motoring, felt that the only answer was to take the battle to Ecurie Ecosse.

They formed Border Reivers (the ancient name of a bunch of marauding Scots) to provide Jim Clark with the support he needed to establish himself. After a career spanning a mere five races, Clark found himself at the wheel of a Jaguar D-Type; with it he became the first sports car driver to lap any post-war British circuit at over 100 mph. That was at Charterhall, but a venture across the North Sea to Spa-Francorchamps proved the comparative irrelevance of racing in local events. This was

serious motor racing and Clark found it a moving experience in more ways than one.

Apart from having to face the magnitude of the circuit's reputation and the challenge it presented, Clark also came up against the sport's unpleasant side when Archie Scott Brown was killed. A fellow Scot, and a remarkable character to boot, his loss in a fiery accident made a strong impression on Clark, one which would never leave him.

He came to detest Spa-Francorchamps, and yet the Belgian circuit, along with Zandvoort in Holland, would give him more success than any other Grand Prix track, a supreme irony with which Clark never came to terms. The remainder of his races in 1958, however, took place at home, and the most significant occurred right at the end, on Boxing Day, at Brands Hatch.

Lotus had just produced the Elite, and Border Reivers bought one of the first from the production line. It was delivered just in time for the Boxing Day meeting and Clark would step into it for the first time and race against, among other notables, Colin Chapman. Clark had never driven at Brands Hatch before but that apparent handicap was forgotten when he heard Chapman and another Elite driver, Mike Costin, discussing whose turn it was to win. On behalf of Border Reivers, Clark was determined to sort out these Sassenachs.

Chapman was no sluggard, particularly in one of his own creations, but Clark took the lead and on a greasy Club Circuit began to pull away. Had it not been for a wayward back-marker, Clark would have won. In the event, Chapman had been able to witness at first hand a raw talent which he would later help mould into something very special.

The Border Reivers continued their good work, much to the consternation of Ecurie Ecosse. Time and again Clark embarrassed the established team and it was clear that the two forces really ought to combine. That happened in August 1959 when Clark was asked by Ecurie Ecosse to share a Tojeiro-Jaguar with Masten Gregory in the Tourist Trophy at Goodwood.

Gregory was something of a hero to Clark and Jimmy's confidence received an

enormous and unexpected boost when he found he was as fast as the bespectacled American. Quite why Clark should have looked up to Gregory is not certain. Masten was quick enough all right but more often than not ended his races spectacularly, usually by vacating his car before it had crashed to a standstill. The TT was no exception, Gregory arriving at a corner too quickly, whereupon he stood on the seat and was flung to safety as the Tojeiro-Jaguar rammed the bank head-on.

Suitably fortified – mentally, if not by hard results – Clark accepted the offer of a test drive with Aston Martin. The big, powerful sports car appealed to him but Clark was not entirely sure he was ready to go along with Aston Martin's plans for Formula 1. He signed, but the Grand Prix programme never got into its stride, which was just as well since Chapman had plans for Jimmy in that direction.

Clark had also driven a Formula Junior Lotus on the same day as the Aston Martin test and he agreed to race with Lotus in Formula Junior and Formula 2 in 1960. It was to be the start of an outstanding relationship, one which remained unique. Clark would drive for no other Grand Prix team and his career in Formula 1 got off the ground sooner than he – but perhaps not Chapman – had anticipated.

At the time, Innes Ireland and John Surtees constituted the 1960 Formula 1 team, so when Surtees had a clashing motor cycle commitment at the time of the Dutch Grand Prix, Clark was offered the drive. It was an impressive debut, the Scotsman running in fourth place before retiring. Chapman had no hesitation in persuading Clark that he was ready for Grand Prix racing on a full-time basis.

The full implications of this new commitment came two weeks later at Spa-Francorchamps. Mindful of his experience there two years before, Clark's reticence was justified when he rounded a corner in time to see marshals removing the body of the Englishman Chris Bristow. That was bad enough, but Clark was later appalled to discover that his friend Alan Stacey had also

Inch-perfect with the Lotus 33 on his way to another victory, this time at Silverstone in 1965.

been killed, after a bird had flown into his face. On top of that, Stirling Moss had suffered serious injuries during practice and Michael Taylor had crashed when the steering broke on his Lotus. It did nothing for Jim Clark's feelings about this unforgiving circuit.

If Jimmy hated Spa-Francorchamps, then he loved Monaco. In 1961 Lotus introduced a new car, the 21, at this race and Clark put it onto the front row, but his hopes were dashed when an ignition lead came loose after a couple of laps. It was an omen of things to come at Monaco, but such mechanical problems would be minor when compared with the political drama surrounding the Italian Grand Prix that year.

Lotus were up against the sharknose Ferrari, and to keep pace Clark needed to tuck the slim Lotus into the slipstream of these powerful cars, a tactic which was particularly appropriate at Monza. Clark did just that when pursuing Wolfgang von Trips and the two cars touched as Clark pulled alongside, von Trips clearly unaware of his presence. Both spun off, the Ferrari crashing into a fence, killing the driver and 14 spectators. Stunned by the tragedy, Clark also had to endure the strain of facing an Italian law which placed responsibility on the driver in any fatal accident. In all, the past 18 months had been a severe test for a man who still considered himself to be more of a farmer than a racing driver.

Things looked up with the introduction of the Lotus 25 in 1962. The car, with its revolutionary monocoque body, got off to a shaky start by retiring with mechanical problems at Zandvoort and, needless to say, Monaco. Next came Spa-Francorchamps, and this would prove to be a fine test of Clark's quiet determination.

Trouble during practice meant very few laps and a start from the fifth row. This did little for his confidence since he wished to conquer his fear of the place, and yet he was about to go racing at an average of more than 130 mph without having the benefit of adequate practice. His tactic would be to acclimatise himself fully during the opening laps, weigh things up and go on from there.

up some of his other activities in that year.

Chapman had decided to take a Lotus to Indianapolis and challenge the establishment. America was not Clark's cup of tea and he disliked the informality, the immediate use of first-name terms and the general assumption that they knew best – particularly at Indianapolis.

One piece of procedure which he resented was the need to complete a rookie test. Clark may have been a modest man but he had his pride and he found it humiliating to have to lap at predetermined speeds, increasing pace as directed in the manner of a novice. All of this merely strengthened his resolve to beat the Americans at their own game. He nearly did it first time out, but unfamiliarity with the rules conspired against him.

The rear-engined Lotus, a greyhound among the lumbering front-engined cart-horses, was the quickest car by far and the use of petrol rather than alcohol-based fuel allowed Clark to make one less pit stop. He was catching Parnelli Jones with ease when the roadster began to drop oil in large quantities. The teams had been told beforehand that anyone dropping so much as a smidgeon of oil would be blackflagged. But this did not take into account a certain amount of Brickyard prejudice.

The man with the black flag prevaricated and, unusually, Chapman did not make a fuss. He did not think Jones would make it to the finish. It was a mistake on two counts. Jones won and many observers felt Chapman should have stood his ground. No matter, it merely increased the desire to return and do a proper job.

Clark led in 1964 until a manufacturing fault caused a rear tyre to throw its tread. The following year – with the majority of runners now using rear-engined machinery – Clark walked off with the $170,000 first prize. Niggled by the thinly veiled criticism of the British invasion two years before, Clark had answered the comments in the best possible way. More than that, he had earned respect and a special place in their affections. The Indy 500 was not a race he enjoyed but it was different, a challenge,

His first flying lap was five seconds faster than his best lap during practice. He was in fifth place, calmly sitting behind the leading bunch. After seven laps, he decided he had learned the circuit in the Lotus 25 and he set the fastest lap of the race thus far as he moved easily into second place. Trevor Taylor, in the lead at the time, waved his team-mate through and Clark simply disappeared into the distance. Pressing on faster than was perhaps necessary, Clark nailed his apprehension and banished his emotions from the cockpit. It was his first Grand Prix win – and a deeply significant one from a personal point of view.

Clark went on to win two more Grands Prix that year and was in the running for the championship until, during the final round in South Africa, the engine lost its oil when a bolt fell out of the distributor drive housing. Few people, though, were willing to bet on anything but a Clark rout in 1963.

And so it proved, as a record-breaking seven races in a season fell to Clark and Lotus. Among them was Spa-Francorchamps. Monaco, once again, was absent from the list, the gearbox being the culprit on this attempt. It almost goes without saying that Clark had been leading at the time.

He settled his first world title at Monza, but the celebrations were tarnished by investigations and accusations over the accident two years before. It was a messy ending to the championship, which rather summed and the brute power of the 4.2-litre Ford V8 was certainly something to savour. But the razzmatazz you could keep. And to think that he had missed the Monaco Grand Prix to do it.

Not that it mattered. In 1965, Clark won the world championship for a second time and there were suggestions that this might be a good moment to retire. Lotus did not have a decent engine in the offing for the change to the 3-litre formula in 1966 and there was the feeling that Jim would marry his longtime girlfriend, Sally Stokes, and return to Edington Mains, the family farm having been in his charge for some time. Jimmy had been asked frequently about marriage but he fobbed the press off with the response that racing was a single man's occupation. Now, perhaps, was the moment to change his lifestyle.

In fact, the relationship with Sally petered out and in 1967 she married Dutch driver, Ed Swart. By then, Jim Clark was more committed to racing than ever. He had become a tax exile, spending much of his time in a flat in Paris and busying himself with Formula 1, Formula 2 and Indianapolis. This was to be his last season of Grand Prix racing and, although he was not to win the championship that year, Clark's driving reached even greater heights of easy perfection.

It had frequently been said that Jim Clark's success came through the possession of the best car on the grid. That may have been true of the Lotus 25 in 1963 but Clark had the ability to use it to the maximum. At Reims, for instance, Clark found that the Lotus was quicker through the curved section but slower than the serious opposition on the straights which predominated. He knew he had to break clear of his pursuers immediately and extend his lead through the curved section if he was to avoid being embroiled in the slipstreaming endemic to that track.

Pictures show the start and, within a few hundred metres, Clark was already several lengths ahead, glancing in his mirror at the wheel-to-wheel mob jostling for position. By the end of the lap, he was 2.7 seconds

ahead. His second lap, always a Clark speciality, was quicker still. The opposition was destroyed. Similarly, in 1966, Clark did things with the 2-litre Lotus 33 which his rivals with 3-litre engines could not hope to emulate.

But, in 1967, he had a problem of a different nature entirely. Chapman introduced the Lotus 49 and the Ford-Cosworth DFV. The V8 engine went on to become the mainstay of Formula 1 but in these early stages it was as difficult to drive as it was impressive, the power coming in a lump at around 6,500 rpm.

Clark tamed that car, winning first time out at Zandvoort and then using its vices to invoke glorious power slides around Silverstone. Clark won that race too, and they towed him round the circuit on a tractor and trailer for a lap of honour. The impeccably behaved crowd flocked to the edge of the track and applauded him all the way.

He had made the race boring but there was something about Jim Clark which was instantly compelling. He had the appearance of a little boy lost; a shy, good-looking superstar who appeared to have difficulty living the part out of the car. That, of course, was the great attraction. Little did the British enthusiasts know that this would be the last time they would see their hero at close quarters.

He won two more Grands Prix that year and produced perhaps one of his greatest drives after stopping to replace a punctured tyre at Monza, unlapping himself and working his way back into the lead – only to run out of fuel. On New Year's Day Clark opened his account for 1968 by winning the South African Grand Prix, a significant result in many respects.

It was Clark's 25th win – a record at the time – and this race marked the last occasion a Lotus would be seen in its traditional

green with the broad yellow stripe. Not long afterwards, Chapman introduced tobacco advertising to his team, the Lotus Grand Prix cars appearing in the garish scheme of Gold Leaf. Clark never got to race the Formula 1 car in those colours.

On 7 April, he was booked to take part in the Formula 2 race at Hockenheim in Germany. He was never on the pace that weekend, the grey, dull Sunday seemingly matching his introspective mood. Lying eighth and neither threatening nor being threatened, Clark's Lotus 48 suddenly left the road on the long curve leading to the top end of the circuit.

A number of theories were put forward and the most likely seemed to be that a deflating tyre had come off the rim. Whatever the cause, the absence of any barriers allowed the Lotus to smash broadside into a tree. Clark was killed outright.

The effect of this was stunning. When the news broke, people simply could not take it in. Not only had this happened during a relatively minor event on a circuit few people knew anything about, it had removed a safe, gifted driver who had seemed indestructible. Motor sport was suddenly vulnerable and without a leader.

It was front page news in all the morning papers. The facts spoke for themselves. He had started 72 Grands Prix and won 25 of them. He had started from pole position 33 times, led for 6,331 miles and set the fastest lap 28 times.

His many fans knew all of that. But what they remembered was the grace and the fluency in a Formula 1 car, the special moments when he relaxed by driving a Lotus Cortina in a manner which took the breath away. They recalled the time in 1962 when, driving a twin-cam 1,500 cc Lotus at the Nürburgring, he finished the first lap of the world sports car championship race almost a minute ahead of the rest of the field. By the time fumes from a broken exhaust manifold finally overpowered him, he was 2½ minutes ahead of the best the likes of Ferrari could provide.

Then there was the day at Oulton Park in 1964 when he stepped into a GT car, a sports car and a saloon car in turn and won all three races. Or the incident at the same circuit in 1966 when he arrived at Old Hall, sideways in his Lotus Cortina, to find a massive Ford Galaxie having a huge accident. Clark swiftly changed direction and went through the gap between the bank and the tail of the steaming Galaxie, foot hard on the power, glancing in his mirror and grinning as he went. There were but inches to spare on either side.

People also remember the time he took himself off to Rockingham and drove in a NASCAR race just for the hell of it. Or the pleasure he gave while hurling a Lotus Cortina through the forests during the 1966 RAC Rally. They still talk about it at Boreham and the way that, once his rally was over courtesy of a stout tree, Jimmy kept turning up at the Ford service areas and on special stages, just to join in the fun.

More than that, though, this was the man the public could relate to: the international star who spoke with a soft Scottish burr, chewed his fingernails to the bone and disliked pushing forward at airports to avail himself of the VIP treatment which was there for the asking.

In the final months, Clark had developed a decidedly more mature look. When he rolled the green Lotus into the winner's enclosure at Kyalami, the late-afternoon sun picked out the relaxed features of a man who clearly found the business easy. Indeed, the sojourn in Paris had given Clark a taste for the cosmopolitan life. He enjoyed it and, contrary to the widely held view, it was unlikely that Jimmy would have returned to farming at Edington Mains.

He would never have relinquished his past, though. Indeed, at Hockenheim he had said he was looking forward to visiting Scotland for the first time in many months and much of this had to do with the feeling of well-being imbued each time he returned to Chirnside. In the early days, nothing pleased him more than exchanging his crash helmet and overalls for a tweed cap and flannels. That explained why his unassuming nature was not tainted by success.

In Duns and Chirnside, the season and its rewards are determined by nature and tractor-power rather than tyre grip and brake-horsepower. The locals knew Clark was an excellent driver, but a successful lambing at Edington Mains meant more to them than a win at Monza and Indianapolis. Sure, they were proud, very proud, of his achievements. But in the Borders, you don't boast. You simply do your best and say nothing about it. Quiet pride is the motivating force here.

It is the same in that grey stone building housing the mementoes and trophies. There is no need for garish neon and rampant commercialism. Just a gentle guiding hand should you need it. It is the perfect approach. Of the 250,000 or so who have travelled from all corners of the world to pay their respects, the vast majority had never met Jim Clark and yet, somehow, they felt they knew him very well indeed.

The Dutch Grand Prix

The Zandvoort circuit, host to a round of the world championship in the Netherlands between 1952 and 1985, frequently produced one of the most exciting races of the season. The 1964 Dutch Grand Prix, however, was not one of them.

It was a tedious race insofar as Jim Clark led every lap. But, on this day, his immaculate performance placed him in a completely different class from the rest. He may have won the race as he pleased, but he did it in a manner which underscored his artistry and confidence. It was a splendid example of how he had become the man to beat.

It was not a matter of the Lotus being head and shoulders above the competition. Clark was not on pole, although, according to the general consensus in the pit lane, he should have been. This, of course, was in the days before computerised timing, and it was felt that the time-keepers had been confused by Clark and Dan Gurney running in close company when they recorded their respective quick laps.

Not that an error would have made much difference since the Brabham and the Lotus were only a tenth of a second apart and, in any case, Clark was unable to improve on his time during the remaining practice ses-

Trouble looming. Jim Clark is escorted from the rostrum in 1965 while the police are not far behind Colin Chapman, the troublesome armband clearly attached to his belt.

sions. For good measure, Graham Hill's BRM was but a whisker away from them both.

So, a win for Clark was not a foregone conclusion. Yet, before the start he had enough conviction in his own ability that he reached an agreement with Colin Chapman over the information to be relayed on his pit board. Assuming everything went according to plan and he took the lead, Clark asked simply to have the gap to the next man displayed on the board. Nothing else. Almost as an aside, he told Chapman that when the gap reached 45 seconds, he would ease off. It was not a confidence-boosting boast. He meant it.

And he carried it out to the letter. Chapman studied his stop watch with increasing admiration as the lead extended little by little with each lap: three seconds after five laps, four seconds after ten laps, five seconds after 15 laps, almost ten seconds after 20 laps.

Gurney, meanwhile, was in trouble; the spokes of his steering wheel had cracked at the hub and he had to abandon the race when the Brabham team were unable to find a spare wheel. Hill was suffering from fuel vaporisation, John Surtees then moving his Ferrari into second place. After 40 laps, Clark was 29 seconds ahead.

At 50 laps he was 40 seconds to the good and, on lap 55, he reached the required figure. Chapman duly showed 45 seconds on the board and Clark eased off for the remaining 25 laps, his times never varying by more than a second despite being in cruise mode. It looked easy and faultless but, in fact, that was not quite true.

Watching at the corner behind the pits, Denis Jenkinson of *Motor Sport* noted that Clark, on one occasion, bumped the inside kerb; not the sort of thing Jimmy would have done in the normal course of events. Clark later explained the reason to Jenkinson.

Leaving nothing to chance, and remembering the hazard presented by wind-blown sand at this circuit, Clark had taken precautions to seal round the edge of his goggles. To make sure they were a close fit, he had adjusted the strap – too tight, as it turned out. During the race, the goggles began to dig into his face and press on his forehead, the result being a splitting headache.

It was during a moment of acute pain that he missed his apex and clouted the kerb. In fact, the headache was so bad at one stage that he almost wished the car would break down but, perversely, it kept going for the required two hours seven minutes and 35.4

seconds. Indeed, it did not miss a beat and Clark had no complaints with it.

'That's the infuriating thing about Jimmy,' observed Chapman afterwards. 'He goes like a clock and, when I ask how the car was, he just says "Oh, fine", and leaves it to me to decide how to improve it for the next race.'

Chapman need not have had any worries on that score. Or, at least, not at Zandvoort. Clark won there the following year, making it three on the trot in Holland, and when the Dutch Grand Prix finally disappeared from the calendar, it was Clark who had won the most races at the circuit, having taken the Lotus 49 to victory in 1967. During the years, as we shall see on the following pages, Clark had one or two stressful moments at Zandvoort but, by and large, he subscribed to the view that it was a pleasant and rather unusual place to hold a race.

The circuit had been laid out in the sand dunes close by the seaside town of the same name. The layout had been the responsibility of John Hugenholtz, one of the very few specialists in circuit design. A Bachelor of Law at the University of Utrecht, Hugenholtz had been the President of the International Federation of Vintage Car Clubs. As a keen sporting motorist, he knew exactly what was required to make a circuit successful from a driver's point of view and Zandvoort epitomised that.

Hugenholtz maintained that a circuit should have several fast corners and a slow one, and the latter he put at the end of the long straight. As the principal place for overtaking, it guaranteed dramatic racing as the drivers positioned themselves to advantage on the fast run past the pits and prepared for frantic outbraking on the approach to the gently banked hairpin.

Known as Tarzan, this corner, and the deeds of daring it encouraged, quickly entered the folklore of motor racing. From there, the drivers went through a fast left and into a tight but fairly quick right at Gerlachbocht, before jumping on the brakes for a 180-degree left-hander. This was directly behind the pits and therefore a popular vantage point, particularly as there would fre-

quently be lurid tyre-smoking moments into it and invigorating opposite-lock slides on the exit as power was applied for the brief climb up Hunze Rug.

Now followed a glorious succession of sweeping bends, rising and falling with the contours of the dunes and leading to a blind but very fast rise through Scheivlak, before the road fell away immediately on the other side. With the North Sea a few hundred yards to the left, the track rushed through a fast right, over Tunnel Oost and on to the rise leading to a sweeping right at Pulleveld. This was critical since a quick exit determined the speed through the gentle curve leading onto the main straight. It was a simple circuit, but a very effective one.

The 2.6-mile track was built in the years immediately after the Second World War, but, since the Dutch were short on both experience and racing machinery, the British Racing Drivers' Club was asked to venture across and christen the circuit in 1948. The first major meeting took place the following year, the main event for Formula 1 cars consisting of two heats and a final. Luigi Villoresi's Ferrari won the first heat, Reg Parnell took the second and, in the final, Alberto Ascari looked like winning until his Ferrari lost a wheel five laps from the end. Victory in the so-called Zandvoort Grand Prix eventually went to Villoresi.

For the next two years, the major race at Zandvoort was known as the Netherlands Grand Prix although it did not form part of the championship. On each occasion it was won by the elderly Talbot of Louis Rosier but, when the stakes were raised and the Grand Prix was recognised as a round of the championship in 1952, the race became serious.

Unfortunately for the Dutch, this was the year of Formula 2 and total domination by Ascari. Zandvoort was no exception and he led from start to finish, clinching the championship in the process. It was a tedious affair and, apart from the lively intervention of Mike Hawthorn in his Cooper-Bristol in the opening stages, the order of the leaders remained unchanged for 90 laps. It did little

for Zandvoort's somewhat parochial image and matters were not helped when Ascari repeated the performance in 1953.

In February 1954 there were hints that the Dutch Grand Prix might not be held that year, the reasons varying from the need to carry out extensive repairs to the track, to the absence of Mercedes-Benz (who would not be ready to make their comeback) which might 'rob the race of much of its international character'. A few weeks later the organisers confirmed their intention to opt out of the championship.

They might have done so in 1955 as well had the race been scheduled a month or so later. The date fell on the weekend following the Le Mans tragedy and, in the general unrest and overreaction which followed, there was muttering about races being cancelled left, right and centre. The immediate worry for the Dutch, however, was the rumoured withdrawal by Mercedes-Benz following their part in the Le Mans accident, but the Rennabteilung duly turned out and totally destroyed the opposition. Fangio and Moss, running nose to tail for 100 laps, were never headed, the only interference with their dominance being fastest lap to the Maserati of Roberto Mieres, the Argentine driver receiving a large Delft china windmill for his trouble. It was touches like that which made this Grand Prix a popular one, although the Dutch in general, still mindful of events ten years before, were probably delighted to have someone other than the Germans receive an award.

Financial difficulties led to the cancellation of the Grand Prix in 1956 and, when the same thing happened no more than a month before the proposed date in 1957, there was an undercurrent of dissatisfaction in the motoring press – as much displeasure as you were ever likely to see in those more conservative and gentle days. The organisers blamed a failure to reach a financial accommodation with the fuel companies, and it said much for the race's popularity that it was accepted as a round of the 1958 world championship. For those British enthusiasts who had made the short hop

across the North Sea, it was a memorable day as Stirling Moss led all the way in his Vanwall, green cars filling five of the top six places. The best Ferrari could manage was fifth – and that was down to an English driver, Mike Hawthorn.

There was further jubilation in the British camp in 1959 when Joakim Bonnier gave BRM their first and, after such a long wait, rather emotional victory. Bonnier had been headed briefly by the Cooper-Climax of Stirling Moss until gearbox trouble forced a pit stop, but otherwise it was a well-deserved result. The BRM team celebrated in the nearby Bouwes Hotel that night, the hosts, Mr and Mrs Louis Stanley, basking grandly in their moment of triumph.

BRM did not have much say in the 1960 Dutch Grand Prix. This turned out to be a Brabham/Moss benefit, Stirling adopting a conservative policy which, ironically, led to his downfall. Tired of criticism that he pushed too hard in his determination to lead at all times and win by the largest possible margin, Moss found himself behind Brabham's Cooper and decided to stay there, pacing himself rather than fighting to take the lead and pull away.

On the 17th lap Brabham put a wheel on the dirt, as was his wont, and dislodged a flat granite square, sunk into the sand to mark the edge of the track. The stone broke in two and the Cooper's rear wheel flicked a sizeable piece in Moss's direction. It smashed a wheel on the Lotus and punctured a tyre, forcing Moss to endure not only a slow drive back to the pits but also a minor pantomime as the Rob Walker mechanics stuggled with the jack and then went through the ridiculous but necessary

business of dismantling the hub in order to change the wheel. The only positive thing to be said was that it sparked off a typical Moss comeback drive as he raced into fourth place. Brabham won easily, the Cooper being followed home by Ireland's Lotus and the BRM of Graham Hill.

At the end, though, there was a sad note when it was learned that a teenage boy had been killed. During the race, a rear brake pipe had failed on Dan Gurney's BRM as he reached the end of the main straight. With only his front brakes operational at 160 mph, Gurney was barely able to slow the car before it ploughed straight on at Tarzan, smashed through a fence and flew through the air before landing on a pathway below. Gurney was shocked but unhurt.

British euphoria was rampant 12 months later when the Dutch race fell eight days after Moss's brilliant defeat of the Ferraris at Monaco. Zandvoort, however, would provide a more suitable stage for the power of the 'sharknose', all three Ferraris occupying front row of the grid. Phil Hill was on pole but Wolfgang von Trips took the lead at the start and was never headed, largely because Hill had his hands full while dealing with an impudent challenge by Jim Clark.

This was the Scotsman's first Grand Prix, not that you would have known it as he overtook six cars on the first lap and tucked in behind Hill. The four-cylinder Climax was no match for the V6 but what the Lotus lacked in power it more than matched the Ferrari in handling. Hill could ease away on the straight, only to have Clark revel in the precision of the Lotus through the quick curves on the far side of the circuit. In the

Peter Collins at Silverstone: very British but at home with Ferrari.

Overleaf: 1958 Dutch Grand Prix: Mike Hawthorn's Ferrari tackles the start of Hunze Rug at the back of the Zandvoort pits.

Left: Stirling Moss and Vanwall: riding the Karussel at the Nürburgring in 1958.

Top: Peter Collins negotiates Station Hairpin at Monaco in 1958, now the location of the Loews Hotel.

Above: Tony Brooks labours in vain after engine trouble had put his Vanwall out of the 1958 Monaco Grand Prix. Graham Hill, racing at Monaco for the first time, flashes past in his Lotus on the climb to Casino.

Left: The awesome brick-faced North Curve at Avus, scene of the German Grand Prix in 1959.

Above: The fast right after the pits in the open expanses of Reims in 1960. The original circuit runs straight on.

**Stirling Moss prepares for action in a Rob
Walker Cooper, the number 7 and a Union
Jack in evidence as usual.**

**Jackie Stewart: making his name in the Ken
Tyrrell Cooper-BMC Formula 3 car in 1964.**

Top: Not at home. Jim Clark speeds past a natural hazard on his way to a fourth victory at Spa-Francorchamps, a circuit he detested.

Left: Graham Hill had to fight for everything, particularly in his early days with Lotus.

Above: Jim Clark: inveterate nail-biter and natural genius.

Top: John Surtees on his way to victory with the Cooper-Maserati at Mexico in 1966.

Above: The sublime and the ridiculous. Jochen Rindt leads at Barcelona's magnificent Montjuich Park not long before the high-wing Lotus crashed out of the 1969 Spanish Grand Prix.

Right: Jim Clark leads the field out of Club Corner and into the Esses at Kyalami in 1968. High in the background, the grandstand and control tower on the main straight. The South African Grand Prix was to be Clark's last.

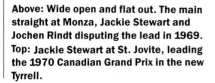

Above: Wide open and flat out. The main straight at Monza, Jackie Stewart and Jochen Rindt disputing the lead in 1969.
Top: Jackie Stewart at St. Jovite, leading the 1970 Canadian Grand Prix in the new Tyrrell.

Right: The Renaissance Centre towers over the pit straight at Detroit, home for the US Grand Prix for seven years.

John Surtees would have been more successful had he concentrated solely on driving.

Peter Gethin: the fastest winner.

Jackie Stewart: at a brilliant peak in 1973.

James Hunt: hero and villain.

John Watson: a gentle touch in a rough business.

Nigel Mansell: supremely quick and spectacular but his own worst enemy.

end, though, horsepower plus Hill's skill and experience won the day, but Clark was well satisfied with third place and the fastest lap.

Normally, on a Grand Prix debut, a driver would be told to take it easy, concentrate on a finish and gain experience. 'Do that,' a team manager would say, 'and you may pick up a point or two when those ahead of you drop out.' It was just as well Clark did not adopt that tactic since, in this race, all 15 starters finished. And not one of them made a pit stop. It is a remarkable statistic, unlikely to be equalled.

It was a different story in 1962 when half of the 20 starters retired, Clark among them. But his name was on everyone's lips once more because he had led for 11 laps with the striking new Lotus 25 before gearbox trouble intervened and left the way clear for Graham Hill to score his first Grand Prix win. Clark struck back with a vengeance the following year as he lapped the entire field. That was not the only way he made the news.

During the final practice session on Saturday, Clark seemed so secure on pole position that he wandered over to the corner behind the pits to watch the competition struggle to match his time. A policeman approached and asked to see Clark's pass. Upon being presented with the necessary accreditation, the policeman insisted it was not good enough and ordered Clark to move from a spot which was regularly frequented by pressmen and photographers alike.

When Clark refused, the officer grabbed Jim by the lapels of his windcheater and dragged him to the pits where a horrified official hurriedly stepped in. The policeman marched off without offering an apology, causing great embarrassment all round since, two days before, the Dutch organisers had received the Grand Prix Drivers' Association award for the best-run Grand Prix of 1962.

This was not to be the last brush between a member of Team Lotus and the Dutch police. And on this occasion, the custodians of the law got their own back by refusing to grant Clark and Chapman permission to enter the press enclosure to conduct a post-race radio interview.

There was more media work necessary in 1964 following Clark's flag-to-flag performance, and again in 1965, when Jimmy won his fourth Grand Prix in succession that year. The daily press, however, were more interested in the turn of events as the police closed in on the Lotus pit immediately after the race.

Trouble had started when an auxiliary policeman, charged with clearing the grid, failed to see Colin Chapman's pass and told him to leave. When attempts were made to remove the Lotus boss forcibly, Chapman responded by decking the policeman with a very fine left-hook. He thought no more about it until after the race when a deputation arrived to make an arrest. A struggle ensued, the Lotus mechanics holding Colin by the feet while the police tugged his arms and Hazel Chapman grabbed one of the officers by the hair. In the end, the law had its way and Chapman was put in the local jail for the night, his only accompaniment being bawdy songs courtesy of a motley group of Lotus supporters, fresh from their celebrations and gathered outside the police station. Chapman was eventually released after a successful court hearing a few days later.

The advent of the 3-litre formula in 1966, and talk of a subsequent increase in performance, prompted the Dutch organisers to move their pit and control buildings 20 feet further back from the main straight and extend the paddock towards Tarzan. With Brabham having made the most of the change in regulations with his 3-litre Repco engine, he was expected to repeat his Brands Hatch victory of the previous weekend. But that did not anticipate perhaps one of the greatest drives of Jim Clark's career.

Saddled with a 2-litre Climax V8 while Lotus waited, almost in vain, for the 3-litre BRM engine, Clark nevertheless relied on this being a driver's circuit to take the battle to Brabham and his team-mate Denny Hulme. It was a superb contest, Clark somehow managing to lead for 49 laps and, when he was not, he had to put up with a splendid piece of team driving as Hulme did his best to defend Brabham's lead. It ended when a vibration damper on the front of the crankshaft broke and smashed a water pump outlet on Clark's car, leaving Brabham untroubled for the rest of the afternoon.

Lotus leapt back to serious contention in 1967 and they chose Zandvoort for the debut of their new car, the 49. Clark had not so much as set eyes on the 49 when he arrived at Zandvoort and his initial acclimatisation took place during practice. Graham Hill, on the other hand, at least had the benefit of some test laps and he knew something about the manner in which the considerable power of the Ford-Cosworth engine kicked in at around 6,500 rpm. He put the Lotus on pole. Clark was eighth.

Hill led until problems with the camshaft drive brought retirement on lap 11. Getting into his stride, Clark began to move forward and he took the lead and maintained it to the finish despite the Ford engine being far from perfect at the end of 90 laps.

The performance of the Ford-Cosworth DFV that day prompted a spectating Ken Tyrrell to place an order for the following year and, appropriately enough, his car won the Dutch Grand Prix. This victory, though, had more to do with the choice of tyres and the delicate touch of the driver.

For once Zandvoort, normally blessed with dry weather at Grand Prix time, was faced with drizzle on race day. Most drivers thought the rain would ease and accordingly fitted dry tyres. Jackie Stewart compromised by selecting dries, but with a hand-cut drainage channel in the middle. When the drizzle became serious not long after the start, Stewart was perfectly equipped and he came through to take the lead from Hill. For the rest of the afternoon – and it was a long one, the race lasting for two and three-quarter hours in these conditions – Stewart stroked the Tyrrell-Matra towards a victory he had not truly expected at the start of the weekend.

It took Stewart just over two hours to repeat the result in 1969, only on this occasion it had nothing to do with a tyre advantage. Pacing himself carefully, Stewart waited for the Lotus of Jochen Rindt to retire before taking the lead and setting a new lap record *en route* to his third win of the season. It reminded Stewart of how pleasant this place could be, but all that would change 12 months later.

This race was won by Jochen Rindt, a significant victory since it marked the beginning of a new era for the wedge-shaped Lotus 72. But Rindt's forlorn features as he stood on the rostrum spoke of something else.

On the 23rd lap, Piers Courage had crashed at the back of the circuit, his de Tomaso leaving the road at high speed and careering into a sand dune, where it caught fire. They were unable to remove Courage from the inferno and the loss of this most dashing and popular young Englishman hit the Formula 1 circus very badly. It did little for Zandvoort's reputation either, which was further damaged by appalling scenes at the same circuit three years later.

But in 1971 the Dutch Grand Prix produced one of its more memorable races, even if the weather was best forgotten. Pouring rain favoured Firestone tyres and it so happened that two wet-weather experts, Jacky Ickx and Pedro Rodriguez, were so equipped. The rest, on this freaky day, were literally nowhere.

For almost two hours the Ferrari and the BRM ran in close company, Ickx leading for 48 laps, Rodriguez for 22, the pair of them trading places and thoroughly enjoying the intensely fought battle. Eventually, Rodriguez had to give best when the BRM V12 refused to run cleanly at low revs, but even then he was only eight seconds adrift at the finishing line. The third-place man, meanwhile, was more than three miles behind.

Doubts over the future of the circuit and an inability to bring it up to the required safety standards led to the cancellation of the Grand Prix in 1972, but the work had been completed by the July deadline 12 months later. This included the introduction of a new corner – Panorama-bocht, a slow right-hander with a wider left-hand exit just before the curve leading towards the main straight. It was a reasonable alteration, but not enough had been done in other departments.

The record books show that this was Jackie Stewart's 26th victory, thus taking him past Jim Clark's previously unbeaten total, but the Tyrrell driver, as a leading safety campaigner, had other things on his mind that evening.

Half-way round the eighth lap, Roger Williamson's March had crashed at the exit of a fast, fifth-gear right-hander. The barrier on the outside of the corner had bent backwards on impact to form a launching ramp, which threw the March to the opposite side of the track, where it landed, upside-down against the armco, and caught fire.

David Purley, who had been running in close company with Williamson, stopped and ran back. Single-handed, he tried to pull the March upright. Then he attempted to get underneath and release the trapped driver. All the while, Purley was pleading for assistance. There was none.

When the fire suddenly erupted into vastly more serious proportions, Purley was beside himself as he tried in vain to summon help for his friend. Eventually the fire was extinguished but, by then, the young English driver was dead. The miserable scene had been caught by the television cameras. Grand Prix racing in general, and the Zandvoort rescue services in particular, were in total disgrace.

The 1974 Grand Prix, by comparison, was trouble-free. The organisers, stung by the inevitable criticism, had redoubled their efforts and a fleet of rescue vehicles was positioned at regular intervals around the track. Niki Lauda enjoyed an effortless win for Ferrari. When he was fastest in every practice session the following year, it seemed a repeat performance was in store. A shower of rain at the start changed everything.

Lauda took the lead, but as the racing line began to dry, James Hunt made the brave decision to stop before everyone else and change to slicks. It would turn out to be one of the best tactical moves of his career. Lauda stayed out for another six laps and, as he returned, he was overtaken by Hunt, now firmly in the groove and fully *au fait* with the remaining hazards of running slicks on a track which was still damp in parts.

Lauda, in fact, dropped two or three places, but he soon recovered and, with 20 laps to go, he was on the tail of Hunt's Hesketh. Now another shrewd move by the Englishman came into play. Hunt had set up his car for dry conditions; Lauda had compromised slightly and, while that had paid off in the wet, he was suffering a straightline disadvantage at this crucial stage. Hunt held him off, the portly figure of Lord Hesketh wobbling with joy as the white car, with its red and blue stripes, crossed the line to give James his first Grand Prix win.

Another victory for Hunt the following year proved to be a vital part of his championship battle for McLaren, but in 1977, he became involved in a controversial manoeuvre with Mario Andretti at Tarzan, the two cars touching and Hunt's McLaren crash-landing into retirement. Lauda and Ferrari, meanwhile, were waiting to profit from this folly.

In 1978 Ferrari were not in contention, for this was the year of the Lotus 79 and nowhere was this more evident than at Zandvoort. The black-and-gold cars of Mario Andretti and Ronnie Peterson filled the front row and ran in tandem throughout, Peterson dutifully playing Number Two as Andretti racked up further points for his championship. The following year, however, the Dutch Grand Prix was as eventful as the race in 1978 had been predictable.

After a false start to the season, the Williams team had got into their stride and Alan Jones was seen as the favourite. The race developed into a tremendous battle between the Australian and Gilles Villeneuve as the French-Canadian made the most of a slightly softer tyre on his Ferrari. Gilles, showing his usual daring, snatched

the lead by running round the outside of Jones at Tarzan. He pulled away but, as his Michelins began to lose their edge, Jones closed in.

The drivers, worried about speeds on the back section of the circuit, had asked to have a chicane inserted. It was designed by a committee – and looked it. Dubbed the Scheckter Chicane in dubious honour of its principal architect, it was a tight left and right which simply did not flow. Coming through here on lap 47, Villeneuve – who, ironically, was Scheckter's team-mate – spun but, typically, kept the engine running and carried on as though nothing had happened.

Villeneuve had a punctured left-rear but did not know it. Thinking his tyres had gone off he signalled his intention to make a pit stop at the end of the next lap. At the same moment, the tyre exploded. Villeneuve kept the car roughly in a straight line before spinning to a halt at Tarzan.

Then, to the astonishment of all and sundry, the rear wheels kicked into life as Villeneuve restarted and he set off to complete the two and a half mile journey to the pits. He reckoned that so long as there was life in the car, it was worth continuing. By the time the three-wheeler reached the pits,

the tyre had gone and the wheel and suspension were a heap of metal trailing behind the car. He received a round of delighted applause from his mechanics but the car was too far gone for anything else. Jones, meanwhile, won easily.

Jones might have repeated the exercise in 1980 had he not made a simple mistake as he led the field on lap 2. Allowing the Williams to run over a kerb at Hunze Rug, he damaged a sliding side-skirt, and the subsequent pit stop not only cost time but also allowed Nelson Piquet, Jones's main championship rival, to score maximum points with his Brabham-Ford. Jones was in the thick of the action once again in 1981, but ultimately the Ford-Cosworth-powered Williams was no match for the Renault turbo of Alain Prost, the Frenchman soaking up the pressure to take his second of many Grand Prix wins.

Didier Pironi won for Ferrari in July 1982 and a fairly dull race was made memorable by a spectacular crash when the left-front wheel of René Arnoux's Renault parted company as he braked for Tarzan. The Frenchman rammed the tyre barrier at high speed but failed to break the altitude record set two years before when a brake problem on Derek Daly's Tyrrell sent the

Irishman cart-wheeling into the air before landing without injury to the driver. When it came to shunts of this nature, Daly did not do things by halves.

Arnoux enjoyed a faultless run to victory in a Ferrari the following year, although his success was due to the championship contenders, Prost and Piquet, colliding while disputing the lead. The incident happened at Tarzan (where else) and Piquet was forced to retire his Brabham-BMW on the spot, Prost running out of road later in the lap as a result of the damage sustained to his Renault.

That race had been significant for the first appearance of the McLaren-TAG turbo. It did not take Prost and Lauda long to hone the new combination into competitiveness in 1984, and Zandvoort marked a record-breaking ninth win in one season as Prost crossed the line ahead of Lauda. The Austrian had made the wrong tyre choice that day, but in 1985 he got it right. Or, at least, he timed his pit stop to perfection and found himself leading Prost.

The race was between these two, and they drove the final three laps as though it were a Formula Ford dice – wheels on the dirt, ducking and weaving, brakes locking. In the end, and exhilarated by the heat of this battle, Lauda kept the young pretender at bay. It had been a consuming battle of tactics and skill.

And it was the last we were to see at Zandvoort. The financial strain was telling and moves were afoot to sell off part of what had become a prime site. Eventually, the track was more or less cut by half and the Grand Prix never went back.

It has been greatly missed. The location, a 30-minute train ride from Amsterdam, had its appeal and the race was invariably exciting, if only because of that long haul down to Tarzan and the furious activity it encouraged. Zandvoort, with its salty taste and sand under foot, lacked grandeur. It had its faults and the marshalling could either be officious or inept; sometimes both. But, overall, the Dutch track was a pleasant place to be and worthy of inclusion in any international calendar.

Stewart put on a brilliant display during his first visit with the BRM to Spa-Francorchamps in 1965, the only driver capable of challenging Clark. A year later, in similar conditions, his views on the circuit would be changed under dramatic circumstances.

There was the occasion when a journalist thought he was recording an interview. It was a lengthy and lucid affair, as serious discussions with Jackie Stewart invariably are, and the writer was pleased with the way it had gone. To his horror, he later discovered that the tape had not recorded a single word.

What to do? Try and remember what had been said? Not a chance; there had been too much careful analysis and too few brief replies. Forget it altogether? No, given his organised mind, Stewart was likely to ask how the story was progressing when next they met. The time allocated for the interview had been a valuable slot during a busy weekend at a Grand Prix. The only answer was to come clean, confess the incompetence and apologise for wasting his time.

'No problem,' said Stewart. 'You can come with me in my car to the airport when this is all over and we'll do it again.'

Sure enough, Stewart was as good as his word and patiently went through the routine for a second time, even pausing at the airport to finish the full interview. Of course the answers were, in many cases, carefully rehearsed; some of the questions had been asked, one way or another, many times before.

But that was not the point. There had been no need for such an accommodating response to the writer's dilemma. Stewart had done his bit at a time when he had other worries, such as trying to win the race and the championship. It was not even as if the journalist represented a prestige publication (he was working for a struggling British monthly). In the eyes of some drivers, the man would have been nothing but an impediment the first time; a gross irritation the second.

Stewart has always been acutely conscious of image, massaging it and working it to the maximum. There is a healthy ego at work here. Overall, he ought to be insufferable, yet he is not. The ability to poke fun at himself and others overrides the threat of self-importance. He will have made light of the botched interview by, from time to time, cheerfully reminding the journalist of his inefficacy, usually in mixed company, but always without malice.

The incident occured in 1973. It could be that Stewart's generous attitude was coloured by the private knowledge that he was planning to retire at the end of the year, but such a suggestion would do an injustice to the professional standards he attached to every aspect of his nine seasons in Grand Prix racing.

During that time, he won three world championships and set a record of 27 wins from 99 starts. When Jim Clark was killed in 1968, it was Stewart who stepped forward as the man to beat, another Scot with the canny ability to cope with the pressures associated with conducting a racing car faster than anyone else.

Originally John Young Stewart thought he might be a footballer. Born in Milton, Dumbartonshire, on 11 June 1939, his only connection with cars was the family's Austin (and later, Jaguar) dealership, handily placed at Dumbuck on the Glasgow–Inverness road. His fancy for soccer began to be superseded by an interest in racing when he accompanied his elder brother Jimmy to motoring events.

Jimmy drove sports cars for Ecurie Ecosse and he was soon quick enough to find himself racing a Cooper-Bristol in the 1953 British Grand Prix. He lost sixth place that day when he spun off during the closing stages and it was a fair indication that Jimmy was not over-endowed with luck. When he later broke his arm in the same place for a second time, doctors advised him to abandon a promising career. Jimmy duly devoted his time to the family business.

Jackie's curiosity had led him to experiment with cars on the snow-covered forecourt of the garage. Barely able to see over the wheel of an elderly Austin, he found he could make the tail slide with excessive use of the throttle. Better still, he could control it with opposite lock. It was a thrill which would never leave him. The thought of going racing had occurred but, having witnessed at first hand his mother's anguish over Jimmy's activities, Jackie decided it would be best to try a less hazardous sport.

Jackie's grandfather had been a gamekeeper for Lord Weir, a local landowner, and this association instilled in the Stewart family a love of shooting and fishing. Jackie applied those skills to trap shooting. He was an excellent shot; too proficient, in fact, for his own good. Certain of a place in the British team for the 1960 Olympics, he lost out through complacency when it came to the final selection. It was a shattering blow, but a serious lesson had been learned and it stood him in good stead when finally the lure of racing proved irresistible.

R. P. Stewart & Sons of Dumbuck had among their customers a wealthy motor racing enthusiast, Barry Filer, who entrusted the garage with the preparation of his cars. Jackie worked on the AC Bristol and the Porsche Super 90. As would become his hallmark, he considered no detail too small for his attention. Under family pressure to quit racing and impressed by the immaculate turn-out of his cars, Filer offered Stewart a drive in the Porsche at a sprint meeting near Ayr. That was the start of it.

For fear of upsetting his mother, Jackie raced under the unoriginal name of 'A. N. Other', but soon the word was out. By then, he had established a considerable reputation in Scottish club events as he urged the Porsche and a particularly ugly Marcos GT into places where they had no right to be. With parental approval, he expanded his activities to include racing the company's Jaguar E-Type demonstrator, a move which helped to attract the attention of Ecurie Ecosse.

The heady days of Le Mans in the Fifties had since passed and the Scottish team's venerable Cooper Monaco was proof of that. Nonetheless, Stewart used this sports car to astonishing effect, particularly when it was noted that, due to rather haphazard repairs after an earlier shunt, the suspension was not exactly spot-on and one wheel was always higher than the other three.

Stewart was eventually to put this car out of its misery against a tree at Oulton Park.

By then, he had impressed many, including Robin McKay, the track manager at Goodwood. When McKay discovered that Ken Tyrrell was looking for someone to drive in his Formula 3 team in 1964, McKay suggested he give Stewart a trial.

In the light of what was to follow, it would turn out to be a historic event, one which would instantly earn Tyrrell a reputation as a talent-spotter. 'That's rubbish,' says Ken in his customary unambiguous manner. 'If you couldn't see, on that day, that Jackie Stewart was a natural, then you were an idiot.'

Stewart, who was more or less unknown to Tyrrell, had never driven a single-seater before. Ken delivered a lecture, saying there was no need to try too hard; they had all day. Bruce McLaren, then the works Cooper driver in Formula 1, was on hand to

establish a time in the Formula 3 car. On his third lap, Stewart equalled it. Another lecture followed. McLaren got back in the car and went faster. Stewart went quicker still, but without so much as working up a sweat. Tyrrell signed him on the spot.

Stewart was to have a sensational year. He won all but two of the Formula 3 races in 1964 and, now that he was a full-time professional, he raced anything he could lay his hands on. In 53 starts he drove 16 different cars, won 19 times, finished second twice and third five times. Formula 3 taught him to drive smoothly and get the most out of a relatively underpowered car. A subsequent step into Formula 2 brought his first experience of strong, relentless competition and the need to employ racecraft and sometimes to bide your time.

Remarkably, he came second in his first

Formula 2 race. Even more exceptional was the fact that he had been asked to drive a Formula 1 car on the same weekend – and this barely a few months after he had first sat in a single-seater. The offer came from Lotus, and Stewart turned down the chance of a non-championship race in preference to taking one step at a time. It was a typically cautious and measured move and, as ever, it was the correct one; offers of Formula 1 contracts for 1965 came regardless.

Cooper, Lotus and BRM were interested. Cooper were in some disarray following the departure of Bruce McLaren to set up his own team and the temporary absence of John Cooper in the aftermath of a road accident. Lotus was tempting, particularly as Colin Chapman had already allowed Stewart his first taste of Formula 1 by offering him a couple of laps of Brands Hatch during practice at the British Grand Prix meeting. But working with Chapman would not be easy and a Number Two post at Lotus had never proved to be a bed of roses, particularly with Chapman concentrating his efforts on Clark. BRM, on the other hand, had a potent car, the promise of valuable testing and the guidance of an amenable (and, dare it be said, possibly beatable) Number One in Graham Hill. Stewart chose the latter.

It was a sign of those comparatively relaxed times that BRM agreed readily to a request by Chapman to have Stewart stand in for Clark (who had slipped a disc while throwing snowballs) in a non-championship race in South Africa at the end of the year. The thought that it would be useful experience turned out to be correct, Stewart suffering the disappointment of a broken driveshaft at the start of the first heat and the elation of winning the second.

The remarkable story continued into 1965. In his first season of Grand Prix racing, he scored a point in the opening race, won the non-championship International Trophy, finished third at Monaco, then second at Spa-Francorchamps and Clermont-Ferrand. When Hill drifted wide at Monza and the second BRM was ready to snap up the nine points, no-one, except perhaps

Stewart himself, was unduly surprised. It seemed so easy.

At the end of the year, he was third in the championship, a remarkable achievement and one which led effortlessly into a victory at Monaco, the first race of the 1966 season. On his first – and only – visit to Indianapolis, he was leading by a lap when the engine broke. Then the bubble burst. The next race at Spa-Francorchamps almost killed him.

On the first lap, he was not alone in being caught out by rain and Stewart, now saturated in fuel, was trapped in the cockpit while Hill and another driver feverishly worked to release him from a wreck which threatened to burst into flames any second.

There was worse to follow. The medical facilities were as good as useless, Stewart being taken to a first aid tent where they could do little to ease the pain from a broken shoulder, a cracked rib, petrol burns and heavy bruising. The ambulance, when it arrived, provided a bumpy and haphazard journey as the driver got lost, twice, on his way to the hospital.

All this fashioned Stewart's resolve to do something about making the circuits safer in the event of an accident. If a driver made a mistake, then that was his fault. But the least he could expect was decent back-up from the moment the car left the straight and narrow. Stewart would campaign vigorously to bring about an awareness of the problem in a sport seemingly content with past values. It was not the done thing to discuss safety, and his views, which were considered to be extreme, made him very unpopular with the establishment. He could not have cared less, such was the depth of his feelings on the matter.

There was one problem, however. His credibility was weakened as each race went by without a win. Stewart had recovered in time to take part in the British Grand Prix but he scored points just once during the remainder of the season.

The future held out little hope since, by staying with BRM for 1967, he was lumbered with the H-16, an engine which could not match its complexity with power. Since

the accident at Spa, he had insisted on having a spanner taped inside the cockpit to facilitate quick release of the steering wheel; he was the first to have a seat harness fitted to his car. There was the suggestion that he had lost his bottle, that the accident had wiped out an unfettered brilliance fed by the naïvety of a novice.

Proof of his commitment came, fittingly enough, at Spa-Francorchamps when he took the BRM into second place while holding the big car in gear for most of the way. At the best of times Spa required two hands on the wheel, and this performance banished any thought that the circuit and its past would compromise his driving. But it brought him no closer to a win.

The following year, he was leading the Belgian Grand Prix before making a late stop for fuel. Then, after a drought lasting two years and one month, he finally won the Dutch Grand Prix.

Now he was at the wheel of a Matra, the French aerospace company having previously worked with Tyrrell in Formula 2. On the basis that the Formula 2 chassis was one of the best he had ever driven, Jackie was happy to go along with Tyrrell's plan to work with Matra when Ken took the step into Grand Prix racing. This was typical of Stewart. It would demonstrate that making the right decision at the right time is a vital part of the racing driver's art. Tyrrell was new to Formula 1 but Stewart knew the team and he was familiar with their capabilities.

It was to be a brilliant partnership, rounded off by the Ford-Cosworth engine

and Dunlop tyres which Jackie had painstakingly developed. Stewart won two more Grands Prix that year, his performance at the Nürburgring being one of the most commanding and memorable of his career. In rain and mist he simply left the rest standing. There was no-one in his class, in those conditions, on that particular circuit. By the time he had finished, vacated his car and mounted the rostrum, the second-place man had just emerged from the gloom to take the flag. Jackie had always wanted to savour the achievement of winning at the Nürburgring – but not under terrifying conditions such as these.

He finished second in the championship that year and, for 1969, Matra produced the MS80, a superb Grand Prix car, one which Stewart would enjoy driving more than any

other. It showed in a succession of consummate performances as he walked off with his first world championship.

Along the way, however, he staged an unforgettable battle with Jochen Rindt at Silverstone, the pair of them racing wheel-to-wheel, first the Matra leading, then the Lotus. The incredible pace eventually took its toll on Rindt's car but, when the 84 laps were over, the thrill of such a clean chase marked this race down as another for Jackie to savour.

He had need of such memories to sustain him through 1970. Motor industry politics determined that Tyrrell could no longer use the Matra chassis if they wanted to retain the Ford-Cosworth engine, and no-one wanted to provide a car to such a lethal combination as Tyrrell and Stewart. No-one except March, the fledgling company welcoming the world champions (and their money) with open arms.

It was an appalling car, even though Stewart somehow managed to coax it to victory in Spain. By mid-season he was in despair, since not even his expertise could wring a sensible performance from such a wilful machine. The only answer was for Tyrrell to build his own car and, from the moment it first appeared towards the end of the season, it was clear that J.Y. Stewart would soon be back on the winning trail.

The first victory of 1971 came in Spain and, by the time the British Grand Prix arrived, the combination was so refined that Stewart was able to reduce the race to tedium as he walked off with his fourth win of the year. By August, he had his second championship thanks to scoring almost twice as many points as the next man.

It all seemed so straightforward, particularly when he won the opening race of the 1972 season. So when he made an uncharacteristic error in Spain and then spun in the wet at Monaco, there was clearly something amiss. An ulcer was diagnosed and he had to forgo the Belgian Grand Prix. The reprieve for his rivals did not last long; he won the next Grand Prix and rounded off the season with two more victories. The ulcer, by this time, was just as celebrated.

Certainly, the illness heightened his already keen notions about being in peak physical condition. Stewart may have been a mere 5 ft 6½ in in his flame-proof socks, but his broad shoulders told of the physical strength which would help him to a remarkable victory in a super-stars fitness competition not long after he had retired. A personal supply of All-Bran was regarded as a piece of equipment just as vital as his overalls and helmet. He fussed greatly over the constituents in his food, hardly ever drank alcohol and never smoked.

His strict regime may have been the butt of paddock humour but he literally seemed to bounce with health. His jaunty walk, up on the balls of his feet, smacked of confidence from the minute he arrived in the paddock. Rarely did he seem, in public anyway, to be fretting over the likes of roll bar settings and tyre compounds. It was most disconcerting for rivals, and in 1973 there was no let-up.

With little to choose between the Lotus-Fords and the latest Tyrrell, Emerson Fittipaldi won the first two races, Stewart took the third, Fittipaldi won the fourth, with Stewart claiming the fifth.

Round six went to Fittipaldi's teammate, Ronnie Peterson. This was the Swede's long-awaited maiden victory and, with that hurdle overcome, it was felt there would be no stopping a man with such thrilling car control and speed. Sure enough, he was on pole at the next round at Silverstone – and then Stewart simply cut the feet from under him.

Peterson led through Copse and into the fast left at Maggotts. Going into Becketts, however, Stewart arrived on the inside, going at an entirely different sort of speed. It almost seemed as though his brakes had failed. With one easy, positive movement, he snatched the lead. Poor Ronnie could only shake his head in disbelief. For the rest of that lap, Stewart put the hammer down. This was in the days before the Woodcote chicane and Stewart came through there in one long, glorious arcing drift. Peterson was destroyed.

Then they stopped the race following a

multiple collision. Stewart had it all to do again. As the drivers waited in the pits and tried to control their pent-up emotions, Stewart casually wandered past Peterson. 'Well,' he grinned, 'you know about Becketts now, Ronnie. I'll have to try somewhere else next time.' And off he went, chuckling and bouncing. Peterson was seriously nonplussed. As it happened, Ronnie would have the last laugh because Stewart was to spin off while attempting a similar move at Stowe.

There were no mistakes at the Nürburgring as Stewart led every lap. Once again, he made it look easy as he remembered every corner and committed himself to each with cast-iron confidence. It was only after others had later driven the 1973 Tyrrell that it became clear what a nervous and difficult car he had mastered during his march into a third world title.

That win, on such a perilous track, was to be his last and yet, when asked to name his most memorable races, it does not come into the reckoning. Jackie quotes three: the Nürburgring in 1968, Silverstone in 1969 – and Monza, his penultimate Grand Prix.

The records show that he finished fourth that day in Italy but they do not begin to describe Stewart's drive. Delayed by a puncture early in the race, Stewart lost over a minute in the pits. He rejoined in 19th place and, on his first flying lap, he went faster than he had done during practice. This was a startling indication that he had cast all inhibitions to one side and was cer-tainly not about to be depressed by his new-found circumstances.

By half distance, he was into eighth place, slicing between one and two seconds per lap off the leaders. When he caught and passed Mike Hailwood at a chicane to take sixth, the Tyrrell disappeared so quickly that Mike thought Jackie must have spun off. And so it went on, the race running out just as he was closing on third place. The final bonus was that the points were enough to assure Stewart of the championship.

Driving at Monza was relatively easy – and that was the beauty of this perfor-mance. Because of its straightforward nature, the circuit demanded total perfec-tion if a driver was to make up ground. He had to be technically correct all the time. A careless moment and that fraction of neces-sary extra speed would be lost.

And there was another aspect to this drive. Some months before, Jackie had decided to retire. He told no-one except Ken Tyrrell and Walter Hayes of Ford. Knowing that to be the case, it would have been easy to cruise home. But Stewart could not resist the challenge presented by such long odds and the personal pleasure to be gained from controlling a racing car at its limit.

The down-side of the sport was to smack Jackie in the face just as he was heading towards the exit door. The United States Grand Prix would not only be his last but also his 100th. During practice, his dashing young team-mate, François Cevert, was kil-led under appalling circumstances and the team withdrew. Jackie made public his retirement three days after attending Cevert's funeral.

Stewart was thus forced to leave with a bitter reminder of the sport's ability to devastate. It revived thoughts of 1970, a desperately low period when three top-line drivers were killed, a time when the sadness seemed never-ending. The accident at Wat-kins Glen made his safety campaigning seem fruitless and worthwhile at one and the same time. More than that, it under-scored the fact that he had emerged from all of this never having spilt a drop of blood.

The question was asked whether he would be tempted to make a comeback. After all, he was only 34 and, by his own admission, he was burnt-out, in need of a break and time to recharge. But what would he do then? Surely he would miss the unique excitement provided by a high-adrenalin lifestyle which he had developed into a first-class art.

A series of track tests for a magazine arti-cle in 1978 suggested that some part of his make-up was in need of attention, be it plain curiosity or polishing a dulled ego with the knowledge that he was just as quick as before. One thing was sure; there was no talk of a return and he did not do the track tests for money.

At an early stage in his career, financial expediency had prompted him to move to a beautiful home overlooking Lac Leman in Switzerland. If anything, he was soon earn-ing more 'in retirement' than he ever did while racing.

Stewart's world today is defined by air-craft, hotel rooms and car-phones; he thrives on being busy and the more com-plex the job in hand the better he likes it. As a consultant and spokesman for tyre com-panies, motor manufacturers and what he describes as 'blue chip companies', his schedule is tied in with commitments to his son's racing team, checking progress at his shooting school in Gleneagles, making pub-lic appearances and giving interviews. Punctual to a fault, dressed smartly to suit every occasion, Stewart is just as well known now as he was when racing more than two decades ago.

If something of note happens in Formula 1 and an opinion is required, then Stewart is always poised with an informed and easily understood comment. He has the credibil-ity to back it up and he is a master of the motor racing 'word-bite'. He knew exactly what he wanted out of racing and now he understands fully the requirements of the media. Indeed, as the incident with the recalcitrant tape recorder proved, it was always thus. Jackie Stewart was, and still is, the consummate professional in a world that is largely peopled by mere amateurs.

The Spanish Grand Prix

everything about Jackie Stewart's win in the 1971 Spanish Grand Prix was as close to perfect as you could wish. If Stewart's definition of a successful driver called for the subtle amalgamation of many talents, then this race was proof of it. Victory on 18 April 1971 required skill, speed, judgement and applied thought. And all of these had to be utilised on one of the most dramatically spectacular circuits ever used, not just in the history of the Spanish Grand Prix, but in relation to the sport as a whole.

Montjuich Park was a stunning place, everything about it having a magical, if sometimes ethereal, quality. It made a wonderful circuit, but somehow you felt it would never last, even though the majority of drivers relished the challenge it pre-

sented. It was almost too good to be true.

Located in Barcelona's largest park, it was easy to reach and overlooked this majestic city. The circuit, measuring 2.35 miles, started at the highest part, corkscrewed its way to the bottom, swept past the palace and then picked up pace through some fast uphill sweeps on the return leg.

The best section, for spectators if not the drivers, came immediately after the pits. In top gear, the cars crested a rise – barriers, trees and a lamp-standard on the left; barriers, trees and imposing buildings on the right – before walloping back onto the track and immediately plunging downhill towards a very tight left-hand hairpin at the bottom. And, for good measure, the track curved gently to the left at this point. It called for perfect positioning of the car before the jump then vicious braking and swift

A Maserati, Peugeot and Bugatti wait for the start at San Sebastian in 1930. The Maserati of the winner, Varzi, is on the second row, behind the Bugatti.

down-changing. It tested everything, from the strength of the car to the durability of the driver's nerve. And it also represented one of the few places on the circuit where overtaking could be carried out. A steely place, Montjuich Park.

When Jackie Stewart arrived in April 1971, this was the second round of the championship. Contrary to the usual run of business for the Tyrrell driver, a win was not a foregone conclusion. Indeed, he had been without maximum points for exactly a year, representing a serious drought for someone of Stewart's expectations. The team were feeling their way with their first car, introduced the previous September, and the pressure was now on to produce the results. Tyrrell had opted to run with Goodyear tyres, but the American firm had also been without a win for 12 months.

Furthermore, it was suggested that the Ford-Cosworth DFV was past its best; a fine engine and all that, but not enough cylinders. The flat-12 Ferrari was enjoying a run of success and when Jacky Ickx put his on pole, with Clay Regazzoni's similar car in the middle of the front row and the V12 Matra of Chris Amon on the outside, only a blind man could fail to see the writing on the wall. As if racing at Montjuich Park was not difficult enough at the best of times, Stewart also had to contend with such paddock scuttlebutt.

He was on the inside of row two, but with a plan of attack in mind. Stewart knew that the Ferraris were not at their best with a full load of fuel. It was imperative, therefore, that he get to the front early and build a cushion against the inevitable attack later in the race.

He managed to overtake Regazzoni on the first lap and set about closing the 1.6-second gap on Ickx. Within a couple of laps he was right on the tail of the Ferrari, pushing and probing, generally trying to unsettle the Belgian as he struggled with the handling.

The tactic worked. At the end of lap 5, Ickx ran wide very slightly as he came through the fast corner leading onto the pit straight. Stewart lined himself up and began to squeeze alongside as they headed at full speed for the crest of the hill. With no room for error by either driver, the cars went dangerously light before hitting the deck with full force, Stewart hard on the brakes – but on the inside line for the hairpin which followed. It was a bold but necessary move. At the end of the next lap, he was one second ahead and going away.

Half-way through the 75 laps, Stewart was 8.5 seconds in front and the gap increased slightly until there were 20 laps remaining. Then the attack came, Ickx equalling his pole-position time and reducing the deficit to 6.2 seconds. Stewart responded by dipping below his best practice effort but Ickx kept coming: 4.4 seconds, then down to 2.8 when Stewart was held up by a back-marker with exactly ten laps to go. Two laps later and Stewart went faster than Ickx's pole time; the gap was 3.9 seconds.

Ickx gave one final push, setting the fastest lap of the race – almost a second quicker than pole – and edging to within 2.4 seconds of the Tyrrell. It was as close as he would get, but neither driver relaxed for a moment, Stewart crossing the line 3.4 seconds to the good. It had been a superb contest which truly matched the surroundings. Stewart had given Tyrrell their first Grand Prix win and he had been made to work hard for it.

This had been the fifth world championship Grand Prix in Spain since the Second World War and, indeed, only the second visit to Montjuich Park. The background to the Spanish Grand Prix runs much deeper than that. It is a confusing assortment of events and circuits, their various histories intertwined in a *mélange* of unimportant meetings and full-blown international motor races, sometimes held at the same circuit within a matter of days.

For the record, the first major race in Spain was held at Sitges in 1909, the so-called Catalan Cup won by Jules Goux in a Lion-Peugeot. The first Spanish Grand Prix as such is credited to a touring car race, held at Guadarrama in 1913 and won by Carlo de Salamano in no less a vehicle than a Rolls-Royce.

In 1923, the Autodrome de Terramar (the remains of which were still visible 50 years later) was opened near Sitges by the King of Spain, but international attention was focused on the Lasarte circuit near San Sebastian on the north coast. The 11 miles of country roads were narrow, twisty and poorly surfaced and, in 1924, there was the additional hazard of drizzle throughout the San Sebastian Grand Prix. Henry Segrave played a waiting game while others crashed and, at the end of an arduous race lasting just over six hours, the Englishman was first to cross the line in his Sunbeam. He was also the last to do so in a British car (in a Grand Prix) until Tony Brooks won for Connaught in Syracuse in 1955.

In 1925, the San Sebastian Grand Prix was won by Albert Divo, who is also credited with winning the Spanish Grand Prix two years before on the banked Autodrome de Terramar. Just to confuse matters further, the race at San Sebastian in 1926 was also known as the European Grand Prix but, whatever the title, it was a punishing event, Goux in the winning Bugatti having to put up with blazing sun and the effects of the scorching Sirocco.

Materassi's Bugatti claimed the San Sebastian Grand Prix in 1927 but he was less successful in the Spanish Grand Prix, spinning off. Robert Benoist stopped to ensure that his rival was unharmed before going on to win for Delage. Both the Spanish and the San Sebastian Grands Prix became the property of Louis Chiron's Bugatti in 1928, after which the latter race disappeared from the international calendar even though the Lasarte circuit continued occasionally to host what had become the national Grand Prix.

Achille Varzi set a record lap at 91 mph to win for Alfa Romeo in 1930, after which the Spanish Grand Prix was not held for a couple of years. The revival at Lasarte in 1933 saw Chiron win the Formula Libre event for Alfa Romeo and, the following year, there was a fine battle between Mercedes-Benz and Bugatti, Fagioli and Caracciola eventually giving the Germans the first two places. Mercedes-Benz made it a clean sweep in 1935, the last year the Spanish Grand Prix was held before the Civil War brought such activities to a halt.

Meanwhile, Penya Rhin, a private society formed in Barcelona to encourage all forms of motor sport in Catalonia, had been running their own Grand Prix. Starting in 1921 at Vilafranca del Penedés, a triangular 9.1-mile track on public roads some 25 miles from Barcelona, the Penya Rhin Grand Prix had moved, in 1933, to Montjuich. The race was held there for four years. When racing was restored at the end of the Second World War, they chose to run their Grand Prix in 1946, 1948 and 1950 on

the Pedralbes street circuit on the western outskirts of the city. This became the location for the Spanish Grand Prix in 1951.

It was an important race as it constituted the final round of the championship, on which depended the title fight between Fangio, Ascari and Gonzalez. Ascari, who had won at Pedralbes the previous year, used his experience to take pole, his Ferrari some two seconds faster than Fangio's Alfa Romeo. Ascari looked strong but Ferrari were to make a disastrous tactical decision.

It was decided to use a smaller wheel size in the interests of superior performance but this did not take into account the high-speed nature of the 3.9-mile circuit with its broad avenues and wide streets. An average speed of over 100 mph caused havoc with the tyres and a number of unscheduled pit stops played into the hands of Alfa Romeo, giving Fangio the race and, with it, the championship.

The Spanish Grand Prix, after a brief absence, returned to the calendar in 1954 and, once again, Pedralbes hosted the final race of the season. The championship had been settled but, happily for the organisers, the race attracted one of the best entries seen all year. Most notable, perhaps, was the long-awaited appearance of the Lancia V8, Ascari putting his on pole position.

The Italian led for a few laps in a brave show which some felt may have been helped by a light fuel load. That left Schell (Maserati), Hawthorn (Ferrari) and Trintignant (Ferrari) free to engage in a superb cut-and-thrust battle which lasted for almost 20 laps. Schell, also with a light fuel load, ran out of road before eventually retiring with broken transmission and Trintignant stopped with engine failure. After that, Hawthorn was able to win as he pleased. It was the last time Grand Prix cars would blast down the Avenida del Generalísimo Franco. Indeed, it was to be the last Spanish Grand Prix for some time.

There was no serious activity until the mid-Sixties when John Hugenholtz, designer of the Zandvoort and Suzuka circuits, was asked to visit a dusty piece of land bordering the main road between Madrid and Burgos. The Royal Automobile Club of Spain wished to build a sporting complex with a race track being the focal point. In fact, it did not quite work out like that, the area devoted to the circuit being less than originally planned and, as a result, the layout was a poor compromise. Known as Járama, the track was basically too slow and too tight.

There was a Formula 2 race and a non-championship Formula 1 Grand Prix in 1967 (both won by Jim Clark). That was enough to gain the seal of approval from the governing body for a round of the championship the following year. The drivers had other ideas and there were last-minute demands for additional catch-fencing and other modifications in the interests of safety. Furthermore, the proposed admission of two local drivers caused a dispute, and there was serious talk of a boycott. The race did take place, but few turned out to watch Graham Hill scoring a morale-boosting win for Lotus just over a month after the death of Jim Clark.

The activity in this part of Spain had stirred the Real Automovil de Cataluna into action and they asked to have the 1969 Grand Prix staged at Montjuich Park. After struggling at Járama, the teams were only too happy to comply, although, on the day, safety once again dominated discussion. The circuit itself was deemed to be satisfactory, the organisers having resurfaced the track and lined it with metal barriers – a prudent move as things would turn out. The main fear centred on the cars and the increasing hazard of high-mounted wings.

The wings themselves, as history has since proved, were based on a sound principle; not so their location as they wobbled on slim stalks attached, in most cases, to the rear suspension, some teams choosing to mount them on the front as well. They seemed perilously frail, particularly when the cars swept over the hump leading to the hairpin.

On the ninth lap, Graham Hill's rear wing buckled as he flew over the jump, the sudden loss of downforce sending the car out of control and smashing it into the

Museo Etnológico

barrier on the right-hand side. Hill was unhurt and quickly surmised that if something had broken, it was likely to have been the wing. His team-mate, Jochen Rindt, was leading at the time and Hill, spotting the first signs of another failure, sent word back to the Lotus pit.

Too late. The same thing happened as Rindt crested the rise for the 20th time, his car careering down the slope, crashing into Hill's wreck and turning over. Hill was on hand to help pull a battered and bruised Rindt from the cockpit. In the light of such excitement, no-one seemed to notice that the spectators were crowded against a waist-high fence, a few feet behind the barrier.

Chris Amon, meanwhile, was in the lead and pulling away from Stewart's Matra-Ford. For 36 laps he stayed there, driving beautifully and controlling the race with ease. Then the Ferrari's engine seized. No-one was less surprised than Amon, this being another part of his wretched luck. Stewart was left to cruise to the flag.

The Scotsman won again when the race returned to Járama in 1970 and his flag-to-flag run was the simplest part of the weekend. Elsewhere, the organisation descended into chaos. Confusion over new rules governing qualification procedures led to much unpleasantness on the grid when, at the last minute, the race stewards revoked an earlier agreement to let everyone start, qualified or not. As they attempted to remove cars some of which already had their drivers strapped in and ready to go, punch-ups ensued.

After a delayed start, there was further trouble on the first lap when the brakes failed on Jackie Oliver's BRM and he T-boned the Ferrari of Jacky Ickx at a hairpin bend. Neither driver was seriously hurt but when both cars caught fire the marshals were unable to do anything other than douse the cars and the circuit with a mixture of water, foam and cement. With only five cars destined to finish, the organisers would have been better off letting everyone start in the first place.

Stewart's win with the Tyrrell-entered March-Ford flattered to deceive, the uncompetitive car failing to do anything of note for the rest of the year. Such a depressing state of affairs for the reigning world champions led, of course, to the construction of their own car and Stewart used it with impressive effect at Montjuich the following year.

In 1972, therefore, it was back to Járama where the organisation was only marginally better than before. Stewart led briefly but had to make way for a dominant Emerson Fittipaldi as the Lotus driver went on to score his second Grand Prix win. He gave Lotus their 50th win a year later at Montjuich Park, and it counted as one of his most fortunate ever. Team-mate Ronnie Peterson had stormed into the lead only to retire with gearbox trouble. Fittipaldi should then have been untroubled, but a slow puncture in his left-rear tyre left him easy prey for Carlos Reutemann. Just as the Brabham driver was poised to lead a Grand Prix for the first time, a CV joint failed and Fittipaldi was free to nurse his car home.

The Ferraris had been nowhere that year, but at Járama in 1974 they came good. In a race which went from wet to dry, the Italian team not only amazed everyone by pulling off quick pit stops, but they also provided Niki Lauda with the equipment to score his first Grand Prix win. With Clay Regazzoni finishing second for Maranello, it was to be the start of a superb relationship – although that did not seem to be the case a year later during a highly charged weekend at Montjuich Park.

There was trouble right from the start. The crash barriers, recently increased to three layers, were found to be loose and, in some cases, not bolted at all. Some sections of armco were old and worn, pieces did not fit properly, there were gaps and sections threatened to open if hit by a car. This did little for the drivers' sense of well-being and it aggravated growing unease over the general standards of safety. While the Grand Prix Drivers' Association got together and argued, Jacky Ickx, not a member of the association, took his Lotus out to practice. The organisers promised the necessary work would be done overnight.

On Saturday morning the drivers inspected the repairs and found them to be cosmetic. They refused to go out. Ickx, accompanied by the BRM of Bob Evans and Roelof Wunderink in an Ensign, took to the track once more. Until now, the team managers had avoided any confrontation – some of them even tried in vain to help by working on the barriers – but matters reached a head early on Saturday afternoon.

The circuit had been given the blessing of the CSI. The teams were, therefore, in breach of their contract and, since all the transporters and motorhomes were neatly housed in a derelict stadium, they were easy meat should legal action ensue. The team managers waded in and made their presence felt.

One by one the drivers climbed into their cars and went to work, only Emerson Fittipaldi remaining defiant as he completed the legal requirement of a few timed laps, albeit dangerously slow ones with his fist raised above his head, before parking his McLaren and walking away to jeers from the long-suffering crowd. The entire affair left everyone on edge. What desperate dramas would the race hold – particularly on a circuit such as this?

The pack poured over the crest of the hill seconds after the start, the Ferraris of Lauda and Regazzoni leading the charge. Unbelievably, Lauda's car then turned sharp right and aimed for his team-mate. As 23 cars bore down on the Ferraris, the worst fears of the weekend seemed likely to be realised in the most terrible way.

Lauda shoved Regazzoni into the barrier on the right and, fortunately, both cars stayed out of harm's way as they rattled expensively down the armco. The rest of the field, or most them anyway, streamed through. Lauda had been tapped by Mario Andretti who, in turn, had been hit by Vittorio Brambilla as the March driver tried an opportunistic move. In the midst of this, two more cars touched, making for all sorts of chaos as the field scrambled through the hairpin. Meanwhile Arturo Merzario, with no intention of racing anyway, rolled to a halt and lit up a cigarette. And there were

supposed to be 75 laps of this. Nervous systems, on edge all weekend, reached breaking point.

In fact, the race settled down, James Hunt (Hesketh-Ford) leading for six laps before Andretti took charge in his Parnelli-Ford. Then Rolf Stommelen (Lola-Ford) led, Carlos Pace (Brabham-Ford) took his turn for one lap before Stommelen moved back in front. Exciting stuff.

It all went wrong at the beginning of lap 26. Stommelen crossed the line with Pace right on his tail. As they reached at least 150 mph, the carbon fibre support snapped under the rear wing on Stommelen's car. The Lola veered left, cannoned into the barrier – which bent back under such a colossal impact. This flung the car towards the opposite side of the track – just at the point where the road fell sharply away to begin the descent down the hill. The Lola became airborne and skimmed the top of the triple-layer barrier before crashing into a prohibited area, where several people were mown down, four of them fatally.

Now there was further dithering and indecision on the part of the beleaguered organisers. The race ran for three more laps before they called a halt. Jochen Mass, whose McLaren was leading at the time, was declared the winner and awarded half-points.

Stommelen survived, but racing at Montjuich did not. The irony was that the incident had nothing to do with any deficiencies, real or imagined, the circuit

may have had. Now it was back to the less attractive alternative presented by Járama.

There was drama of an entirely different kind in 1976 when James Hunt's winning McLaren was found to be 1.8 cm too wide. The ensuing controversy was an unfortunate end to what had been a splendid race by both Hunt and his great rival Lauda but, sometime later, a court of appeal reinstated Hunt as the winner. The following two years were ruled by Andretti and Lotus, while the race in 1979 was one of those rare occasions when Ligier could do no wrong, Patrick Depailler running away with his first and only win for the French team.

In 1980, however, the race was dominated, not by man and machine, but by lawyers and politics. This was at the height of the war between the teams and the governing body over the control of the sport – or, to be precise, its finances – and Alan Jones was recorded as the winner of a Grand Prix which was declared illegal and thrown out of the championship.

Sport reigned supreme the following year when Gilles Villeneuve scored the most amazing victory as he refused to be beaten in a cumbersome Ferrari turbo which had no right to run in the rarefied air at the front of the field. For 67 laps, he resisted attack from a frustrated mob of pursuers; it was car-control and tenacity at its very best, the first five finishers covered by just 1.24 seconds. It was also a demonstration of how Járama was too narrow and tight for a

decent Grand Prix. It had become down-at-heel and no-one was sorry when Formula 1 gave Spain a miss for four years.

There was a complete change of scene in 1986 when the Spanish Grand Prix moved south to Jerez, the aim of the new circuit being the promotion of this famous sherry-producing region. Tucked in the only hills for miles around, the track was compact enough but it lacked places to overtake and, more significantly, it lacked spectators. While the motor cycle races could draw vast crowds, the motor racing Grands Prix were entirely devoid of atmosphere. And, in 1986, the absentees missed one of the closest finishes in the sport's history. Nigel Mansell's Williams-Honda was comfortably ahead of Ayrton Senna's Lotus-Renault until tyre wear forced a very late pit stop. With eight laps left and 19.4s to make up, Mansell put on a thrilling charge, but failed in his attempt by 0.014s.

Mansell made up for that by destroying the opposition in 1987 and then giving energetic chase to the winning McLaren-Honda of Alain Prost the following year. In 1989 Mansell, having left Williams for Ferrari, was banned from taking part following an alleged misdemeanour in Portugal the week before, thus leaving Senna to win more or less as he pleased. Senna looked like making it two in a row in 1990 until a punctured radiator on his McLaren-Honda left the way clear for Prost to score for Ferrari. The result, though, almost seemed irrelevant.

During practice, Martin Donnelly had crashed heavily when the suspension failed on his Lotus-Lamborghini going into one of the fastest corners. The car disintegrated, flinging the Ulsterman onto the track. His survival was nothing short of a miracle and, regrettably, that proved to be the only happening of note in the short history of this circuit.

For 1991, a new track was opened at Montmelo to the north of Barcelona, thus taking the Spanish Grand Prix close to what is, in many respects, its spiritual home. Nothing, though, seems likely ever to match the heady days at Montjuich Park.

Gethin abandoned Formula 2 for Formula 5000 and the Church Farm McLaren in 1969. It was a perfect move.

n 1973 *Competition Car* magazine ran a caption contest each month. One picture showed Mike Hailwood wearing a wicked grin and looking down at what appeared to be a small diary in his hands as he walked away from a group of attractive, smiling women. The captions were predictable enough, sexual innuendo abounding. But the winning line was superb. It said simply: 'I wonder if Gethin knows I've got his little black book …'.

If nothing else, it summed up the popular image of Peter Kenneth Gethin. Here was a driver with a twinkle in his eye, someone who enjoyed his racing and the spin-offs associated with his profession. By 1973 Gethin's reputation as a driver just about matched his repute as a lady's man, which is to say he was a racer of considerable poise and speed, even if his career, if you will pardon the expression, had many ups and downs.

Both summaries were rather unfair. He had perhaps milked the Jack-the-Lad image for all it was worth but, underneath, Peter Gethin was serious about a Formula 1 career which had been relatively brief and, by 1973, had lost its way. As a consequence, his single victory, in the 1971 Italian Grand Prix, was considered by some to be a fluke. It had, in fact, been a beautifully managed and courageous piece of work, even though his casual, laid-back image tended to understate that. Peter Gethin had materialised quietly onto the Grand Prix scene and he would disappear with equal restraint.

Becoming world champion had never been a truly burning ambition. That was hardly surprising since his father, Ken Gethin, was a flat-racing jockey and later a trainer of note in and around the Epsom area, close by where Peter was born in February 1940. Gethin Junior gave up horse riding when he was about 12 years old because he considered it to be too dangerous, but the removal of such a time-consuming diversion did little to improve his academic studies. He emerged from school in Leatherhead, Surrey, with just one GCE O-Level to his name.

Four years were spent as a Ford apprentice and an interest in motor racing led, midway through 1962, to the purchase of a Lotus 7. He entered it at Brands Hatch and, to his great surprise, won pole position and a valuable lesson as he subsequently spun off in the wet while leading. A couple of wins followed, all of which encouraged Peter to buy a Lotus 23 sports racer for 1963.

It was a disastrous year largely because the car was so badly set up – something which Gethin did not discover until near the end of the season when Tony Hegbourne, a more experienced driver, took a brief test drive and was immediately appalled. After that, there was no stopping Gethin and he won race after race.

During 1964 Peter raced occasionally against Charles Lucas, and 'Luke' offered Gethin a place in his newly formed Formula 3 team for the following season. Peter later joked that he got the drive simply because Lucas fancied his girlfriend, but, whatever the reason, the deal did him no favours, the Lotus and Brabham put his way being less than competitive. The name 'Gethin' appeared more often as a retirement than a finisher.

A move to Rodney Bloor's Sports Motors Manchester-based team in 1966 did little to improve the failure rate. Nevertheless when he was up and running, Peter began to feel that he was good enough to make his mark and perhaps go all the way to Formula 1. In 1968 he enjoyed the occasional Formula 2 outing, and a brilliant drive at Albi in France, where he finished second in a Frank Lithgoe Racing Brabham BT23C after leading the likes of Rindt and Pescarolo, did much for his reputation. It was not enough, though, when it came to putting together a Formula 2 deal for 1969.

For a while he appeared to have reached a dead-end. Then an avenue suddenly opened which would take him right to the top. This was the inaugural year of Formula 5000, the single-seater category based on lusty 5-litre engines. Bruce McLaren had taken a great interest in the technical and sales possibilities of the series. Gethin was asked to drive the semi-works McLaren-Chevrolet M10A, entered by the Church Farm Racing team and run by 'Colonel' Bernard Hender, Derek Bell's stepfather. Gethin had no hesitation in accepting.

Peter reckoned that this would do more for his reputation than struggling along in Formula 2. He felt he had the best car and an excellent chance of winning the championship; it would keep his name to the fore. More than that, the McLaren had been tested and developed by Bruce himself, whom Gethin liked and respected enormously. It had to be the correct decision. So it proved, Peter winning the title with a clean, quick style which suggested he could cope with the step to Formula 1.

That came out of the blue in May 1970. When Denny Hulme suffered burns to his hands at Indianapolis, Bruce had no hesitation in drafting Gethin into the Formula 1 team for the Belgian Grand Prix. He never took part in that race, disaster overwhelming the team in the biggest possible way.

Peter had turned up at Goodwood on 2 June to have his first test in the McLaren M14 and he had just been strapped into the cockpit when a pall of smoke arose from the far side of the circuit. McLaren, driving his CanAm car, had crashed into a marshal's post at 170 mph. Gethin was among the first on the scene and what he saw was to make a lasting impression. Bruce had been killed instantly.

Peter's first Grand Prix turned out to be the Dutch, the team giving the race at Spa-Francorchamps a miss in the wake of this tragedy. With the loss of Bruce, Gethin was without a supportive link to the management and his relationship with Teddy Mayer did not gel. The best Peter could do was sixth in Canada, two laps behind the winner.

Matters were not helped in 1971 by the introduction of the M19. The new car gave false hope when, but for a bolt dropping out of the rear suspension, Denny Hulme would have won the first race in South Africa. After that the car, with its rising-rate suspension, proved extremely difficult to set up and Gethin was totally at sea – as were

the team if only they cared to admit it.

Mayer eventually decided to call in Roger Penske and Mark Donohue to help solve these problems, using Gethin's car. Peter was told that his services would not be required after the Italian Grand Prix in September. Certain he was the 'fall guy', Gethin felt bitter about the whole affair. He was sure that, had Bruce been there, things would not have reached such a state and the car would have been sorted out sooner rather than later.

Then Pedro Rodriguez was killed in a sports car race in July, leaving BRM without a driver. Louis Stanley, who had talked to Gethin in the past about a drive, was quickly on the telephone, asking if he would be free to join BRM in Austria, one race before his sell-by date at McLaren. Peter accepted with alacrity and took great pleasure in telling Teddy Mayer what to do with his rising-rate suspension.

The Austrian Grand Prix was won by Jo Siffert in his BRM and, despite being plagued by a misfire, Gethin went to Monza feeling better than he had all season. The V12, he reckoned, might be just the job for the slipstreaming battle which lay in store.

Gethin was 11th-fastest in practice but, proving grid positions did not count for a great deal at Monza, Clay Regazzoni took an immediate lead. He had started his Ferrari from the fourth row.

The race was true to form, the lead changing four times in the first ten laps, Gethin keeping in touch from around tenth place. Then he became involved with a brief scrap with Jackie Oliver – his replacement at McLaren – and that coupled with lapping back-markers, meant the BRM lost contact with the leading group. Having finally shaken off Oliver, Gethin went motoring.

Charging along on his own and using 500 rpm more than was recommended, he took every corner at the maximum, on every lap. Gradually he reduced the gap to the leading bunch of five and, to his amazement, the slipstream began to work when he was about four seconds behind. In the space of the next lap he had hauled right up to the tail of a group comprising Peterson

(March), Hailwood (Surtees), Cevert (Tyrrell), Ganley (BRM) and Amon (Matra).

Amon dropped from contention when he tried to pull a rip-off from his visor and succeeded in tearing off the whole lot. Gethin was fifth with seven laps to go and, having got this far, he was determined not simply to finish fifth. He could see no reason why he could not win. The trick, he knew, would be to manoeuvre himself into one of the first two places coming out of the final corner.

In the event, Gethin's cause was helped when Peterson outbraked Cevert and slid wide briefly, Peter then diving inside them both, his brakes locked, the BRM now into a big slide. Utterly determined not to lift off, Gethin kept his foot to the floor and came out of the Curva Parabolica marginally in front. But Peterson was coming back, the red March moving up on Gethin's left shoulder, Cevert outside Peterson with

Hailwood just a yard or so behind as they fanned out onto the broad finishing straight.

Peterson was surging forward and Gethin knew there would be nothing in it as they reached the flag. Working on the assumption that emotion and basic logic would probably apply in the absence of sophisticated photographic equipment on the finishing line, Gethin thrust his right arm in the air to help the officials make up their minds. The March nosed ahead of the BRM – but about 20 yards too late. Peter Gethin won the Italian Grand Prix by 0.01s.

Cevert, who felt *he* should have won, claimed Gethin had edged him onto the loose stuff at the last corner, but Peter was past caring. And, to make his day complete, Oliver's McLaren had finished a distant seventh.

Louis Stanley was delighted and, as was Mr Stanley's way, Gethin found himself

The fastest race and the closest finish. Gethin thrusts his arm in the air as Peterson, flanked by Cevert, edges alongside the BRM. Hailwood is tucked in behind the March as the leading quartet laps Bonnier's McLaren for the fourth time.

elevated on the seating plan at the dinner table that night, an ironic state of affairs since Peter had watched Stanley wining and dining Cevert the previous evening in a fruitless attempt to woo the talented Frenchman to BRM for 1972.

On this occasion, though, Peter Gethin was The Man. And he enjoyed every minute of it. Not so the journey back to Villa d'Este, the expensive and lavish hotel by Lake Como. The Stanleys' chauffeur-driven limousine picked up a puncture shortly after leaving the restaurant and Gethin found himself to be the only person present capable of changing the wheel. So there was the winner of the Italian Grand Prix on his hands and knees, in the gutter, at midnight, with Louis Stanley towering over him and chortling: 'Ho, ho, ho, who would have believed it ... the winner at Monza ... ho, ho, ho ...'

At least, as Peter pointed out, the man

had a sense of humour. He also had an acute appreciation of money, Gethin receiving the princely sum of £800 for his day's work – and about £300 of it went towards paying his bill at Villa d'Este. There were no more pay days at the Grands Prix that season although Gethin did win the non-championship Victory Race at Brands Hatch, a result which was utterly overshadowed by the death of Siffert when his BRM left the road and caught fire on the approach to Hawthorn Bend.

Gethin's Italian victory went some way towards persuading Marlboro to back BRM in 1972, which, ironically, allowed Stanley to launch ambitious plans that dragged the team to its knees. By running a vast and variable number of cars, Stanley gave drivers from different nations the chance to come and achieve very little.

A confident prediction by Stanley that he expected BRM to win at least four world

championship races proved to be wide of the mark as the shambling team quickly lost cohesion. Gethin soon lost interest and his contract was not renewed for 1973. Apart from a one-off appearance for BRM in the Canadian Grand Prix and a drive for Graham Hill's team the following year at Brands Hatch, Peter's role as a Grand Prix driver had ended.

He drove for Chevron in Formula 5000 (scoring a surprise win in the 1973 Race of Champions at Brands Hatch) and the Belgian VDS team (winning the 1973/74 Tasman series) before finally calling it a day in 1977. Tired of the travel, especially the transatlantic trips while competing in the CanAm series for VDS, he wanted to spend more time in his village home in West Sussex, particularly following the birth of his son in July of that year.

Nevertheless, in 1978, he was off again, this time running a Formula 2 team for a pair of wealthy Americans whose prowess on the track did not match the magnificent Peterbilt truck which towed the ensemble around Europe. The struggle to qualify for, never mind finish, races was demoralising for all concerned and the project was wound up at the season's end.

A move to the United States in 1980 was not a success either, the job as public relations consultant for VDS being easily within his personable scope but the time spent in Texas proving just how much he missed the rolling countryside of West Sussex. He could not get his wife, son and dog home quickly enough.

After a period spent dabbling in property, Gethin's wide-ranging experience in racing was applied to working with Mike Earle's Formula 2 team and sorting out the wild but quick Beppe Gabbiani. When the Italian started winning and driving with consistency, Peter seemed to be just the man to help the Toleman Grand Prix team get into their stride now that they had a certain Ayrton Senna on their books for 1984.

He stayed as team manager for 18 months, an interesting but turbulent period which proved that Formula 1 was no longer the fun place it had been. Unbelievable

Gethin receives advice from Denny Hulme at Monza in 1970, shortly after Peter had joined the McLaren Grand Prix team.

political dramas over fundamental matters such as the supply of tyres soured Gethin's opinion as he helped put together the take-over deal with Benetton. Once that was complete Peter moved out, keen to finish with Grand Prix racing.

Better, he thought, to run a Formula 3000 team. That would at least be like motor racing as he remembered it. Alas, that also proved to be disappointing, his driver that year choosing to blame the poor performances on the car rather than accept

that his limited ability might have played a part. Following further problems with a manager in his employ, Peter lost what little interest he had remaining and decided to try something else.

Fortunately, he was able to turn his hand to a subject in which he was more than adequately qualified: he began running driving courses at Goodwood. It was an idea he had been considering before the Tole-man offer came along; in recent years the company has proved highly successful. Comprehensive road and circuit training courses have attracted private individuals as well as major clients like IBM and Mercedes-Benz. There is a permanent staff of

eight, with more than 30 instructors on call, and the whole operation is held together by Gethin's experience and relaxed manner.

Motor racing today has little appeal for him but it can never detract from the immense enjoyment drawn from his time spent at the wheel. The records show that during his Grand Prix career Peter Gethin spent a mere ten miles at the front – in fact, given the chopping and changing throughout a single lap at Monza, it may be even less than that – but nothing can alter the fact that he led the most dramatic and fastest few yards in the history of the sport. As that photograph caption suggested in 1973, he always did have a certain degree of style.

The Italian Grand Prix

The start at Monza in 1931.

eter Gethin's narrow victory at Monza in 1971 marked the end of an era. This was the last of the great slipstreaming battles, the ultimate in a thrilling format which did not permit accurate forecasting of the winner until the last few hundred yards of the final lap. Even then, there would be doubt.

Fears over the increase in speed brought the inevitable countermeasure: the introduction of chicanes. They cut the heart out of the place, denied the long straights and fast curves their life-blood which had made Monza a magical name. And yet it refused to die. There was simply too much history here to be suppressed by the blandness of modern thinking. The circuit and its surroundings had begun to crumble and decay; perversely, the more they did so, the greater the sense of history which seemed to prevail at every turn.

Monza is brimful of memories, some thrilling, others desperately sad. This circuit, to the north of Milan, has more or less been the permanent home of the Italian Grand Prix for 70 years and has brought

moments of high drama and tragedy, all of them acted out before one of the most knowledgeable and partisan motor racing audiences anywhere in the world.

Other circuits come close, but none can match the highly charged atmosphere of Monza on a hot September afternoon. At a time when motor racing is cutting itself off from the past, allegedly in the interests of progress, Monza retains a vibrant legacy which stretches back to 1922.

The first Italian Grand Prix had been held the year before, on a triangular road circuit of some ten miles near Brescia. Since there were only six starters it is surprising to record that three of them reached the finish 322 miles later, Jules Goux leading the way in an eight-cylinder Ballot.

Meanwhile, the Italian motor industry felt it should have a permanent and enclosed racing circuit, and the park adjoining the royal villa in Monza was chosen as the most suitable site. There was controversy right from the start.

A few days after the first sod had been turned by Vincenzo Lancia and Felice Nazzaro on 26 February 1922, work was

brought to a halt as protests from environmentalists and other such lobbies grew. When the plans were adjusted and finally approved, more than 3,000 men set to work and completed the job in 110 days. The result of their endeavours was an exciting combination of road circuit and banked track measuring 6.21 miles and incorporating very fine grandstands, pits and a network of service roads. On 10 September 100,000 spectators turned out in pouring rain to witness Pietro Bordino take his Fiat to victory in the 497-mile Italian Grand Prix.

The absence of Sunbeam in 1923 (Segrave having won the French Grand Prix that year) gave a slightly hollow ring to Fiat's victory as Salamono led home the similar car of Nazzaro. The entry was not much better a year later, not even the postponement of the race by more than a month improving the quality of the field, the Alfa Romeo of Antonio Ascari dominating. The Italian team repeated this result in 1925 despite the loss of Ascari some months

previously in the French Grand Prix.

The introduction of a new formula in 1926 brought with it dull racing as many manufacturers, unable or unwilling to foot the research and development costs, withdrew. Bugattis filled the first two places, but 1927 was the year of Delage as Benoist added the Italian Grand Prix to his impressive list of achievements. Chiron's win in a Bugatti in 1928 was marred by catastrophe, Materassi's Talbot having crashed through the flimsy barriers, killing the driver and 27 spectators. As a result, major steps were taken to improve spectator safety and the Italian Grand Prix was absent from the calendar for two years.

The return in 1931 coincided with the introduction of a change of formula requiring the races to last for a minimum of ten hours, and Campari and Nuvolari had to share the winning Alfa Romeo. A reduction to five hours the following year allowed Nuvolari to have it his own way.

Nuvolari left the Ferrari-run Alfa Romeo team in 1933 to join Maserati, and the Italian Grand Prix that year developed into a needle match between these two teams, victory going to Fagioli's Alfa Romeo after Nuvolari had run into tyre trouble in the closing stages. The date was 10 September and the day would be remembered for the tragedy later in the afternoon during the course of the Monza Grand Prix.

The race, run in three heats and a final, took place on a combination of the banking and track which made a high-speed oval. Oil and water on one of the curves was not cleaned up properly and Baconin Borzacchini and Guiseppe Campari were both killed when their cars skidded and overturned. Then, in the final, the same piece of banking also took the life of Count Czaykowski.

Monza's critics seized their chance and the organisers abandoned, for the time being, the 6.21-mile combination and the high-speed oval. Overreacting slightly, the Monza authorities introduced a strange combination for 1934. Run in an anticlockwise direction, the 2.69-mile circuit used the outer banked curve, a link road

leading onto the back straight of the circuit as we know it today, which brought the cars through Vedano (later to be known as the Curva Parabolica) and onto the pit straight. From there they completed a U-turn and ran in the opposite direction towards the banking again, the opposing pieces of track being separated by shin-high marker boards. To round it off and slow the cars down even further, chicanes were added on both of the fast curves.

Much of this was prompted by the arrival of very fast machinery from Mercedes-Benz and Auto Union, but the circuit in this form proved so tiring that the winning Mercedes-Benz had to be shared by Caracciola and Fagioli. The track layout was not a success and the authorities tried again.

This time, they used most of the road circuit – run in the accepted clockwise direction – but took the cars onto the banking for the final mile or so, thus avoiding Vedano. For good measure, they added another three chicanes (made from straw bales) in various parts of the circuit to match the existing one on the South Curve. Hans von Stuck proved to be the 1935 winner on this 4.28-mile circuit, his Auto Union being one of the few cars to last the 73 laps. The same layout was used in 1936, the absence of Mercedes-Benz helping Rosemeyer and Auto Union to victory.

Politics are never far from the surface in Italian motor racing and the switching of the Italian Grand Prix from Monza to Livorno in 1937 is a fine example of this. It so happened that the great Nuvolari, driving an Alfa Romeo, had defeated the German teams in the Coppa Ciano race held on this circuit in 1936. The thought occurred to the Italians that he could do it again.

The circuit at Livorno, known to the British as Leghorn, ran for 4.48 miles alongside the Mediterranean coast before returning inland to the small town of Ardenza. In the event, the plan for an Italian victory against the might of the German onslaught failed to work, Caracciola winning for Mercedes-Benz.

It was back to Monza for 1938, the so-called Florio circuit now without the three

1935 chicanes. Nuvolari, although driving for Auto Union, at least gave the crowd something to cheer for as he won the last pre-war Italian Grand Prix at an average of 96.76 mph.

Monza became a military dumping ground during hostilities and, when racing resumed in 1947, a 1.75-mile circuit for the Italian Grand Prix was mapped out around the Milan fairgrounds. By this stage, Alfa Romeo were such a professional force that they could afford to indulge in choosing who would win, a policy which did not sit well with Count Felice Trossi as he slowed on the final lap, his goggles raised, to indicate the farcical nature of 'beating' Varzi.

The scene switched in 1948 to a very tight circuit in Turin's Valentino Park. Although Wimille won for Alfa Romeo, the race was notable for the debut of the Ferrari V12. When racing returned to the Monza road circuit in 1948 Wimille won again, but the following year Ferrari benefited from Alfa Romeo's temporary withdrawal, Ascari winning on the 3.91-mile circuit at an average of more than 105 mph.

In 1950 Alfa Romeo were back, ready to engage Ferrari in some momentous racing. At Monza, Alfa won to clinch the first world championship for Farina. In 1951 however, Ferrari came good as the fuel-guzzling Alfa Romeos found difficulty in matching the

unblown V12s from Maranello. There was a right royal set-to in their home Grand Prix, but in the end the Alfas could not beat Ascari even though the team, and Fangio, won the championship.

The move to Formula 2 in 1952 meant that Ascari and Ferrari were virtually unopposed, although that was to change in 1953 as Maserati began to provide stiff opposition, their first Grand Prix victory coming, appropriately enough, at Monza. The result was not all that clear-cut, however.

For the entire length of the race the Ferraris of Ascari and Farina waged a thrilling battle with Fangio's Maserati, the similar car of Marimon running with them

although several laps down after a spin and a pit stop. Coming through Vedano for the last time, Ascari appeared to have victory within his grasp. Then he spun, taking his team-mate with him, Marimon crashing into Ascari in the confusion. Typically, Fangio found a gap and motored alone up the pit straight to take the flag. Except there was none, the official so surprised that he forgot to wave it, and Fangio completed another lap, just to make sure.

Ferrari were defeated again in 1954, this time by Fangio and Mercedes-Benz, but not before the German team had been given a run for their money, Stirling Moss leading convincingly for 19 laps until the oil tank

split on his privately entered Maserati.

There was much to report at Monza in 1955. On 26 May Italy went into deep shock when it was learned that Alberto Ascari had been killed while testing a Ferrari sports car at Monza. He had not been due to drive the car at all and onlookers were surprised when he asked to have a run. Mystery still surrounds the cause of the accident at the fast Vialone curve leading onto the back straight.

The Monza authorities, meanwhile, had been building new banking and they put it to full use for the Italian Grand Prix, Fangio winning for Mercedes-Benz on the 6.21-mile track. Despite the remedial work, the uneven surface on the banking took its toll in 1956 as several cars suffered steering failures, most notably the leading Lancia-Ferrari of Musso. That let the Maserati of Moss back into the lead, despite having run out of petrol some laps before; he had been saved thanks to a friendly push into the pits by the privately entered Maserati of Piotti.

There were two world championship rounds in Italy in 1957, the Pescara Grand Prix taking place three weeks before Monza. Run on a magnificent triangular combination of long straights and a hilly section, the 16-mile public road circuit by the Adriatic served warning of what was to come at Monza as Moss gave Vanwall victory. For the Italian Grand Prix the locals had to stomach not one but three green cars on the front row. It was too much to take; overnight, the officials decided the front row could accommodate four cars, Fangio's red Maserati joining the Vanwalls.

The organisers had abandoned the banking and, for the first 20 laps or so on the super-fast road course, the pace was breathtaking as two Maseratis swapped the lead with the British cars. Then, one by one, the contenders succumbed to the pace, leaving Fangio to fight with Moss. But on this day and on this circuit the Maserati was no match for the Vanwall despite Fangio's total determination not to be outdone.

A year later, though, Vanwall looked like being beaten by Ferrari during this crucial round of the championship struggle bet-

ween Moss and Hawthorn. When Moss went out with gearbox trouble, the Ferrari seemed set to take maximum points. In the closing stages, however, the legacy of clutch trouble at the start reduced Hawthorn's pace and he had no answer to a brilliant charge by Tony Brooks as the Vanwall driver made up for time lost in the pits investigating an oil leak.

By 1959 Vanwall were out of racing and the era of the rear-engined Cooper had arrived. The Ferraris, with their front engines, were cumbersome but the team hoped to benefit from an important weakness in their rival. The high speeds at Monza were certain to require tyre changes, in which case the Coopers, with their bolt-on wheels, would be in trouble. The works Coopers, and the privately entered Rob Walker team, went along with the game, practising wheel changes when their inten-

tion was actually to nurse their tyres and run non-stop. And that is what happened, Moss winning for Walker, although Jack Brabham's works Cooper eventually had to give best to the hard-charging Ferrari of Phil Hill.

The British frowned upon a decision to return to the bumpy banking for the 1960 Italian Grand Prix, and their boycott of the race left the way clear for Ferrari, led by Phil Hill, to fill the first three places. The British view was that the high-speed circuit was used purely as a means of giving the front-engined Ferraris a rare advantage, but the following year the combined road and banked circuit was still in use and every car on the grid was rear-engined.

The British duly turned up this time even though it was accepted that they were likely to be thrashed by Ferrari, the Italian team having been more than adequately pre-

Fiat Abarth 131 Rally

pared for the advent of the 1.5-litre formula. Sure enough, Phil Hill won with the magnificent 'sharknose', yet this victory brought him no pleasure. On the second lap, a collision between Jim Clark's Lotus and Wolfgang von Trips on the approach to the Curva Parabolica had resulted in the Ferrari smashing into the fencing, killing the driver and 14 spectators.

Although Cooper, Lotus and Brabham had caught up by 1962, the Italian Grand Prix was dominated by BRM, as Graham Hill and Richie Ginther led all the way. Ginther finished second again in 1963, but the BRM had to give best to Clark and Lotus on the road course, the banking having been abandoned the previous year. In the midst of this green supremacy, Italian red made a brief return in 1964 as Surtees won for Ferrari on his way to the world title. Twelve months later, however, the British

were once again a major force at Monza, Jackie Stewart scoring his first Grand Prix victory at the wheel of a BRM.

The arrival of the 3-litre formula in 1966 did not favour BRM and their 16-cylinder engine and rarely suited the Ferrari V12 either. But the flat-out blind at Monza played into the hands of the red cars, Lodovico Scarfiotti leading home Mike Parkes on one of the few days when Jack Brabham failed to score maximum points. Brabham looked set to put that right the following year but was foiled by a patch of oil, dropped by the previously dominant Lotus of Graham Hill. This was at the last corner and Surtees nipped through to score a surprise win.

The McLaren of Denny Hulme won in 1968. There was an epic struggle the following September as Jackie Stewart and Jochen Rindt battled for 243 miles, the Matra beating the Lotus by 8/100ths of a second. Doubtless that wonderful encounter came to Stewart's mind in 1970 when Rindt lost his life during practice. A mechanical failure caused the Lotus to go out of control under braking for Parabolica, the front being torn off the car as it hit the barrier. Rindt, drawn into the depths of the cockpit, died as a result of throat injuries inflicted by the seat-belt buckle (he had refused to wear crotch straps). The loss of such an extrovert performer was keenly felt by the Italians as they flocked into the autodrome on Sunday morning, but the race provided the perfect antidote. Clay Regazzoni dramatically shook off his slipstreaming pursuers to win for Ferrari and become a hero overnight.

When Peter Gethin's winning average topped 150 mph in 1971, the Monza authorities became worried. It was all very well having one of the fastest circuits in the championship but the consequences of an accident did not bear thinking about. Accordingly, chicanes were added at the end of the pit straight and at Curva Ascari leading onto the back stretch. These measures reduced the speeds, but they also broke up the racing and induced several minor incidents, one of them robbing Regazzoni of the lead in 1972 when his Fer-

rari collided with a back-marker. Once the Ferrari of Ickx had dropped out with electrical trouble, Emerson Fittipaldi was left to cruise to a victory which would clinch the championship for Lotus.

The chicanes had been seen as a temporary measure, but they were still there in 1973, the year Stewart produced one of his greatest drives as he pulled back a full lap to finish fourth following a pit stop. That gave the Tyrrell driver his third world title on a day when Ronnie Peterson won for Lotus, thereby depriving second-placed Fittipaldi of an opportunity to win the championship for the second year in succession.

Peterson and Fittipaldi were at it once more in 1974, the difference being that Emerson was now in a McLaren as he finished a close second. He was second again in 1975, but as far as the delirious fans were concerned that was of no consequence. Regazzoni had led all the way for Ferrari and third place was good enough to give Niki Lauda the championship, the first for Ferrari in 11 years.

The scenes at the finish were both colourfully dramatic and intensely frightening as the mob scaled the wire fencing and poured onto the track from all directions. This was customary, but, on the occasion of a Ferrari victory, the vigour and sense of purpose shown by the *tifosi* took on a new intensity. They simply outnumbered and overran the officials, Lauda commenting that he felt safer in his car at 170 mph than he did standing still in the midst of such hysteria. It was for this reason that many disliked Monza, yet it was impossible not to be swept along by such incredible fervour.

The mood in 1976 was just as dramatic. Lauda had returned to finish fourth after suffering appalling burns at the Nürburgring just six weeks before. It was as brave a performance as you could wish to see and the crowd loved him for it, Peterson's winning drive in the March being an irrelevance as far as the Ferrari fanatics were concerned.

By now, the 'temporary' chicanes had made way for a series of tight corners of a more permanent nature. They were not

popular in 1976, but the authorities were unmoved and they were still in place the following year as Mario Andretti led all but nine of the 52 laps for Lotus. However, his warm feelings towards Monza would be heavily coloured by events on the first lap of the 1978 Italian Grand Prix.

Starting had always been something of an adventure at Monza. It was fun when it went right – Regazzoni frequently being in second gear as he crossed the line just as the front row cars were about to leave it. When it went wrong it was a total disaster, as it was in 1978.

Intimidated, perhaps, by the urgent drama of Villeneuve's revving Ferrari on the front row, the starter gave the green light long before the back of the grid was in place. Given the wide expanse of track, those back-markers snatched the opportunity to make flying starts, the field being heavily bunched at the point where the track then narrowed to half its width at the blocked-off entrance to the old banking. Added to this, Ronnie Peterson had made a slow start from the third row.

In the mêlée which followed, the Lotus was struck by another car and turned sharp right into the barrier, the impact producing a vivid ball of orange flame. Ten cars were involved and the race was stopped, Peterson being removed to hospital with leg injuries which did not appear from initial reports to be life-threatening.

Andretti finished first, the Lotus narrowly beating Villeneuve but neither of them were to make the rostrum thanks to application of one-minute penalties for jumping the start. Thus the Brabham-Alfa Romeo of Niki Lauda was declared the winner, although Andretti was able to celebrate his one and only world championship. The following morning, however, all of that seemed meaningless when news came through that Peterson had died in hospital. This was to devastate Formula 1 and put into question the erratic starting procedure at Monza.

Everything was satisfactory in 1979 as Jody Scheckter won the race and gave Ferrari the championship. Rounding off the

Amon's Matra leads a slipstreaming bunch into Curva Parabolica in 1971. Gethin's BRM, Oliver's McLaren and the Marches of Galli and Pescarolo follow.

day, Villeneuve finished second for Ferrari and the ever-popular Regazzoni claimed third place in his Williams.

In the background, meanwhile, a struggle between Monza and Imola was resolved in favour of the circuit in Emilia, the teams receiving a pleasant surprise in September 1980 as they sampled the excellent facilities there. The 3.1-mile circuit was good for the drivers, too, Nelson Piquet using his Brabham to full effect by leading most of the way. Imola was adjudged to be such a success some that clever political footwork saw the introduction of the San Marino Grand Prix, leaving Monza free to carry on hosting the Italian Grand Prix on the traditional September date.

A third chicane had appeared on the run to the first Lesmo corner but it did not hurt the top-end power of the Renault turbo sufficiently to prevent Alain Prost from leading every lap in 1981. A light shower of rain, however, put paid to Carlos Reutemann's chances, the Williams driver having produced one of the finest single laps ever seen at Monza as he placed his normally aspirated car on the front row.

On the subject of very fine laps, Mario Andretti opened every emotional vein in the place in 1982 when he made a Formula 1 comeback by not only driving for Ferrari but also taking pole position. It was a scriptwriter's dream and, even though he finished third, the *tifosi* were well satisfied. Patrick Tambay had taken second place for Ferrari behind René Arnoux's Renault, an acceptable result since Enzo Ferrari had announced his intention to run Arnoux in 1983. René was to be denied the thrill of winning at Monza by Piquet's Brabham-BMW, but a trip over a kerb in 1984 cost Piquet his second win in succession, the resulting split radiator allowing Lauda to score for McLaren.

Prost, having lost out with a blown engine that year, came back 12 months later to take a vital nine points for McLaren *en route* to the 1985 World Championship. Luck was not on his side at Monza in 1986, however. Although on the front row, alternator trouble forced him to vacate his car on the grid and dash back for the spare McLaren. The pole-position man was also absent, as last-minute problems with Teo Fabi's Benetton sent the Italian to the back of the grid.

Thus, the 1986 Grand Prix started minus the front row, victory going to Nelson Piquet in a Williams-Honda. He won again in 1987, but only after Ayrton Senna's Lotus had slithered off the track while lapping a back-marker a few laps from home. At least he finished second.

In 1988 a spectacular brush while lapping Jean-Louis Schlesser (substituting for an indisposed Mansell at Williams) resulted in Senna not merely losing the lead but also the chance of a clean-sweep, McLaren having won every race thus far in the season. More than that, the incident allowed the Ferraris of Gerhard Berger and Michele Alboreto to sweep past for an unexpected one-two.

There was little sympathy to be found for Senna anywhere inside the Monza Parco that day, nor was there any 12 months later in September 1989. On that occasion Senna's McLaren blew up while leading, handing victory to Prost, soon to leave McLaren for Ferrari.

But the 1989 race will be remembered more for its aftermath as Prost, to the disbelief of Ron Dennis, handed the winner's silverware to the crowd and then proceeded to complain about the second-rate treatment he had been receiving from McLaren and Honda. The alleged deficiencies did not stop Prost from going on to win the championship, but McLaren and Senna extracted their revenge at Monza the following year by leading all the way, Prost's Ferrari finishing second.

After years of prevarication, the Monza authorities pleading a lack of planning permission, the new pits and administration buildings were completed in 1990, replacing the peeling concrete structure which had long since outlived its purpose. Several years before that, the paddock had been extended and the use of the garage block, some distance from the pits, abandoned. Security, a perennial problem at Monza, had been stepped up, but theft remained a major hazard.

Somehow, though, the underlying tension created by all of this merely adds to the unique atmosphere of Monza. With the steep and now badly cracked and overgrown banking remaining as a monument to past glories and follies, the sense of tradition is pervasive.

It is impossible not to be moved by a visit to the Autodromo Nazionale di Monza. Either you like it or you don't. But if you do, then there is no finer theatre of motor racing, particularly on a warm and hazy Sunday afternoon in early September as another highly charged chapter is added to the history of the Italian Grand Prix.

Moment of controversy at Brands Hatch in 1976 as Hunt's McLaren is launched onto two wheels.

The *Daily Express* called him 'Britain's Golden Boy'. *The Sunday Times* purred in patronising fashion that he was 'Master James'. In every publication, James Hunt was simply good news.

This was around the time of a rollercoaster ride to victory in the 1976 world championship. Hunt's progress thus far had been nothing short of sensational, a never-ending series of sometimes ridiculous protests, brilliant drives and disappointing results – all of them crammed into nine months between the first race in Brazil and the final, hugely theatrical, shoot-out in the teeming rain in Japan.

When it was all over and the novelty value had worn off, Hunt became the *enfant terrible* of the press. *Vogue* called him *l'anti seducteur*, a typically striking cover using his fulsome blond locks to frame a bored and slightly arrogant look.

The winter of 1976/77 and the spring which followed became open season on James Simon Wallis Hunt, son of a stockbroker, ex-public schoolboy and dashing sportsman who frequently shouted off his mouth with flowing use of a plummy accent. He was, allegedly, ill-kempt and ill-mannered. And he seemed to love it. The more indifferent he became to the views of the media, the more hostile the world at large seemed to become.

The impression was that he was intolerant. That bit was true. Ever a pragmatist, James Hunt wanted to win by the most direct method available. If he did not succeed then, yes, he became angry with those around him. More than anything, though, he became extremely annoyed with himself. And it was that absence of self-pity which would carry him through impossible odds simply to make it into Formula 1 in the first place and eventually to become world champion.

Hunt's gangling, hunched appearance militated against him from an early age. He was rejected as a bus conductor because he was too tall, this potential line of business being one of the many he explored as a means of raising enough cash to purchase and prepare a Mini and take up racing.

To the dismay of his parents, James's future ambitions were diverted by a visit to Silverstone in 1965 and he subsequently abandoned plans to go to medical school. The aim of the trip had been to celebrate his 18th birthday; the outcome was an immediate attraction to a branch of sport in which, hitherto, he had taken no interest whatsoever. But, typically and without bragging, James felt it was something he could do rather well.

Tennis had first highlighted his sporting ability and he subsequently claimed with justification that he could have been a squash champion. All of that became irrelevant when, at the age of 21, he sat in a single-seater for the first time and discovered straightaway that he could drive quite quickly. He had no idea why – but that was unimportant; he simply had a feel for the business of motor racing.

With an Alexis bought on hire-purchase, he began hesitantly, learning enough to confirm the feeling that he could make a name for himself, and then moved into Formula 3 during 1969. Racing a two-year-old Brabham powered by an engine which was more elderly still, Hunt did enough to permit the purchase of a Lotus and lay claim to some sponsorship for the following season.

As ever the money was nowhere near sufficient, particularly as James had now embarked on a hand-to-mouth tour of Europe. He scored two wins and several reasonable placings, the shortage of cash imposing worthwhile restraint on his driving. Hunt hardly ever crashed (that would soon change) and he reckoned his repair bill for the season came to no more than £600. A large slice of that had been accounted for by a well-publicised incident at the Crystal Palace circuit in south London.

Hunt became locked in combat with

Dave Morgan, another young charger with more than reasonable talent even if his wild brake-locking moments did not suggest it on this October afternoon. The battle was for third place and, at the exit of the last corner, Morgan tried an impossible move. The result was two wrecked cars, Hunt's Lotus beached in the middle of the track with both right-hand wheels missing. James sprang from the wreck, marched over to Morgan and, in full view of the nation's viewers, promptly thumped his startled adversary.

It was the first public hint of Hunt's short fuse and a clear indication of his high adrenalin level when in a racing car. Hunt later claimed he drove better that way, his nervous system reaching such a peak that he would vomit into a bucket moments before a Grand Prix and sometimes explode in an uncontrolled release of pent-up emotion when the race was over. And if his race ended prematurely and not in Hunt's favour, then it was best to give him a wide berth, as Dave Morgan learned that Saturday afternoon in 1970.

For the following season, James had a works-supported March at his disposal. It was an average car and his results appeared to reflect it. The truth was that the degree of uniformity of these underpowered Formula 3 cars allowed those without talent to mix disastrously with those who were more generously blessed. Invariably, if Hunt could get clear of the field, he would race into the distance. There were wins at Montlhéry and the Nürburgring. But there were also impressive accidents, particularly at Zandvoort where a collision with another competitor sent James motoring on his head for several hundred feet. The title 'Hunt the Shunt' grew ever more popular.

In 1972 he slithered further downhill, a ride with the works March team ending with an argument at Monaco early in the season. Having progressed no further than Formula 3, his future seemed seriously limited. It appeared to take a turn for the worse when he subsequently joined forces with an unlikely band of racers. In fact, this was to be the beginning of one of the most colourful and romantic episodes in motor racing.

James Hunt was to drive a Dastle Formula 3 car for Lord Alexander Hesketh. His team-mate would be Anthony 'Bubbles' Horsley. It hardly seemed a combination likely to set the Formula 3 world on fire, never mind gaining recognition in the lofty peaks of Formula 1.

'Bubbles' was running the operation for his lordship and he speedily approached Hunt when the rift with March became final. The smirking and the sniggering became widespread when Horsley crashed more often than not and James then had a massive shunt during practice for the support race for the British Grand Prix at Brands Hatch. As was frequently the case, the accident was not Hunt's fault. On this occasion, a car ahead lost control and Hunt, in attempting to avoid a collision, merely succeeded in having an even bigger accident as he turned the Dastle upside-down. For good measure, 'Bubbles' crashed elsewhere on the circuit and James was hospitalised briefly after becoming involved in a road accident on his way home.

It was enough to make anyone give up. But, as Horsley was to note, it was precisely this sort of situation which made James more determined than ever. Presented with a seemingly hopeless cause, Hunt would simply refuse to be defeated. Besides, Lord Hesketh and James got along famously, each sparked the other's passion for racing and matters British.

With backing from 'Hesketh Finance', James raced a Formula 2 March later that year, an excellent drive at Oulton Park giving him third place behind the works cars of Niki Lauda and Ronnie Peterson. One or two good placings in various races elsewhere encouraged Hesketh to make plans for 1973.

The original scheme was to enter the Formula 2 championship, but a brief venture into Formula 1 at the Race of Champions prompted Hesketh to raise his game. The team had hired a Surtees and James used it to finish a very creditable third in the race at Brands Hatch. Having tasted life in this upper echelon, the thought of returning to the more basic world of Formula 2 did not appeal to his lordship.

With typically quirky logic, Hesketh reasoned that if he was to spend a fair sum to get moderate results in Formula 2, he might as well invest the same amount and struggle along in the infinitely more acceptable world of Formula 1. Hesketh and Grand Prix racing would unite at Monaco. All three seemed made for each other.

Not a man to do things by halves, Lord Hesketh attacked his venture with style. A base was established on the 160-foot yacht *Southern Breeze* at anchor in the harbour, while a Bell Jet Ranger and a Rolls-Royce Silver Shadow carried the colourful ensemble hither and thither at all hours of the day and night. Beneath the flaunted opulence lay a strong desire to succeed. If nothing else, the team were intensely serious about their motor racing. All of which suited James admirably.

A March-Ford had been purchased and with it came Dr Harvey Postlethwaite, a talented young engineer whose resonant name alone was enough to have him on board with this band of extroverts. James qualified on the ninth row and was running in sixth place when the engine expired. He had been more than impressive in such elevated company. Monaco 1973 had been the thrilling start of a brief but spectacular journey for the red, white and blue team with their teddy bear emblem.

Postlethwaite's development of the March helped Hunt score his first championship point when he finished sixth in France. At the end of the season, James had 14 points, a tidy sum for the driver and a team – particularly *this* driver and team – in their first season. It underscored the message that Hesketh was worth watching.

Certainly, the gossip columnists thought that to be the case as they found the team from Northamptonshire to be a useful window into a glamorous world which the social writers never fully understood. They did appreciate the marquees at the British Grand Prix, the silver-service lunches, the champagne and the helicopters whisking the gentry back and forth from Hesketh's nearby mansion to this high-octane garden party at Silverstone. Hesketh and Hunt gained Formula 1 more national newspaper coverage outside the sports pages than the rest of the teams put together. The problem was deciding where Hesketh should go next. There was only one option: they had to build their own car.

The Hesketh 308 was ready in time for the 1974 season and the entourage duly returned to Silverstone for the non-championship International Trophy. When James won, it seemed this fairy-tale enterprise knew no bounds. Despite the heady euphoria, Hunt nonetheless had his feet firmly on the ground. The feeling was that the car was workmanlike, but he would be hard-pressed to challenge the likes of McLaren. So it proved.

During the long haul round Europe, Hunt had but a couple of third places to show for his endeavours. Then, improvements to the car at the end of the season brought a fourth in Canada and third place at Watkins Glen. There was the thought that 1975 could be much better.

He led the opening Grand Prix in Argentina for nine laps before the excitement of the moment caused him to spin. A strong recovery brought him into second place, but when he led in Spain and then crashed, paddock opinion had it that James could not deal with motor racing's ultimate pressure. He was to blow that theory apart in the most convincing manner at Zandvoort in June.

In a race run in wet/dry conditions, Hunt not only made a wise tactical move by being the first to change to slick tyres, he also held off a relentless attack by Niki Lauda. Hunt did not make a single mistake and his first Grand Prix win was earned in circumstances which he relished. Now that he had established his credentials, all James needed was a car capable of matching his ability.

The Hesketh 308C was not such a car. It looked the part, a logical development of the Zandvoort-winning machine, but the 308C did nothing to further Hunt's reputation in 1975. And, at the end of the year, the

base of a seemingly bottomless financial pit had been reached. Hesketh had spent close to £1 million on his team but, with no sponsors in sight, he had no option but to make a much regretted departure. For a while, it seemed James would be out of work.

Then, in an extraordinary sequence of events, a vacancy arose within a top team. At the 11th hour, Emerson Fittipaldi told McLaren he would be leaving. Within seconds of receiving the news, Teddy Mayer, the McLaren director, was on the telephone to Hunt. A deal was completed within 36 hours.

The move suited James perfectly. Sponsorship was arranged with Marlboro and, even though he would in effect be racing a car which had won the championship in 1974, it was still reasonably competitive. Hunt's experience with Hesketh had equipped him with the ability to stand on his own two feet and take the knocks which would invariably come with driving for a top-line team. The first test for the new liaison, however, was a particularly tough one.

The opening Grand Prix of the 1976 season was at Interlagos, a sinuous and difficult circuit on the outskirts of São Paulo. The date was 25 January, which meant there had been very little time for James to settle in with the team, let alone drive the car. It showed in many ways, not least in the fact that he did not fit the McLaren properly when he climbed on board for the first official practice session. By the time that had been sorted out, there was little opportunity to work on the car.

The following day, the Ford-Cosworth engine blew up in the first session. Engine changes were a more haphazard affair than they are today and James watched his mechanics at work, not really knowing the full extent of their competence. The feeling was mutual. James knew that in an hour or so he was going to have to get into that car – a car he didn't really know – and wring its neck. After all this frantic effort, the mechanics would expect him to come up with the goods.

James went out and put the McLaren on pole. He immediately had everyone's

respect. The year of Hunt the super-star was under way.

James retired from the race with engine trouble, but not before he had run competitively with Niki Lauda. When he finished second to Lauda's Ferrari in South Africa, it became clear that these two were likely to set the pace although no-one in their right mind would have contemplated such a dramatic turn of events as the season unfolded. Hunt *versus* Lauda would become the sporting catch-line of the year.

James tangled with Patrick Depailler's Tyrrell on the streets of Long Beach, Hunt doing himself no favours by standing on the track and shaking his fist each time the Frenchman came by during the next few laps. The next round in Spain was to prove a critical one.

James claimed pole but Lauda led for 32 laps before the pain from broken ribs sustained in a tractor accident forced him to ease off and let the waiting Hunt through. When James won, it could not have been more satisfactory from his point of view.

Then the scrutineers moved in with their rulers and the McLaren was found to be 1.8 cm too wide across the rear wheels. Hunt was excluded. The arguments began.

A mistake had been made by the team and the penalty had been harsh. But no-one dreamed that any performance advantage could be had from such an infinitesimal amount. And yet, during the races which followed, Hunt was nowhere.

The Spanish Grand Prix had coincided with the introduction of new regulations calling for, among other things, the mounting of the rear wing further forward. The McLaren, in its new guise, had obviously gone well in Spain and now it was handling badly. The only change since then appeared to have been the reduction in width by 1.8 cm.

Not quite. The team had also moved the oil coolers to the side pods for the Spanish race and then, fearing they might be breaking other regulations, they had returned them to the original position beneath the rear wing. That seemed harmless enough but it took the team three races to discover

that the new location for the oil coolers, about an inch further forward than before, was seriously affecting the airflow around the rear wing in its new position. The oil coolers went back to the sidepod – and James Hunt simply flew to victory in France. The British Grand Prix was next.

By now, James Hunt was in the front pages as well as on the back of every tabloid newspaper in Britain. His unconventional manner and casual style of dress either infuriated or delighted the nation. He added grist to the media mill by appearing to behave in a petulant manner on the Tour of Britain, a mixture of racing and rallying which he had won a few years before.

Hunt's much-publicised partnership with Noel Edmonds became national news when James deposited the Vauxhall into the trees on a special stage. The disc-jockey wanted to have the car repaired and carry on; Hunt had simply had enough and said as much. Fleet Street went into overdrive and an unexceptional disagreement was elevated into the ranks of a full-scale quarrel. Brands Hatch, meanwhile, rubbed their hands with promotional glee.

There was a full house on 18 July to see James start from pole. Regazzoni barged through from the second row to challenge Lauda for the lead. To Hunt's amazement and initial delight, he watched the Ferraris tangle at Paddock Hill Bend. Then he realised he was to be a part of the accident as well. The McLaren briefly became airborne, bending the front suspension as it crashed back onto the track. Cars went in all directions. The race was stopped.

The next 30 minutes were totally chaotic as the stewards experienced great difficulty in deciding what interpretation to place on the vague regulations covering these matters. It was announced that any driver who had failed to complete the first lap would be ineligible for the restart. It was also suggested that the use of spare cars would not be permitted.

Either way Hunt was in trouble – but not half as much as the organisers. They became aware of mounting agitation within the spectator enclosures on this hot summer's day; beer cans flew higher and the chanting grew louder. The organisers, showing commendable flexibility to match the mounting need for self-preservation, suddenly found a rule which said Hunt

could start because his car had been moving, albeit slowly, at the time the race was stopped. Everyone, except Ferrari, was happy.

Lauda led for 45 laps but, when Hunt forced his way through, the place erupted. Lauda did not respond and James was left to cruise to one of the most emotional victories of his career. As he motored slowly through Paddock Hill Bend, and up the rise towards Druids, James raised both arms aloft. Arthur Partridge, a spectator perched high in the grandstand, caught the moment on film and that evocative photograph is the only racing picture on display in James's home.

A court of appeal had since returned Hunt's victory in Spain but, even so, Lauda's second place at Brands Hatch meant the gap was still 23 points in the Austrian's favour. There was nothing for it but to battle on, James arriving at the Nürburgring with a desire to win which went beyond the simple accumulation of points. Success at this demanding track would provide immense personal satisfaction and he started off in the best possible way by putting the McLaren on pole. Lauda would

share the front row.

The game plan changed on race day when rain hung in the air and everyone, with the exception of Jochen Mass, started on wet rubber. At the end of the first lap, it was clear Mass had made the correct decision, Hunt leading a number of cars, including Lauda's Ferrari, into the pits for slicks. By the time they rejoined, Mass was into a comfortable lead. But what should have been the driver's day of days was to be interrupted in the most terrible manner.

For some unaccountable reason, Lauda crashed on the far side of the circuit, his Ferrari bursting into flames. The Austrian driver was eventually pulled free by four drivers, but when he reached hospital his burns were considered to be too great to offer hopes for survival. A priest gave Lauda the last rites.

James suddenly realised how much he had depended on Lauda's presence. Feeling helpless but fervently hoping the Austrian would survive, James sent a provocative telegram in the hope that it would both enrage and encourage. Against all predic-

tions, Niki was back in action six weeks later.

In the intervening period, James had finished fourth in Austria and won at Zandvoort. By the time Lauda had returned at Monza, the gap between them was down to two points. The Italian authorities were determined to have their say and Hunt's McLaren was forced to start from the back of the grid as a penalty for an alleged fuel infringement. The resulting battle through the field ended ignominiously when he had an unnecessary collision with another car. Lauda, meanwhile, had finished fourth.

On to Canada now and any hope of a decent confrontation seemed to be demolished when Ferrari's appeal over Brands Hatch was upheld. Nine points were taken away from James; three more were given to Niki.

Hunt responded brilliantly by taking nine points at Mosport while Lauda scored none. James repeated the performance a week later at Watkins Glen. That made it Lauda 68 points and Hunt 65. Only the Japanese Grand Prix remained.

A place on the front row at Mount Fuji would be more important than ever. Hunt, technically minded only when he needed to be, adopted a typically pragmatic approach when it came to sorting his car to suit the 2.7-mile track.

During the first day of practice, he made very little progress. Vain attempts to balance the M23 between oversteer on the fast corners and understeer on the slow ones only succeeded in mystifying James. At the end of the day, he examined the lap times and concluded that the fastest drivers had probably decided to abandon a technical approach. They had either said 'to hell with it' or they didn't care about such complicated matters in the first place. James followed this line of thinking and used sheer willpower and reflexes to hurl the McLaren onto the front row. Lauda was third-fastest. So far, so good.

On race day it rained, as only it can in this part of Japan. There were doubts that the race would be held at all but, after much indecision, suddenly it was on, Hunt powering off the line to take full benefit of his

grid position. He pulled away in inverse proportion to Lauda's progress towards the back of the field. Unhappy with the appalling conditions and possessing a sharper realisation of the dangers involved and the meaning of life – *his* life – Lauda decided to stop even though it meant throwing away the championship. Lauda did not care about that any more than he cared about making his views public. James Hunt had it made.

Then the rain eased, the breeze finally blowing the swollen clouds away and drying the track. With two-thirds of the race completed, Hunt pressed on, Depailler closed in with his Tyrrell and took the lead, and still Hunt pressed on, the team choosing not to give him instructions either way concerning a tyre change. Not even when they could see that he had a punctured rear tyre. With so much at stake, this was a matter for the driver, they reasoned. Lauda may have retired, but if Hunt finished lower than fourth, the title would go to Austria. Better to let James make the decisions.

In the end, the choice was made for him. The left-front tyre suddenly failed, the result of running the wet-weather rubber on the drying track. Luckily for James, the pit entrance was close at hand and he dived in, had all four tyres changed and returned, convinced he was out of the championship. In a state of blind fury, he drove like a man possessed. Along the way, he passed two cars and moved into third place without realising it. At the flag, he was still third and therefore the 1976 World Champion. Everyone knew it except James.

With the famous short fuse now well and truly lit, he charged into the pit lane and tore himself from the cockpit, all the better to give Teddy Mayer a piece of his mind. He was confronted by a sea of smiling faces but such was the density of his red mist that he failed to register what they were saying. And, even when the message got through, he refused to believe it. Later, much later, the soothing flow of a celebratory drink or two allowed the wonderful realisation to dawn.

The winter which followed was an impossible round of functions and public appearances, a difficult job for a well-organised professional such as Jackie Stewart; a chore for someone of Hunt's more relaxed inclination. The gossip columnists, having had their pound of adulation, now picked on every late arrival, every smart occasion seemingly belittled by James's casual attire, every word that was out of place. Hunt was glad to climb on board the plane for Argentina and get down to the business of defending his title.

Just three wins – Silverstone, Watkins Glen and Mount Fuji – do not do justice to either the quality of his driving in 1977 or the fact that the team was struggling to make the McLaren M25 as successful as its predecessor. He finished fifth in the championship with 40 points and 1978 was even worse as he collected a third, a fourth and a fifth place during the 16 races. The glory days of McLaren were over – for the time being. Unable to keep pace with the ground-effect cars which were then *de rigueur*, McLaren had slipped from conten-

tion and they lost Hunt's interest along the way.

For 1979, he joined the Wolf team but he had no enthusiasm for the lack of finesse required by the ground-effect cars and the way that the emphasis was switching to the input of designers and engineers rather than the driver. Always keenly aware of the dangers, and not afraid to admit the fact when necessary, Hunt decided after seven races that he had had enough and quit without further ado.

The sudden departure was totally in keeping with a man who, throughout his career, had been capable of surprises. On his day, he was brilliant. On other less memorable occasions, he was bratish, boorish and belligerent.

In recent years, he has calmed down and matured bringing intelligence, humour and always a touch of controversy to his work as a television commentator. A natural affinity with the off-beat remains, such as his passion for breeding budgerigars and the wearing of bright-green socks with his dinner suit at major functions. His home in Wimbledon, south London is an extraordinary domestic pastiche as sundry characters pass through the lounge to the backdrop of parrots and children fighting for the right to be heard.

When James decided to retire, he confided in Eoin Young, the co-author of Hunt's aptly titled autobiography *Against All Odds*. Young later discussed the retirement in his column in *Autocar*. Summing up the feelings of many who viewed James with a mixture of pleasure, distaste, admiration and indifference, Young wrote:

'What do I think? I think he won 10 Grand Prix races and a World Championship. I've never been able to condone what James does or the way he does it, but I have an idea that I understand why he does it. I'm not excusing him, but then I'm not condemning him either, as most other people tend to do. He is a totally competitive person as he understands the word and in the Hunt dictionary competitive means only one thing – winning.'

The Canadian Grand Prix

The sleepy town of Bowmanville, some 50 miles east of Toronto, became the epicentre of a motor racing storm in 1976. This was the year the media could scarcely believe their luck. The stories, each one dripping with melodrama, seemed never-ending.

According to the sycophantic tabloid press, James Hunt was Britain's underdog in a grim battle against that Austrian, Niki Lauda, and the unsporting Ferrari team from Italy. There had been protests in Spain, protests in Britain. Hunt won at

Járama, then he lost the nine points, then they were given back. He was not allowed to start the British Grand Prix, then he was, then he won, then a protest was rejected.

Lauda crashed heavily in Germany. He was at death's door. Then – and this one took some believing – he came back to continue his fight for the championship. And so it went on, each race fuelling the sports writers like never before. In Canada that year, the stories started before a car had so much as turned a wheel at the Mosport track.

Hunt arrived in Toronto knowing that a

court of appeal was sitting in Paris to discuss Ferrari's protest over his victory at Brands Hatch. He knew he was in the clear. It was, he felt, an open-and-shut case. But, with the governing body, you never could be sure. Consistency had never been a watchword at the FIA.

James went off to play squash and forget about something over which he had no control. As he arrived at the court, there was a message saying there was bad news. He knew immediately what it had to be.

The game of squash turned out to be one of the worst he had ever played. By the time he had finished, the press were waiting to confirm his fears. The Brands Hatch victory had been thrown out; Lauda was now the winner of the British Grand Prix. And the bottom line said that Lauda's championship lead had suddenly stretched from five points to 17. There were three races remaining: Canada, United States and Japan. All Hunt could do was go for broke … talk about long odds.

A war of words began. The agencies reported Lauda's pleasure over 'a correct decision', one which was 'for the good of the sport'. Hunt was angered by that. There was a story which suggested Hunt had said he was not interested in safety, only in racing. He was alleged to have told Lauda that they could take the crash barriers away for all he cared. By the time that particular tale had gathered speed, the two drivers were supposedly at each other's throats.

Lauda and Hunt, outspoken both, had been at the forefront of the safety campaign. Hunt had actually told Lauda that, since the Mosport track was generally agreed to be in poor shape, then Lauda knew what needed to be done and he would not require any help from James. Furthermore, he had asked, and been granted, permission to stand down from safety affairs until someone had sorted out the rules and regulations. Hunt figured he had enough on his plate while trying to win the championship.

Those were the simple facts, none of which involved rancour or intrigue. What reached print bore no relation to the truth, but it made for a good story.

In fact, the slack-jawed reporting suited James admirably. With such a huge points deficit he needed to employ every tactic he could think of; therefore his game plan was to unsettle Lauda by having the Austrian believe that James had, in his words, 'freaked out'. If Lauda thought that the appeal court decision, and his alleged response to it, had unhinged Hunt, then the Englishman's driving might become wild and irrational. In that case, he would best be avoided on the track.

Hunt was trying to neutralise his rival before the action had even started. The effect was to make the little town of Bowmanville crackle with tension as the teams checked in at the Flying Dutchman motel. Reporters did not know which way to turn.

There was substance to worries over the state of Mosport Park and the suggestion that the race might not be held at all. The 2.459-mile circuit had been opened in 1961. Since then the harsh Canadian winters had taken their toll on the track surface. A disagreement over finance had led to the cancellation of the previous year's race and the absence from Mosport merely heightened its shortcomings when the Grand Prix teams returned.

The drivers did agree that the circuit layout, rising and falling through 450 acres of rolling countryside to the north of Lake Ontario, was as testing as any on the championship trail, the downhill Corner 1 being outstanding. Predictably, after much talk on the subject and one or two changes, the deficiencies of the circuit were quickly forgotten once practice got under way.

There was a sharpness to James Hunt's driving and there was no need to ask from where the motivation had come. Using the known and trusted handling qualities of his McLaren to the full, Hunt took pole by four-tenths of a second. He was enjoying the circuit and the car, but the media attention when he left them was something he could have done without. Lauda, meanwhile, was not happy with the handling of his Ferrari; he would start from sixth place.

Glorious autumn weather tempted 85,000 spectators to Mosport for the weekend. On race day, the schedule fell behind when a hectic Formula Ford race called for major rebuilding of some of the crash barriers. The delay raised James Hunt's adrenalin level even more. His tactics were as before in this topsy-turvy season; he simply had to win.

That plan received an immediate setback when Ronnie Peterson made a better start and took the lead. Hunt harassed the Swede for eight laps before finding a way through. Immediately, he pulled out 1.5 seconds on the March-Ford, but any thought that he would be left to get on with scoring maximum points ended four laps later when Patrick Depailler forced his Tyrrell into second place.

Hunt and Depailler had tangled earlier in the year at Long Beach, and, as the season went by the Frenchman had become a serious force. The introduction of the six-wheeled Tyrrell had called for a period of acclimatisation, but by autumn Depailler was flinging the ungainly car into the corners with exhilarating abandon. And Mosport he clearly loved. By quarter-distance, he was less than two seconds behind the McLaren and giving serious signs of wanting to score his first Grand Prix win. Five laps later, he was 1.5 seconds behind, then 1.3, then 0.8. Hunt was being made to work extremely hard. Lauda, meanwhile, was fifth and struggling with the handling.

As the leaders began to work through the back-markers, Hunt employed all of his cunning to keep Depailler at arm's length. By carefully timing his passing moves, James would be hindered for the minimum amount and, if he played it absolutely right, he could leave Patrick to struggle as he attempted to follow through on a difficult section of the track. It was a superb contest of enterprise and daring: Hunt with everything to play for, Depailler chasing the scent of a long-awaited victory.

In fact, Patrick was beginning to sniff something else. A special petrol-filled safety diaphragm had been incorporated in the system to sidestep the need for the dashboard gauge to be fed by petrol. This precaution had been taken to avoid the hazard of routeing fuel into the cockpit – and ironically, by some fluke, the safeguard had gone wrong.

The first sign of trouble came in the final few laps. Until then, Depailler had been able to recover each time Hunt trapped him behind a back-marker. On some occasions he had hauled the Tyrrell right onto the tail of the McLaren; indeed, he was so close at one time that a move to take the lead seemed almost inevitable. With five laps remaining, Hunt sliced past the battle for ninth place. Depailler did likewise and everyone waited for a certain final attack.

It never came. Instead, Depailler began to drop back and, immediately on crossing the line for the 80th and final time, Patrick pulled up sharply, flung off his belts and collapsed by the side of the car. Overcome by petrol fumes, Depailler said he had driven as though on automatic pilot. His left eye was virtually closed; the last five laps had been no more than a blur of scenery and a vague idea of where he was. Until this had happened, he felt sure he could have made a serious effort of relieving the McLaren of first place.

James Hunt had, in that respect, been lucky. But, overall, he had driven perhaps one of the most determined races of his career. And his reaction, as he crossed the line with both arms high in the air, said he had done it when it mattered most. Needless to say, one or two beers were enjoyed in the Flying Dutchman that night.

There were few places to go in celebration since this was a fairly sparse part of Ontario and the Grand Prix itself was short on tradition. The vastness of the country and the isolated pockets of population within it had meant it was difficult for a cohesive form of national racing to evolve.

Mosport Park, in fact, was the first major race track worthy of the name and the inaugural Canadian Grand Prix in 1961 was for sports cars. The advent of the powerful CanAm cars saw victories in later years of Jim Hall (Chaparral) and Mark Donohoue (Lola). The successful running of these two races in particular helped convince the FIA that Canada was ready to host a round of the world championship in 1967. It was no coincidence that this was also Canada's centennial year.

The race was scheduled for the end of August, inconveniently placed between the German and Italian Grands Prix, forcing teams to cross the Atlantic once more for the US Grand Prix in October. Nonetheless, there was virtually a full turn-out, the entry swollen by local drivers, of whom Eppie Weitzes had the third works Lotus put at his disposal. It has not been recorded how he felt when, from the back row of the grid, he could just about see Jim Clark and Graham Hill on the front with their similar cars. Once the race had started Weitzes would have seen nothing, because the first drop of the red-and-white Maple Leaf flag at a Grand Prix coincided with a downpour.

Denny Hulme, no fan of racing in the rain, found more grip than anyone by using the edge of the track and splashed past Clark to take the lead. The sensation of the opening laps, however, was Bruce McLaren as he gave his new BRM-powered car its first airing. Bruce, having recovered from an early spin and climbed from 12th to second, was poised to take the lead. Then the rain stopped and Clark speeded up. The Lotus quickly passed Hulme's Brabham and, when the rain returned, McLaren was expected to come into the reckoning once more. Indeed, he would have done so but for the absence of an alternator (omitted to save weight) which meant there was no way of coping with a flat battery.

When Clark retired with wet electrics and Hulme stopped to change goggles, Jack Brabham inherited a lead he would never lose, Hulme charging back to give the Brabham team a one-two. Thus ended the first Canadian Grand Prix, a crowd of 55,000 leaving damp but apparently happy as they faced horrendous queues on the way home.

The question of unfavourable logistics was neatly solved in 1968 when the Grand Prix was scheduled to coincide with the next round at Watkins Glen. This time, though, there was a change of venue. It was felt that Quebec, very much a separate entity within the country as a whole never mind Canadian motor sport, should have a crack of the whip and Le Circuit Mont-Tremblant, 90 miles north-west of Montreal, was booked for the weekend of 22 September.

Situated in the Laurentians near St Jovite, a superb circuit carved out of rugged terrain was made even more delightful by the mature tints of autumn. Certain safety improvements were suggested by the drivers and quickly implemented, Jacky Ickx putting them to the test when his throttle jammed and pitched the Ferrari into the catch-fencing. The Belgian was considered fortunate to have got away with a broken leg, but it ended his chances of winning the championship.

The circuit, for all its majesty and depth of challenge, was exceedingly bumpy and 90 laps proved a tough test. In the event, only three of the 19 starters managed to run non-stop, victory going to the McLaren-Ford of Denny Hulme. Even he was first to admit that the day had been bought and almost paid for by Chris Amon, the eternally unlucky New Zealander dominating from the start. His clutch had broken on lap 8, but there were no obvious signs of difficulty as he opened a lead of more than a minute. With 18 laps to go, the Ferrari's transmission gave out; another massive dose of 'what-might-have-been' for poor Chris. Ickx, on crutches, was on hand to console his team-mate when he returned to the pits.

Ickx more than made up for the disappointment by winning at Mosport the following year. On his first visit to the circuit, Ickx remarked that it was an 'excellent race course' but added that overtaking would be difficult. He was to prove it while trying to take the lead from Jackie Stewart as they swept downhill and into the very fast Corner 2. The two cars touched, Stewart's Matra spinning to a halt, Ickx continuing on his way to head another one-two for Brabham in Canada. He publicly apologised to Stewart afterwards but added, somewhat cynically, that racing was about leading, not following.

Stewart took him at his word when he streaked into the lead at St Jovite in 1970. This was something of a surprise since he was, for the first time, at the wheel of the new Tyrrell. The impressive honeymoon lasted for 32 laps before a front stub axle broke and, while Stewart and Tyrrell had made their point, the Scotsman must have noted the irony of seeing Ickx of all people take advantage and lead home the similar Ferrari of Clay Regazzoni.

Twelve months is a long time in motor racing terms so, when the teams arrived at Mosport in September 1971, Tyrrell and

Stewart were the combination to beat. Rain on race day, however, threatened to upset form. Sure enough, after leading for a brief period, Stewart had to contend with a dazzling display from Ronnie Peterson. The March, having checked the strength of the barrier on numerous occasions, finally moved ahead, but Stewart's persistence gave him the lead again in the aftermath of another of Ronnie's more lurid moments.

Running in tandem, their battle ended when a back-marker let Stewart through but failed to see Peterson in the spray. The resulting damage to the nose of the March finished Peterson's challenge and Stewart was home, if not dry, when deteriorating conditions caused the race to be halted prematurely after 64 of the scheduled 80 laps had been run.

Meanwhile, there was trouble brewing in Quebec as the owner of Mont-Tremblant fell out with the Canadian motor sport authorities and the circuit, in need of major repairs, began to fall into disuse. Striking while the opposition was down, new management at Mosport gave their place a

facelift, installing new barriers, additional kerbs, a machine shop in the paddock – and acquired a new sponsor in the Labatt Brewing Company. The race, though, was almost a repeat of the previous one.

Rain was not the problem this time but fog which threatened to cause the Grand Prix to be postponed. The supporting races were cancelled, but the weather improved in time to have the race started, albeit an hour late. Once again, Peterson's March provided Stewart with the most serious opposition and, once again, the Tyrrell finished the day as the easy winner after Peterson had tangled with Graham Hill while lapping the Englishman's Brabham.

Rain did fall in 1973 but the trouble arose when it stopped after about 15 laps. As the entire field stumbled into the pits to change to slicks, lap charts went to pieces. Then, just as some semblance of order re-emerged, the officials threw the entire proceedings into confusion.

Plans to use a pace car, a novelty in Formula 1, were brought into force when two cars collided on lap 33. It took three laps for

the pace car to appear and, when it did, it was placed before an Iso Marlboro which – and this was the only thing over which everyone agreed – most certainly was not leading.

In the end, the man with the chequered flag waved it half-heartedly at Peter Revson's McLaren-Ford; the scoreboard, meanwhile, said that Fittipaldi was leading, a fact with which the Lotus team naturally concurred, Colin Chapman having gone so far as to toss his cap in the air in time-honoured fashion. Then Jackie Oliver and Shadow threw their metaphorical hats into the ring by suggesting that they were second and ahead of Revson, who should have been third. The officials stood firm: Revson got the nod and everyone else got the hump. It had been a messy race in every respect.

Niki Lauda came to Canada with a chance of winning the 1974 world championship. It ended when he crashed and lost the lead, having failed to notice dirt which had been scattered on the track by a wayward back-marker. Instead, a victory for Fittipaldi and McLaren assured the Brazi-

lian of his second world title.

With Mosport out of favour in 1975 due to a familiar disagreement over money, McLaren found themselves back in the victory circle in 1976 after James Hunt's exquisite drive and a splendid day's racing. That would not be the case the following year as the Canadian Grand Prix provided every shade of drama, from the ridiculous to the very bad.

It began when Niki Lauda had a row with the Ferrari team, packed his bags and went home. During the first day of practice, Ian Ashley lost control of his Hesketh on the flat-in-fifth brow near the end of the back straight. The car became airborne, somersaulted a few times, cleared the crash barrier and flew into a tubular tower supporting a television camera. The entire structure – which, happily, was unoccupied at the time – collapsed and the Hesketh fell to the ground in a tangle of poles, its engine somehow tucked under the chassis. Ashley's injuries were confined to broken wrists and ankles.

The upshot of the accident was a hue and cry over the absence of a helicopter, an organisational failing which was underscored when, later in the day, Jochen Mass spun off at Corner 1 and the wooden posts supporting the guard rail gave way. The quietly voiced fears of slipping standards at Mosport suddenly became more strident as

the drivers demanded action. There was talk of a boycott but, as ever, unity among the drivers was lacking and the race went ahead.

Victory for Mario Andretti seemed certain once the menacing presence of James Hunt had disappeared in spectacular fashion. Andretti had been leading, Hunt his shadow, when they came to lap the McLaren of Jochen Mass. Andretti was incensed when the German chopped across, forcing him to lift off and allow Hunt to take the lead. Any thought that this might have been team tactics, however, quickly disappeared when Mass proved to be even-handed in these matters and promptly had his teammate into the wall. Andretti, who had a grandstand view, said Mass waved Hunt through and then lost control; Hunt's views were slightly different and infinitely more colourful.

So furious was he that, when a marshal tried to prevent him from crossing the track, Hunt knocked the man down and then received a heavy fine for his trouble. As a result of these blows of various hues, Andretti found himself in control until two laps from the end. Then the engine on his Lotus failed. Jody Scheckter, to his delight and surprise, was next in line, taking a win for Walter Wolf in the oil baron's adopted country. It was a splendid day for Canada. But there was even better to come in 1979.

Mosport Park, unable to keep pace with the requirements of the rapidly developing Grand Prix cars, now belonged to a past era. Just as Mosport had been quick to step in when Mont-Tremblant fell by the wayside, the Quebec motor racing fans returned the compliment when it was announced that the Grand Prix would be held on a manmade island in the St Lawrence.

Designed by Roger Peart, a British motor sport enthusiast resident in Montreal, the 2.9-mile track was based on a perimeter road on Île Notre-Dame, formerly the site of pavilions built for Expo '67 international fair. The island, a short ride by metro from the city centre, had also been used to stage the rowing competitions in the 1976 Olympic Games and the teams were based in the former boat houses at one end of the vast lake.

The Quebec circuit was an idyllic setting and the track itself had a reasonable mixture of corners, although some were considered to be too tight. There was the feeling, though, that nothing would be too much trouble to rectify – which is often the case at a new venue where the organisers are willing to please.

All of this was riding on the back of one man. In 1978 and for the first time, Quebec had a Grand Prix driver truly worthy of the name. This was Gilles Villeneuve's first full season of Formula 1, and he returned to his homeland with a growing reputation for the spectacular. There was genuine talk of him winning his first Grand Prix, right here, in Montreal.

This was also the year of Lotus. Following the tragic loss of Ronnie Peterson at Monza, Jean-Pierre Jarier was drafted in as Andretti's team-mate. Seizing his chance, Jarier took pole and streaked into the lead. Villeneuve, starting from the second row, had to bide his time in fourth place, moving forward when Alan Jones suffered a slow puncture, and then taking second place at the expense of Scheckter's Wolf. Jarier, however, seemed unassailable.

Then an oil leak told of imminent engine failure and a heart-broken Jarier had no alternative but to coast into retirement. What made it worse was the delighted reaction of the crowd as they received the news of his departure. Villeneuve was leading with 20 laps to go. Under no threat, the French-Canadian drove to an emotional victory and congratulations from the prime minister, Pierre Trudeau. It was a dream come true for both Gilles and the race promoters. The future of the Grand Prix at Île Notre-Dame was assured.

Niki Lauda's future was decided on this very track the following year when the Austrian suddenly chose to quit motor racing on the spot. One minute he was practising his Brabham; the next, he was on his way to the airport, his helmet and overalls left on the pit counter. As if that was not enough excitement for one weekend, the race developed into a thrilling encounter between Villeneuve and Alan Jones, two uncompromising racers who thoroughly enjoyed a battle which lasted for the entire 72 laps, victory going to Jones.

There was much more at stake for the Williams driver in 1980 as he arrived for the penultimate round of the championship locked in combat for the title with Nelson Piquet. In theatrical fashion, the Williams and the Brabham started from the front row and then collided at the first curve. The track was blocked in the ensuing confusion and the race stopped.

Piquet took his spare car while, fortuit- ously, the Williams was more or less untouched. Piquet led but the engine (which should have been changed over- night, but was not) failed. Didier Pironi overtook Jones to lead the field, but the Ligier driver had been penalised one minute for jumping the start. Jones was declared the winner – and the 1980 World Champion.

The following September, Jacques Laf- fite won for Ligier-Matra in appalling con- ditions which accounted for 11 drivers either having accidents or spinning off. This was the one complaint about Montreal. The climate at this time of year tended to be chilly and uncomfortable, so when the US Grand Prix was moved to Detroit in June and linked with the Cana- dian Grand Prix, the answer seemed to have been found. By a stange quirk, the weather on 13 June 1982 was unseasonably cold and grey. And that was not the only unsettling thing about this race.

Villeneuve had been killed the previous month and, despite his absence and a trans- port strike in the city, a vast crowd turned out to watch Pironi start his Ferrari from pole. That, at least, is what he should have done. The Frenchman stalled seconds before the green light. The pack swept past but, at the back, Ricardo Paletti was unsighted and he slammed straight into the stationary Ferrari. It took the best part of half an hour to cut the novice free from his Osella; on arrival at a city hospital, Paletti was pronounced dead from massive chest injuries.

The race, of course, had been stopped and by the time it was restarted the after- noon had become even colder and gloomier and, for many, Nelson Piquet's win for Brabham and BMW could not come quick enough.

Apart from time lost when making a pit stop for fuel and tyres, René Arnoux led all the way for Ferrari in 1983, Piquet scoring an equally routine win for Brabham-BMW the following year. Ferrari earned a virtu- ally unchallenged one-two for Michele Alboreto and Stefan Johansson in 1985, yet just 12 months later the red cars were

nowhere. Williams and Honda were now the dominant combination and Nigel Man- sell took one of the most commanding wins of the season, a result he might well have repeated had the Canadian Grand Prix been held in 1987.

The race was back on the schedule in 1988, complete with new pits at the far end of the circuit and a new sponsor, Molson, replacing the long-standing arrangement with their brewing rival, Labatt, and bring- ing the necessary finance to ensure the race's immediate future.

The outcome of all these changes was a race which highlighted the performance of the McLaren-Hondas as they made full use of the turbo's fuel efficiency on a circuit notorious for high consumption figures.

It looked like being a repeat win for Ayr- ton Senna in 1989 but, just three laps short of the chequered flag, his Honda V10 failed. He had driven superbly on a wet track and his absence from the front of the field gave a surprise but welcome victory for Thierry Boutsen and Williams-Renault. Rain again added the element of a lottery in 1990 but, this time, Senna's car did not let him down and he produced the most serene performance on his way to another nine points and, ultimately, his second world championship.

When he arrived for the Grand Prix in 1991, Senna went to great lengths to point out that, just because he had won the first four races of the season, it did not automat- ically mean he was about to clean up in Montreal. His powers of foresight seemed remarkable when, for once, McLaren were not in the reckoning, Senna retiring from third place.

This race belonged to Nigel Mansell. Or, at least, 68½ of the 69 laps did. Less than a mile from home, the Williams-Renault failed him, victory going to an astonished Nelson Piquet and Benetton-Ford. Piquet had won twice before in Canada but this result, along with many of the races in this delightful country, would be memorable through a combination of the bizarre and the dramatically different.

Watson's speed and professional approach stood out when he raced a Crosslé In club events In Ireland.

JOHN WATSON

John Watson came of age in the Heathrow Post House Hotel on Monday 16 August 1976. But in true Irish fashion, rather than grow a beard, he shaved his off. The hirsute image had been Watson's trademark ever since he first appeared at a motor race in England seven years before and yet, on this particular morning, he was more than happy to set to work with his razor. It was a pleasant reminder that he had just won his first Grand Prix the day before.

Watson had come to an agreement with Roger Penske; if John won a Grand Prix then he would remove the bristles which did not quite fit the clean-cut image of the American entrant and his team. When Watson came down to breakfast that morning, Penske did not recognise him. Was this pasty-faced, slightly self-conscious guy really the man who had just won the Austrian Grand Prix?

That it was summed up the curious paradox which had been John Marshall Watson ever since he first sat in a racing car in his native Northern Ireland. He was to become one of the finest exponents of the Grand Prix art and yet he gave the impression of not quite believing that he was as good as he really was.

Curiously, Watson's early appearances at local circuits such as Kirkistown and Bishopscourt smacked of a quiet confidence that matched an obvious natural gift for the business. His professional approach and immediate speed placed him on a higher level than the cheerful amateurs with whom he regularly competed on both sides of the Irish border. It was clear in many minds that there was the stamp of greatness about him. But no-one could be quite sure how the man himself felt about such theories. Brashness never was his way.

It is stange – yet, in Watson's case, it hardly seems surprising at all – that he did not possess a burning desire to be a racing driver as a youngster even though motor racing was his consuming interest from an early age. It was as though he refused to be influenced by the obvious since the sport was an integral part of the household, his father Marshall Watson having regularly raced in the Fifties with cars such as a Formula 2 Alta.

John would accompany his father to the races and, in later years, work in the family business selling new and second-hand cars from a small showroom in Belfast. When John finally decided to try his hand at racing, it was clear from the impeccable method of attack that he had the enthusiastic support of his father; very much, as John put it, 'a dad and lad operation'.

He began with an Austin Healey Sprite, which doubled as a road car, and he then switched to an immaculate Crosslé sports racer. His smooth, relaxed style told how at ease he was in the car, but the big test came when he got his hands on an ex-works Lotus 48 Formula 2 car and travelled to Thruxton with Team Ireland for the Easter International in April 1969.

John had not yet turned 23 and here he was entered alongside the likes of Graham Hill, Jochen Rindt and Jackie Stewart, names he had previously revered but which were now about to provide what could be an embarrassing yardstick for his perceived inadequacies. The Lotus 48 was not considered to be a particularly good car and he had no experience of it. Nor had he seen Thruxton before. All in all, this was not the ideal way to make a frontline début.

He made the middle of the grid for his heat, qualified for the final and was making extraordinary progress from 18th to fifth when he crashed. The car was badly damaged and, despite John's fleeting promise, the accident knocked the stuffing out of the little team and his entrant withdrew. It was back to club racing in Ireland.

The brush with motor racing's high society left a deep impression and the Watsons realised which path they must take if John was to make the most of what was clearly a useful talent. Marshall forked out for a Brabham BT30 and John set off on the European Formula 2 trail in 1970. With no help or guidance, the learning curve was perilously steep as Watson discovered such novelties as slipstreaming and the art of pacing yourself rather going hell-for-leather in the manner of a club race. A bad crash at Rouen resulted in a broken leg and a serious setback, but he returned the following year and scored his first European Formula 2 Championship points by finishing fifth at Mantorp Park in Sweden.

An established member of the racing scene in 1972, John joined the ranks of the many useful drivers without either a car or money, and he picked up drives where he could. The most significant contact came towards the end of the year when he drove a privately entered March Formula 1 car into sixth place in the non-championship Victory Meeting at Brands Hatch. The March was sponsored by Hexagon of Highgate and Paul Michaels, owner of the up-market sports car dealership, was eventually to play a major role in lifting Watson into Grand Prix racing on a permanent basis.

In the meantime, enter Bernard Ecclestone. Bernie had taken over the Brabham team and his astute eye had landed on Watson. Seeing John as a likely lad for the future, but now available at a bargain-basement price, Ecclestone offered a deal which provided a seat in the Brabham Formula 2 team with the occasional Formula 1 drive when there was a car available. In return, Watson would commit himself to a three-year contract with Ecclestone. John accepted with alacrity. And, to fill out his programme, there would be drives with the Gulf long-distance sports car team. The 1973 season looked like being his best ever. It almost ended before it had begun.

Brabham had just introduced the first car designed by Gordon Murray, and John had the happy task of working with the talented South African as the BT42 received its first airing in the Race of Champions. Held at Brands Hatch, this race did not count for the championship but it attracted most of the leading Formula 1 teams. Watson was settling in nicely with the new car during the race when the throttle jammed open on the entry to Stirling's Bend. The Brabham rammed the bank and John broke his leg – the same one which had been fractured at Rouen three years before.

By the time that had healed, the Formula

John made the correct move when he took up racing in Europe in 1970.

2 season had got into its stride and Ecclestone did not think it worth pursuing the championship at such a late stage. Apart from the Gulf sports car drive, there was little to fill Watson's time, although he did make his Grand Prix début at Silverstone in the previous year's works Brabham, now entered by Hexagon. Painted an unattractive shade of brown, this car handled poorly, had a down-on-power engine and retired after 13 laps. Finally, and partially fulfilling his promise, Ecclestone entered Watson in a third works car for the money-rich US Grand Prix, his race lasting for just seven laps before the Ford-Cosworth failed. The future looked bleak since neither Watson nor Ecclestone had sufficient funds to support a Formula 1 drive in 1974.

Paul Michaels stepped into the financial breach by buying one of the BT42s and entering Watson for a full season of Grand Prix racing. It was a major breakthrough. John responded with regular finishes and scored his first world championship point by finishing sixth after hounding Emerson Fittipaldi's McLaren at Monaco.

The BT42 was exchanged mid-season for a BT44 and John used it to take an excellent fourth in Austria after stopping to change a front tyre. His confidence and reputation growing, there was much acclaim when he put the Brabham on the second row of the grid with a quick lap at Monza. Then, as he returned to the pits, a rear wheel casting broke and the BT44 was badly damaged. Ecclestone stepped in with the offer of the spare works Brabham but, since this had been used as a test hack, John suffered various problems and finished seventh.

During the season Watson had driven Formula 2 cars for John Surtees, a task which many saw as being only for the foolhardy. Rather than complain about the difficult working environment as Surtees, in his customary manner, took on too much, Watson simply got down to business. Surtees appreciated that and offered John a Formula 1 drive for 1975, Ecclestone agreeing to the necessary contractual release.

It was hardly a bed of roses. The Surtees TS16 looked to have come from the wrong end of the elegance scale but Watson's belief in his ability allowed him to do remarkable things with the blue-and-yellow car. He finished second in the Race of Champions and, had it not been for a flat-spotted tyre during a thrilling drive at the legendary Montjuich Park, he might have won the Spanish Grand Prix. In many ways, it was frustrating for both the driver and entrant since there was not the money to do racing in the proper manner. Preferring to concentrate his limited resources on building a car for the following season, Surtees withdrew after the Austrian Grand Prix. Watson appeared to have been both risking his neck and wasting his time.

It says much for the astute awareness of Roger Penske that he should call upon Watson in the shocking aftermath of Mark Donohue's death in Austria in August. The American-financed and British-based team, struggling to find their feet in Formula 1, were in a state of flux following the accident. Watson was just the man for the job – even if he did have a beard.

During the winter, Watson formed a strong bond with the team as they prepared for the 1976 season, but once the racing had started it seemed as if Watson would never score a point, never mind winning a race. The Penske PC4 was gradually being brought to a peak of competitiveness and in Austria, a year after Donohue had been

killed, Watson pulled off his first Grand Prix win in a thoroughly convincing manner.

There was a spring in his step as the clean-shaven Watson turned up for the next race at Zandvoort, the confidence boost of that first win lifting his performance to new levels as he threw himself into a cut-and-thrust battle with James Hunt. Watson was driving as quickly as ever but there was now an added touch of controlled aggression. He was a more complete driver. At last, he appeared to have turned the corner. Then Penske decided to close down his Formula 1 operation at the end of the season. It was typical of Watson's misfortune.

Many observers felt he was about to make his own bad luck when he agreed to drive for Brabham in 1977. Powered by the 12-cylinder Alfa Romeo engines, the Brabhams were not regarded as having race-winning potential, but Watson had been impressed by the power when running in company with the Alfas during the latter part of 1976. He also had enormous faith in Gordon Murray.

That belief was to be well-founded. The glorious-sounding red cars were on the pace and, in France, Watson drove in masterly fashion to fend off a lengthy attack from Mario Andretti. Going into the last lap, Watson had it made. Andretti, having tried everything he knew, had resigned himself to second place. Then the Brabham, unable to pick up the last drop of fuel, began to splutter. Watson was utterly helpless as the Lotus swept into the lead and John, fuel permitting, would cheerfully have mown down Colin Chapman as the Lotus boss threw his cap in the air. It had been the cruellest stroke imaginable.

Two weeks later, it happened again. This time Watson had been dealing superbly with Hunt's McLaren at Silverstone, the difference being that the trouble arose earlier in the race, thus reducing the cutting edge of the disappointment. The year was turning out to be a character-building one in many ways. Not long into the season Carlos Pace, the Brabham Number One, had been killed in a flying accident, thus foisting upon John the responsibility of leading the team and sorting the car. Watson's firm response surprised many including, perhaps, the man himself.

In 1978 he had a different sort of challenge to overcome: the menacing presence of Niki Lauda within the team. Again, he rose to the occasion. And, again, his wretched luck continued. At Long Beach, for instance, there was a huge explosion in the cockpit as he held second place. Heat from the brakes had burned through a breather pipe from the oil tank, the vapour then igniting and travelling back to cause chaos in the tank. Naturally, it had never happened before ...

Proving he had the measure of Lauda – in terms of speed in the car, if not in guile and psychological warfare out of it – Watson claimed a place on the front row at Monaco. He led until half-distance, brake trouble then forcing a trip into an escape road. Typ-

ically, though, Lauda won two Grands Prix that season whereas Watson had to make do with minor placings.

There was no doubt over Watson's ability and for 1979 he was chosen by McLaren to replace the departing James Hunt. It was a rather unfortunate scenario for Watson to enter into. The media immediately latched upon John as being the next British golden boy, and the McLaren sponsor Marlboro massaged the theme for all it was worth. Watson changed his hairstyle and adopted a more worldly-wise image. But he never quite carried it off; underneath you knew it was the same likable, modest man. The fact that Marlboro did not appreciate the reality reflected unfavourably on them rather than on their hapless hero.

Meanwhile, Watson's troubles continued on the track. He was involved in a first-corner collision in the opening race and, as the season progressed, it became clear that the performance of the 1979 McLaren-Ford did not match expectations. John claimed a point here and there, and 1980 turned out to be just as bad. McLaren were in deep disarray, but Watson counted himself lucky to be around when the inevitable take-over took place, Ron Dennis and John Barnard arriving to set McLaren on course towards a decade and more of remarkable prosperity.

While Dennis took charge of the organisation, Barnard went to work on a car which would be revolutionary. The introduction of a chassis manufactured entirely from carbon fibre set new standards and it came at a time when Watson was approaching his peak.

As the 1981 season got into its stride, Watson shook off the frustration of the previous two years and reminded himself of the pleasures associated with being in a truly competitive car. Third in Spain, he took second in France and then talked about finishing first at the next race, the British Grand Prix. Everyone knew it was not an idle boast; 'Wattie' was in with a shout at Silverstone.

Luck was on his side, too, for he managed to avoid a multiple pile-up by the skin of his teeth. Not exactly threatening in the early

laps, Watson nevertheless moved cleanly and swiftly through the field as he recovered from the effects of an accident which, given his normal luck, he would have been terminally involved in.

The race was under the control of the Renault team; when they ran into trouble, Watson was poised to strike. The place went berserk when John moved into the lead with eight laps to go and, on this occasion, he stayed there until the very end. It was almost too much for him to take in and, as he crossed the line, he gingerly raised his hand as though expecting the victory to be snatched away.

The reception received on his slowing-down lap was overwhelming, John's self-effacing manner not permitting the belief that this was for *him*. But such had been his appalling luck in the past that the emotion sweeping the enclosures, and indeed the pit lane, was both genuine and heartfelt. There has rarely been a more popular winner on such a widespread scale. Everyone was delighted for dear old 'Wattie', and not many drivers, not even Nigel Mansell in the years to follow, could make such a claim.

Watson went on to finish sixth in the world championship and there was genuine cause to believe 1982 would be his year. The McLaren was improving all the time and, after a slow start to the season, Watson found the perfect race set-up to win the Belgian Grand Prix at Zolder. That result brought mixed emotions for John since the weekend had been darkened by Gilles Villeneuve's fatal accident.

A few weeks later, he was to score an excellent win under happier circumstances as the Grand Prix teams raced for the first time on the streets of Detroit. Not only did Watson actually managed to pass no less than 12 cars, the result put him firmly in charge of the world championship. And there was the added satisfaction of beating his team-mate, Niki Lauda, the Austrian having made a heavily publicised return to the sport which had almost killed him.

On a high now, Watson extended his lead to ten points by finishing third in Canada. After that, the momentum began to die

away: tyre trouble in Holland, a spin when avoiding someone else's accident at Brands Hatch, a broken battery lead in France ... and so the list of problems went on. In fact, Watson failed to score a single point in the next six races, though fourth place in the penultimate round at Monza gave him an outside chance of taking the title in Las Vegas. John drove brilliantly there, slicing through from a mediocre grid position to finish second. But it was not enough. And that would be as close as John Watson would get, although 1983 would have its moments, some of which were very good indeed and some just plain terrible.

The McLaren with its normally aspirated Ford-Cosworth was being outpaced by the turbos, but not even the most powerful of engines could cope with a magnificent drive by Watson at Long Beach. In trouble throughout practice, both Lauda and Watson had started from near the back of the grid.

The race was a different story, the set-up of the McLaren being as near perfect as John could wish. And it was on such occasions that Watson was at his most dangerous. Combining natural skills with sharp aggression, he simply carved his way through the field. After 45 of the 75 laps, he

was in the lead. No-one could touch him.

Watson was just as bemused as the rest of the team. He cared little that the organisers, in a state of some confusion because of such an unexpected result, played the national anthem of the Republic of Ireland rather than 'God Save The Queen'. Standing on the rostrum that March afternoon would literally be the high point of his year. From then on the season went sharply downhill, bottoming out with an excruciating failure to qualify at Monaco and lifting slightly with third places in Detroit and Holland.

The future, though, seemed promising. The TAG turbo had arrived and this, com-

bined with Barnard's skills, would surely return Watson to consistent front-running. John, meanwhile, was waiting for McLaren to open discussions over the terms of his contract for 1984; it was seen as a mere formality. His position of strength, however, was completely undermined when Alain Prost unexpectedly quit Renault. Marlboro and McLaren snapped up the Frenchman and John Watson was suddenly unemployed. The switchboard at McLaren was jammed with abusive and irate calls from John's many fans. But the deed had been done. Watson's career as a frontline Grand Prix driver was effectively finished because of

this late stage in the bargaining season.

During the next two seasons John turned to sports car racing, a discipline which suited his experience and measured style. But it was not Formula 1. When McLaren then asked John to act as a stand-in for the injured Niki Lauda at Brands Hatch in late-1985, it placed him on the horns of a considerable dilemma.

He was being offered one of the best seats in the house since the McLaren was an established pace-setter. But John had not driven a Formula 1 car for two years. And he had as his benchmark Alain Prost, then considered to be one of the quickest drivers in

Unaccustomed as I am: Watson heads for a very popular win at Silverstone in 1981.

the world and completely at home in this car.

In effect, Watson could only lose. If he went quickly, then that was to be expected in such a fine car. If he was not up to speed, then his day had passed. He finished a tidy, undramatic seventh, just fractions of a second away from a championship point. It was his 152nd and final Grand Prix. In many ways the sad episode said everything about a gentle, gifted artist whose huge natural talent was largely squandered and frequently suppressed in what, for him, was a harsh environment.

The Austrian Grand Prix

n 1976 it was the *Raiffeisen Grosser Preis von Österreich*. The following year the Austrian Grand Prix was sponsored by *Gröbel Möbel*. The year after that it was someone else. The wide variety of backers emphasised the hand-to-mouth existence as the organisers of this popular race struggled to survive. But it also meant that, in 1976, John Watson got to keep the winner's trophy.

Nothing could have suited him better. The cup, resident for many years in the lounge of his converted coastguard cottage in Sussex before he moved to a larger house in Oxfordshire, was a majestic affair with a deep bowl, rather like the circuit itself.

The Österreichring had been carved out of the foothills of a wooded mountain range overlooking the town of Zeltweg. The Province of Steiermärk had spent around £500,000 in 1968 and 1969 on the construction of a circuit which made full use of the rolling terrain. The corners were fast, many of them were blind and, at a time when safety was the buzzword, it was a surprise to find a new track which had not gone overboard in the interests of clinical uniformity. Indeed, the Österreichring was anything but bland. The drivers, in the Seventies anyway, loved it.

Part of the pleasure derived from conquering the Österreichring came from the unspoken knowledge that it did not reward mistakes in a kindly manner. On the other hand, it was not the sort of place where a driver wanted to suffer a mechanical failure. Watson and the Penske team were fully aware of that when they arrived in 1976.

Twelve months previously, Mark Donohue had died as the result of injuries received when a deflating tyre sent his car off the road at the very fast Hella-Licht Kurve. Donohue had been driving for Penske and the circuit, despite its grandeur and pleasant surroundings, did not hold agreeable memories. Watson, brought in as Donohue's replacement, had been working all year to help the team recover. A good result here would be the perfect tonic.

With the benefit of a productive test session at this circuit, Penske were better pre-pared than usual and Watson was on the pace straightaway. Which was just as well since the first practice session on Friday morning would turn out to be the quickest, rain spoiling the remaining three.

Watson was on the front row, alongside James Hunt's pole-winning McLaren, with Ronnie Peterson (March) and Gunnar Nilsson (Lotus) filling row two. The Ferrari team, recovering from the shock of Niki Lauda's crash in Germany two weeks before, gave the race a miss and their absence took its toll on the usually healthy number of spectators drawn from across the Italian border.

Those who were present began to wonder if they would see a race at all. Heavy clouds and a sprinkling of rain led to much prevarication. Since the weather seemed unable to make up its mind, the officials and the teams did likewise and the start was delayed.

The appearance of large areas of blue sky, however, prompted positive activity, the cars venturing out on slick tyres even though the track itself was still damp. It had been decided that the race would be stopped if the cars were seen to kick up a reasonable amount of spray and, although this was the case in the opening laps, the officials, wisely as it turned out, restrained themselves. This was particularly good news for John Watson, since the Penske was leading a Grand Prix for the first time.

After four laps, however, Peterson took the lead, Watson content to let the March go since he felt he would have the advantage when the track finally dried out. In any case, John was more concerned about Jody Scheckter as the South African urged his six-wheeled Tyrrell through the field, passing Watson on lap 7 and setting off after Peterson.

Watson had closed up on the leaders just as Scheckter made a lunge at the inside of the March as they swept through a downhill right-hander. The rear of the Tyrrell then stepped out of line, Peterson began to draw alongside and Watson was having a go at passing them both. Ahead, and about to be lapped, a back-marker threatened to dis-rupt everything, all four cars blasting past the pits and rushing up the hill line-abreast. It was a breath-taking moment; Peterson emerged in front, with Watson second.

Then the sun came out, beating strongly on this beautiful landscape and generating further confidence in Watson. On lap 12, he took the lead and pulled away, never to be headed for the rest of the afternoon. With its dry weather settings and a perfectly matched set of tyres, the Penske was handling beautifully, Watson controlling the race with an ease which he found hard to credit.

At the end of 54 laps, he had achieved an ambition which seemed to stun the entire team. And, behind it all was the thought that this result went a considerable way towards expunging the memories of 12 months before. One way or another, it was an emotional day for Citibank Team Penske.

That night, Watson and Penske flew to London while the mechanics, led by crew chief Derrick Walker, prepared for the difficult haul back to base in Dorset. That was the only problem with the Österreichring. Its remote location, in the Styrian region to the north of Klagenfurt, meant a lengthy drive no matter which route you chose. Nevertheless, the circuit itself made the trip to the Austrian Grand Prix worthwhile. That had not always been the case.

In 1957, *Autosport* carried a report on Austrian motor racing. It did not require much space to say that circuit racing was something of a rarity, hill climbing being a more popular discipline, if only because of the plentiful supply of suitable venues. Even so, the last hill climb of a reasonable international standard had been held near Vienna in 1939, won by Hermann Lang in a Mercedes-Benz.

However, in 1957 there was hope for the future. A new group, the Österreicher Automobil Sport Club, had staged an important meeting at Aspern, an aerodrome near Vienna. Thirty thousand spectators turned out to watch six races on a 1.69-mile track utilising most of the two runways and part of the perimeter road. By all accounts, the day was a considerable success, British, Italian, German and Swiss drivers sharing the winning.

At the same time, plans were afoot to run races on a military airfield at Zeltweg, located in the flat valley of the River Mur, just below where the Österreichring was later to be located. The organisers, with assistance from the Austrian Government, were extremely ambitious and from the outset had their eye on finding a place for an Austrian Grand Prix on the international calendar. The circuit, though, did not quite match their lofty aspirations.

L-shaped and running up and down the main runway with a short loop onto a taxiway and around a grass island, the track measured 1.9 very bumpy miles. It saw sports car races in 1957 and 1958 and Formula 2 events, along with two non-championship Formula 1 races, during the next five years.

An application to hold a round of the 1963 World Championship had been rejected, but the Austrian Grand Prix was finally accepted in 1964. The organisers were to find that running a small Formula 1 race was one thing and a full-blown Grand Prix quite another.

The timing beam failed, leaving the officials to use stop-watches, and the resulting times did not always correspond with those recorded by the experienced members of the Grand Prix teams. There was confusion over the validity of passes when a typist's error in the instructions to police rendered many of the armbands ineffectual in the eyes of the law.

The paddock was housed in an aircraft hangar, which was all very well until an engine was started and all conversation had to cease. Added to which, the pits were located in the middle of the runway, the circuit's two main straights passing on each side. It was necessary, therefore, to shuttle everything and everyone into position before track activity could begin.

Steering arms, suspensions and transmissions took a terrible pounding on the corrugated surface. The BRM of Graham Hill was an exception and, after many laps, he took pole position, John Surtees (Fer-

rari), Jim Clark (Lotus-Climax) and Dan Gurney (Brabham-Climax) joining him on the front row.

In fact only six of the 20 starters completed more than 100 laps, the Ferrari of Lorenzo Bandini winning as the Italian controlled the gap to Richie Ginther's BRM. Elsewhere there were many disgruntled drivers, the favourites having gone out with broken driveshafts, collapsed suspension, Rindt's Brabham even managing to jump a tooth on the rack-and-pinion steering.

But the most spectacular retirement of all occurred to Phil Hill as he crashed into a wall of straw bales, the Cooper then catching fire and blazing merrily, the marshals incapable of helping at all. Hill had gone off at the corner leading onto the runway, a tight left-hander made even more difficult by a drainage gutter running across the apex. Because he had crashed at this same corner during practice, he had been forced to use the back-up Cooper, a car of some vintage which showed in its evil handling. All in all, he was glad to be done with both the car and the Zeltweg circuit.

There were promises that the 'track' would be resurfaced, but when sports cars visited Zeltweg the following year the place was found to be as bumpy as ever and the chances of holding another Grand Prix were gone.

Unperturbed by this, the locals laid plans for the Österreichring in the hillside above. When the first international race – a round of the World Sports Car Championship – was held there in 1969, the drivers were surprised and impressed. Comparing this with the airfield was like talking about Kitzbuhel and a municipal ski slope in the same breath. The return of the Austrian Grand Prix in 1970 was keenly anticipated.

From the outset, the Österreichring seemed to possess a strong sense of history. It had a mature look about it without any unattractive standardisation, flat landscapes and high, inhibiting kerbs. The corners were immense in every respect. The Boschkurve, a beautifully cambered downhill right-hander, left no doubt that bravery and skill was necessary to go

through it quickly. With the barrier right on the edge, nothing could be left to chance.

The races were, by and large, significant and more often than not contained a pleasant element of surprise. The pattern was set in 1970.

The Austrians turned out in huge numbers to see their hero, Jochen Rindt. If he won at home then the championship would be his, the first Austrian to win it. That, in itself, was a potential piece of history worth coming a long way to witness. In the event, they were to be disappointed, Rindt's Lotus blowing up as he gave chase to the Ferraris of Jacky Ickx and Clay Regazzoni.

For some time now the red cars had been threatening to dominate and on this day, the first since Rouen in 1968, they had it their own way. As soon as Ickx took the flag, the multitude of Italian fans made their presence felt as they swept onto the track. The paddock was engulfed, Ickx and Regazzoni having to lock themselves away until the mob had subsided. Already, the Österreichring had earned a place in the motor sport annals.

The following year's race was to prove better still. Barely a month after Pedro Rodriguez had been killed, the still-devastated BRM team arrived in Austria, determined to carry on but in need of a psychological boost. Jo Siffert, now carrying the burden of responsibility, rose to the occasion magnificently. Not only did he take pole, the Swiss led every lap. It had been BRM's first win in over a year. Two more unpredictable victories were to follow but, by the time the Austrian Grand Prix came round again, Siffert was dead and the team was starting a long slide into decline.

Tyrrell and Lotus dominated 1972, Jackie Stewart more or less ending his championship run in Austria when the latest Tyrrell proved no match for Fittipaldi's victorious Lotus. The boot was on the other foot in 1973, a fuel leak costing Emerson the lead after his team-mate, Ronnie Peterson, had waved the Brazilian through in the interest of retaining his title.

It was not an easy circuit to master, but once a driver and his engineer had a handle

on the Österreichring and confidence soared, then it was a glorious place to sink your teeth into. Carlos Reutemann was very much that sort of driver. If things were bad, then they were *really* bad. But, when he was up, Carlos was unbeatable. Sunday 18 August 1974 was just such an occasion as Reutemann led every lap with that stunning, graceful style.

No such superlatives, even in a moment of rash enthusiasm, could ever have been applied to Vittorio Brambilla, but the records show that he won this race in 1975. The records, however, do not come close to describing the conditions that day as a thunderstorm of Wagnerian proportions visited the circuit. Vittorio, knowing no fear, was in the lead when the race was stopped. He had never won a Grand Prix before – or since – and the thrill of the moment caught him out, the orange March skating nose-first into the crash barrier as he waved with unconfined joy. It was the one bright moment in an otherwise desperate day.

During the warm-up in the morning, Mark Donohue had left the road as the American went through the very fast Hella-Licht Kurve at the top of the hill above the pits. Donohue's car mowed down several rows of catch-fencing which then gathered beneath the March and raised it high enough to clear the crash barrier. The car severely injured two marshals and then slammed into an advertising hoarding mounted on stout steel poles. One of the poles caught Donohue a sharp blow to the head; although he was conscious before being flown to hospital, he died a few days later. Watson's victory the following year would go towards making amends for Penske.

Niki Lauda had been recovering in hospital, happy to learn that Watson had taken points away from James Hunt, but a year later the Austrian was back and his fellow-countrymen turned out in force to celebrate his recovery and witness a home victory. They came away bitterly disappointed. Lauda not only failed to win, he was beaten by Alan Jones in a Shadow, hardly the front-running combination of the moment.

The truth was that Jones was in the right car at the right time, a rare set of circumstances helped by the retirements of Mario Andretti and James Hunt while leading. The Austrians, meanwhile, were mystified by this strange turn of events.

There was little for them to get worked up about in 1978 either. In a race which was stopped after several laps because of rain and restarted with the track about to dry, Lauda crashed his Brabham while heading for second place. Master of all these condi-

tions, Peterson produced one of his greatest drives for Lotus, his reputation re-established, his name on everyone's lips. It was to be his last Grand Prix win. A month later Ronnie was killed at Monza.

Alan Jones used the excellence of his Williams FW07 to defeat the Renault turbos in 1979 but, a year later, he was no match for Jean-Pierre Jabouille as the Frenchman, against all expectations, nursed his Renault home on one set of tyres. Jabouille's shrewd judgement had a major effect on the out-

come of the 1981 Grand Prix when, in his capacity as adviser to the Ligier team, he chose the perfect tyre compound to enable Jacques Laffite to score a rare victory.

In 1982, there was perhaps the most dramatic finish ever seen at this or, indeed, any other circuit. As temperatures soared on race day, the turbos fell by the wayside leaving the Lotus of Elio de Angelis safely *en route* to his first Grand Prix win.

Then, during the closing laps, two things happened. The Ford-Cosworth began to stutter and Keke Rosberg mounted a stunning charge. Flinging the Williams around the Österreichring as only he could, Rosberg took yards off the Lotus during the final lap. They rushed through the last corner, the white car tucked under the rear wing of the black one. Rosberg darted to his right at the last minute, the two cars crossing the finishing line almost side-by-side. There was hardly anything in it – but nonetheless enough to have a jubilant de Angelis thrust his arm in the air in victory.

A year later, turbos filled the first five places, a calculated win for Alain Prost doing much to bolster the Renault driver's championship chances. Niki Lauda was sixth that day, struggling against long odds with his normally aspirated McLaren; a win at home seemed further away than ever. In 1984, he put that right by winning for McLaren, although there were moments of serious doubt when he lost fourth gear ten laps from home.

The following year, Niki chose the Aust-

rian Grand Prix to announce his impending retirement. Then it looked like there might be a fairy-tale ending as he led the race. But Lauda's hopes were dashed on lap 40 when he was sidelined with turbo trouble, allowing his team-mate Prost to move through for McLaren. Prost won again in 1986 despite having virtually to coast the final few laps, his TAG turbo cutting out. Only his healthy cushion over Alboreto's Ferrari saved the day.

The problems encountered by a driver during a Grand Prix weekend can be manifold but the 1987 race seemed to encapsulate the lot. Nigel Mansell spent every moment out of the car with an ice bag clamped to his jaw following the removal of a wisdom tooth. The discomfort did not prevent him from surviving two aborted starts and a clutch failure to win for Williams-Honda. Then, on the way to the victory podium standing on the official jeep, Mansell was almost knocked out as it passed under a low gantry.

Other headaches were placing the future of the circuit in doubt. Lap averages had risen to beyond 150 mph (and this despite the introduction of a chicane at Hella-Licht in 1977) and there was concern over the lack of run-off area in certain places. Security fell under suspicion, too, Stefan Johansson colliding with a deer and doing much damage to his McLaren.

On race day the narrow pit straight was blamed for the aborted starts, the second being caused by a pile-up involving ten cars. Besides, although not mentioned officially, the area around Zeltweg and Knittelfeld, for all its natural beauty, was not considered to be up-market enough for the increasingly influential corporate guests and their need for convenience and luxury. No-one was particularly surprised when the race was dropped from the calendar. The absence of the Österreichring left a vacuum not quickly filled and the drivers, their complaints apart, were sorry to see it go.

John Watson put his finger on it: 'I'm glad I won there,' he said. 'It was not what you would call a classic Grand Prix. But it was certainly a classic circuit.'

Following the death of Colin Chapman, Mansell's progress was hampered by a clash of personalities at Lotus.

The first public hint of dissension came when the facsimile machine clicked into life. The date was 11 October 1986. The place, Mexico City. Stuttering laboriously through the machine came a copy of a feature written by James Hunt, published in *The Times* that morning. It was a profile of Nigel Mansell, the man who, with the right result in Mexico, could become the first British world champion since Hunt himself ten years before. The piece claimed that such a thing would not be well received by those inside Formula 1. The feeling, according to the story, was that Mansell was not fit to be a worthy champion.

The receipt of this story was greeted initially in stunned silence. Here was one of the top British sportsmen of the moment being gently but firmly torn apart just as he was on the point of achieving lasting greatness. There was immediate outrage, particularly among those who had been paid to come to Mexico to sing his praises.

Then there was the creeping realisation that others quietly shared Hunt's views but no-one had dared articulate them. Certainly not in print. It was almost a betrayal, the exposure of a skeleton in the cupboard just as the world's spotlight was focused on the front door of the family home.

The subsequent heated discussions within were divisive. You either supported Mansell or you did not. And that, on reflection, has always been the way. Not a man of half-measures, either in the car or out of it, Nigel Ernest James Mansell has been the most excitingly controversial British driver ever to win a Grand Prix. He has been more contentious, even, than James Hunt.

To quote the popular aphorism, you knew where Hunt was coming from. He would be outrageous but that was expected, and you half understood why. Mansell's frequently belligerent actions were confusing. They would also be intensely frustrating because, more often than not, they were compromising one of the quickest racing drivers this country has ever produced.

On his day, Nigel Mansell is simply outstanding and it is that knowledge which has

driven him ever onward from the grim period when the only believers were his wife, Rosanne, and a small group of supporters. This enlightened band must take great credit because unlike Moss, Clark or Stewart, Mansell possessed no obvious signs of the brilliance to come. His climb from obscurity to one of the world's highest paid sportsmen is the stuff of which bestsellers are made. But, throughout, you doubted if this story would ever have a satisfactory ending.

The beginning was simple enough. Karting provided the introduction but the equipment was basic, Mansell urging himself on in a world which he knew little about. His fundamental skills were good enough to earn a place on the British Junior Team and this first acquaintance with the international arena brought a new dimension; simple enjoyment was replaced by the intoxicating pull of serious competition. By moving into a more sophisticated class, he found he could go quicker still. After that, motor racing was the obvious step.

Now came the first of many familiar hurdles. He had no money. Nigel had qualified as an engineer with Lucas Aerospace and his parents were urging circumspection, a steady job seeming more secure than a dubious existence as a racing driver. Besides, Nigel was married and had responsibilities. He also had an understanding wife and friend in Rosanne and, when the future was discussed, she had no hesitation in agreeing that if he wanted to try racing, then he should.

He continued working as an engineer while raising money for racing by selling off guns and paintings. A six-year-old Formula

Ford Hawke seemed a poor exchange for £1,000. Budgetary considerations meant a maximum of eight races; he won five of them and finished second once. He had also overspent. Now the road car had to go.

The knowledge that he could win was sufficient to override any concern about security. The turning point came in May 1977 when he won a race at Thruxton in a Crosslé 25F, which he followed up by doing a deal to race a 32F. During practice for his first race with the new Crosslé, a slower car crossed his path and deposited Nigel into the bank. The car was written off and so, according to the doctors, was the immediate career of this young driver – and a professional driver to boot, since he had given up his job three weeks before.

A broken neck and a crushed vertebra were diagnosed; he would need to be flat on his back for six months. It that was the case, Mansell knew he would also be flat broke. So he quietly discharged himself and had a friend take him home. Six weeks later, heavily strapped and collared, he was back at the wheel and on his way to winning eight races and a championship. Formula Ford offers flooded in. He turned them all down. Formula 3 had to be the next step.

That would, of course, cost considerably more money. So Nigel and Rosanne sold their house and gave most of the proceeds to March. In his young and naïve way, Mansell thought the rest of the season would take care of itself as sponsors formed a queue at his door. Instead, it was costing between £2,000 and £3,000 per race and he was getting nowhere. When 1978 ended, Nigel committed himself to 15 hours a day as a work study engineer in order to repay his massive debts. Rosanne hardly saw her husband all winter.

In the following spring, a drive was offered in the Unipart Formula 3 team. The Dolomite engine was fine in the wet and Mansell won his first race at Silverstone, having finished second a few weeks before at Thruxton. The 1979 season was not as bad as the previous one but it was dismal nonetheless. It suddenly seemed much worse on 15 September when Andrea de

Cesaris piled into the side of Nigel's car at Oulton Park and put Mansell on his head, severely injuring his back. It was a dreadful time for Nigel and Rosanne. There had been no money, no holidays, no luxuries, nothing. And here he was, confined to bed.

Ten days later the telephone rang. It was Team Lotus, unaware of the full extent of his injuries, wanting to know if Nigel would be free to test drive their Formula 1 car at Paul Ricard. Mansell said he had never felt better, which, in a manner of speaking, was true. He duly presented himself with helmet, overalls and pain-killing tablets. He had a quiet and difficult struggle climbing on board but, once under way, the thrill and exhilaration blanked out the pain. Well, most of it, anyway. Four weeks later he signed a testing contract.

Throwing everything into each mile, Mansell set out to impress and make the most of this opportunity. He knew he had succeeded when Lotus entered a third car for the 1980 Austrian Grand Prix. Mansell qualified and that seemed to be the main hurdle of the weekend overcome. In fact, it turned out to be the easy part.

As the mechanics topped up Mansell's fuel tank on the grid, some of the petrol slopped down his back. He had to grin and bear it. For Mansell there was no alternative; he was not about to consider walking away from the very thing he had dreamed about. The petrol did its work and when an engine failure brought merciful relief, Mansell was already badly burned about his buttocks. His critics would later say that a pain in the backside was an appropriate way for Nigel to begin his frequently tempestuous career in Formula 1.

At first, though, he made remarkable progress by going faster than anyone thought possible. That continued into 1981 when he was third-quickest during practice at Monaco and scored his first points by driving a nicely controlled race at Zolder in Belgium. The following year was made difficult by a car which was not easy to set up, but the crucial blow occurred in December.

When Colin Chapman died of a heart attack, Mansell lost his most staunch sup-

porter. Nigel looked upon the mercurial Lotus boss almost as a father-figure, Chapman instilling great confidence and massaging Mansell's delicate ego. Chapman's successors were not of that persuasion and Nigel, rightly or wrongly, developed a healthy persecution complex.

That, in turn, produced an almost desperate pressure to succeed; a need to show these people that they were *wrong*. Monaco in 1984 was the most public example. In teeming rain, on a circuit he loved, Mansell found himself leading a Grand Prix for the first time. And he was pulling away from Prost's McLaren. But, rather than reduce speed, he went even quicker. Going up the hill towards Casino, the black-and-gold Lotus got away from him, clouted the barrier and damaged his reputation just as much as the car.

The error was understandable. But the insistence that it was not his fault, that a white line was to blame, was difficult to swallow, and a festering distrust between Mansell and the media was born. With each succeeding race, he seemed to get worse, emotion corrupting his talent for going quickly. The fact that he had not been handled sympathetically was proven when he joined Williams in 1985.

Under the expert tutelage of Peter Collins, the team manager and a self-confessed Mansell fan, Nigel was taught to ignore what others said and simply do what he knew best. Portugal, the second race of the season, was a turning point. After crashing on his way to the grid, Mansell faced a start from the pit lane. It was raining hard and the Williams-Honda was not the easiest car to drive, the fierce characteristics of the turbo acting like an on/off switch. Mansell finished fifth; not much on paper but a brilliant personal milestone. He began to believe in himself again.

As the season progressed, so did Nigel, and second place at Spa-Francorchamps in September marked the beginning of an extraordinary metamorphosis. He came to the European Grand Prix believing he could win and, on an emotional day at Brands Hatch, with a touch of luck on his side, he

did just that. The sheer joy on Rosanne's face said it all for only she knew the incredible hardship which had led to this.

Now he was up and running and another win followed in South Africa. Into 1986 now and a win at Spa-Francorchamps. But most impressive of all was a totally dominant display in Canada. Finally, it seemed, he had rid himself of all doubts, victories in France and at Brands Hatch coming easily despite intense pressure at the latter from his team-mate, Nelson Piquet.

There was talk now of the championship and a stunning drive to victory in Portugal confirmed it. There were two races left, Mexico and Australia, and a win in either might do the trick, depending on how Piquet and Alain Prost finished.

With almost gloomy foreboding, Hunt's article arrived and Mansell threw away his chances by failing to put the car into gear on the line. Naturally, he would not admit it. On to Adelaide, where third place would do. He had it made when that now infamous left-rear tyre blew on the main straight and, overnight, Nigel Mansell became a British hero, a classic underdog, a brilliant loser.

He was voted Sports Personality of the Year in every competition worthy of the name. Sympathy was in copious supply. But the media were running out of patience. A badly managed press conference – the only press conference that winter – indicated that perhaps Nigel was making the mistake of believing too much of his own publicity. It seemed he was having difficulty in handling the transition from star to superstar. The tragedy was that he was unable, or was not *allowed*, to see that fatal flaw. Anyway, why should he worry when the 1987 Williams-Honda was even better than its predecessor? As his coterie of advis-ers constantly told him, he was the best and the world loved him.

The world did not know what to make of it when he collided with Ayrton Senna in Belgium and then tried to throttle the Brazilian. But the world most certainly did love him when he produced the most electric performance to win at home. It was a truly breath-taking drive combining all of Nigel's star qualities: daring, skill and a refusal to give up. Once again, the championship looked like running to the wire but Mansell brought it to a premature conclusion when he crashed during practice in Japan. And Nigel being Nigel, his exit was spectacular as he shared his pain with the world at large.

'There's always a story when Our Nige is around' had become a popular cliché among the press. And so it had seemed, Austria that year being a fine example as he arrived with his wisdom teeth in a bag and

Nigel usually excels at Monaco. He tackles the Loews Hairpin with the Williams-Honda in 1986, the year he should have won the championship.

A keen eye for financial matters. Nigel opened a Ferrari dealership in Dorset in 1989.

an ice pack at his jaw. He won the race and, on the way to the rostrum in an open jeep, Mansell stood up too soon and was almost knocked unconscious by an overhead girder. As always, he wore the bruises well. His ability for the spectacular action saw him save Peter Collins from drowning in the vicious currents off Rio, while in 1986 he answered a Mayday call in his helicopter by landing at the scene of a crash and pulling the pilot from his aircraft.

There were few stories in 1988, however, when Williams lost the Honda turbo. Nigel's move to Ferrari at the end of that season opened a package of intrigue, politics and thrilling performances. It was hard to imagine a meat-and-two-veg Englishman mixing with this volatile team.

He won them over from the start by giving 100 per cent in his usual manner, and a victory first time out in Brazil sealed the

alliance. He was immediately on top of Gerhard Berger and established his position by winning twice more, the overtaking move in Hungary being a Mansell classic. From the start, Nigel had seen 1989 as a formative year with Ferrari; in 1990 he would win the championship.

That plan did not take into account the arrival of Alain Prost, Mansell having to give up his Number One status and more besides as the Frenchman set about making the team his own. Once again Mansell's need for total support showed itself as a weakness and his motivation suffered. In addition, he was plagued with mechanical failures, not all of which were of his own making, but the breakdown at Silverstone proved too much.

In full flood of emotion, he told the world he had had enough. He would retire at the end of the year. That seemed logical

enough, for Mansell had plenty to live for. Understandably, he wanted to spend more time with his three children, indulge in a passion for golf and use his private jet to flit between beautiful homes in Portugal and the Isle of Man. The question was, would they fill the vacuum? Williams moved in, played beautifully to his ego and persuaded a return which had always been on the cards, even if Nigel chose to delude himself and mislead the press.

Nonetheless, it was a welcome turn of events. A Grand Prix without Nigel Mansell is a race without a talking point. Whatever he does, Mansell is news, be it a thrilling drive or the overreaction at the end of a controversial one. In 1989 he was banned from the Spanish Grand Prix, a ridiculous decision which did not match the alleged crime of ignoring a black flag in Portugal the week before. It prompted familiar

emotional behaviour as Nigel threatened to retire, but, more than anything, his absence from a tedious Spanish Grand Prix proved how necessary was his exciting presence. The British press were at a loss all weekend.

For 1991, however, the media reported Mansell's claim that he now had all he needed at Williams-Renault. Here was a team which would give him their full backing, the exclusive use of a spare car and the impetus of a chassis and engine combination on the point of success. Hardly any mention was made of Riccardo Patrese, Nigel's team-mate.

In the first six races, Patrese out-qualified Mansell every time and beat him in Mexico. Nigel had plenty of mechanical problems to account for this, but it was clear that Patrese's remarkable performances were taking their toll. Mansell's battered confidence received a timely boost with a superb victory in France. Until then, he had been confused since he seemed to be driving better than ever and yet he was being defeated by a so-called journeyman driver earning a seventh of Nigel's fees.

Financial awareness was the one factor

which Mansell had under control from the start. His desperate shortage of money in the past had fostered a keen appreciation of what it could do. During an interview at his rented home in a suburb of Birmingham in May 1981, Nigel spoke of looking forward to the time when he could afford to move into the country, have an indoor pool and a small piece of land.

On the weekend of the 1991 Mexican Grand Prix, the *Financial Times* carried an advertisement for the sale of his house on the Isle of Man. Set in 200 acres on a cliff top at Port Erin, the purpose-built seven-bedroom mansion boasted a swimming pool, gymnasium, sauna, rifle range, helicopter garage and housekeeper's cottage.

The asking price was £4 million. It was a fair indication of his worth, but the fact that Mansell was leaving for Florida also suggested a man not at one with himself, someone still searching for a nirvana which does not exist. Or, at least, not in a private world where even the mildest form of criticism is seen as personally destructive.

As James Hunt pointed out in his article in 1986, the constant employment of defen-

Mansell's triumphant domination at Silverstone in 1991 made up for the disappointment of his last-lap failure in Canada.

sive tactics brought Mansell a reputation as a whinger inside the business. Outside, though, he remains a national hero, one who has done more for the image of Grand Prix racing than all of the British drivers of recent times.

Mansell can be a warm and decent man, a brilliant performer with an almost obsessive will to succeed. Sometimes, though, a strange need to go beyond that takes him into the realms of the impossible. In the car, he gets away with it often enough to indicate a raw, courageous brilliance. But outside the cockpit it simply translates into irrational behaviour riddled with unconscious humour. It is that, just as much as his achievements on the race track, which will make Nigel Mansell the most talked about British winner for years to come, a driver perfectly capable of winning the championship. Whether he is actually fit to hold the title is something which James Hunt might dispute.

The South African Grand Prix

There was always an agreeable feel to the South African Grand Prix. If it represented one of the opening races, then this warm and hospitable country made a pleasant escape from the European winter. And if South Africa marked the latter stages of the season, then there were few better places in which either to unwind or, if necessary, to settle the championship.

In 1985, it was the penultimate round. The title had been decided at the previous race, an emotional occasion in more ways than one since the European Grand Prix had also provided Nigel Mansell with his first victory. He came to South Africa much relieved, the bogey of being a 'nearly man' having been put down after 72 Grands Prix. There was still the unspoken thought that the result at Brands Hatch may have been a

flash in the pan. South Africa would prove otherwise in the best possible manner – starting with practice.

The Kyalami circuit was a place where the driver and his car could get into their stride. Crowthorne, the right-hander at the end of the long, dipping straight, had to be taken cleanly because it led into a plunging downhill curve through Barbeque, followed by a flat-out rise and a deceptively quick left-hander known as the Jukskei Sweep.

Then on towards Sunset, a long but very fast right before the medium-speed left at Clubhouse. The short straight which followed led into the esses and a sharp rise towards Leeukop, the final right-hander. This was a tight corner with a difficult uphill entry, but the exit was vital since it fed onto the main straight and the gradual

climb towards the pits. Although it was not a particularly difficult track, the average speed for the 2.55 miles exceeded 135 mph and it held the drivers' attention in many places – as Mansell discovered on that October afternoon.

Qualifying had boiled down to a battle between Nelson Piquet's Brabham-BMW and the Williams-Hondas of Mansell and Keke Rosberg. Rosberg had been quickest on the first day but, in the final session, Mansell produced a lap fast enough to gain pole and Rosberg's total respect, a certain

Trevor Taylor leads Jim Clark and Stirling Moss at the start of the 1961 South African Grand Prix at East London. A spin by Clark as he avoided a stalled back-marker led to a superb comeback as the Lotus caught and passed Moss to take the lead.

Bitter disappointment for John Love and the home crowd at Kyalami in 1967 as the Cooper-Climax lost certain victory through a late stop for fuel. The Rhodesian driver leads Dan Gurney's Eagle into the esses.

indication of the bravery involved.

Mansell had touched 206.996 mph on the run towards Crowthorne and he did not want to lose such valuable momentum. On the very limit through Jukskei, he snatched sixth briefly before slamming back to fifth and taking Sunset without braking – a move which caused him to grow pale while discussing it later. On through Clubhouse and the esses. So far, so good.

Coming into Leeukop, however, the Williams began to understeer. Rather than back off, Mansell decided to drive through the problem. The car ran wide on the exit, mounted the kerb and narrowly missed the concrete wall, Mansell not lifting off for a moment as the Williams kicked up the dust. He got away with it and pole, only the second of his Formula 1 career, was just reward.

The new-found confidence carried into the race as Mansell streaked into the lead, Rosberg working his way through from fifth place after a bad start. By lap 9 he was on Mansell's tail and looking for a way through, Nigel obligingly waving him past, confident that he would be in a position to attack later in the race. It was a mature move which would pay dividends sooner than expected.

At the end of the next lap, Piercarlo Ghinzani's Toleman-Hart blew up at Crowthorne and Rosberg was the first to find the oil. The Finn flew off the road, Mansell receiving a fraction more warning and teetering through the corner. Rosberg somehow recovered but a typically dramatic drive, involving full use of the track and most of the grass verges, could not bring him close enough to prevent Mansell from winning his second Grand Prix in succession. On his penultimate lap, Rosberg established a new record for Kyalami and it would remain for ever. The 1985 South African Grand Prix turned out to be the 19th and last to be held on the Kyalami circuit in that form.

The first had been staged in 1967 but, seven years before that, a 2.4-mile circuit at East London had returned South Africa to the international map. This track, crossing the local rifle range and laid out in parkland bordering the Indian Ocean, used parts of the 15-mile Prince George road circuit which, in turn, had drawn foreign participation in the very first South African Grand Prix in 1934.

Won by Whitney Straight in a Maserati, this handicap event was continued in 1936 (the Bugattis of 'Mario' Massacurati and Jean-Pierre Wimille finishing first and second on a circuit reduced to 11.7 miles) and ran for three more years, Meyer's Riley finishing second to Pat Fairfield's ERA in 1937 before winning outright the following year. Victory for Villoresi's Maserati in 1939 marked the final South African Grand Prix before the outbreak of the Second World War.

In the meantime, there had been various races of note, such as the Grosvenor Grand Prix, first held in 1937 on the 4.6-mile Pollsmoor road circuit on the outskirts of Capetown and won by Ernst von Delius in an Auto Union, and the Rand Grand Prix, run in the same year in Johannesburg for the prime benefit of Fairfield's ERA. Yet, despite this serious activity, international racing was to make a very slow comeback following the return to normality. There was much rejoicing in motoring circles when the South African Grand Prix was scheduled for East London on 1 January 1960.

This was a Formula Libre event outside the world championship and the Cooper-Borgward of Stirling Moss headed an entry list which included an extraordinary assortment of single-seaters, sports cars and one-off specials such as a Netuar Special which, perhaps mercifully, blew up and failed to start. Moss led until a misfire prompted a pit stop and allowed the Cooper-Climax of Paul Frere to win with ease.

Moss returned at the end of the year with a Formula 2 Porsche, winning the Cape Grand Prix at the Killarney circuit just outside Cape Town before moving back to East London. There, on 27 December, he dominated the second South African Grand Prix to be held that year. Once again, it was open to all-comers, Moss sharing the track with weird and wonderful machinery like a front-engined Cooper-Chevrolet whose driver had to grapple with a steering wheel which looked as though it had been borrowed from a bus. Moss lapped this vehicle ten times.

The local problem continued into 1961 when, with the South African Grand Prix barely ten minutes old, the leaders were already in among the back-markers. Jim Clark, finding a stalled Cooper in his path with the driver attempting to push it, spun in avoidance and lost the lead to Moss. At least his comeback gave the race some interest, Clark's Lotus 21 eventually catching and passing Moss's more elderly Lotus 18. Clark and his team-mate Trevor Taylor made a habit of winning the various Grands Prix in the so-called Springbok Series but Jimmy failed to take the one which mattered most.

On 29 December 1962 the South African Grand Prix at East London was, for the first time, a part of the world championship. To the delight of the organisers, it would settle the series in favour of either Clark or Graham Hill. The 90,000-strong crowd was reported to be the second largest to have attended a sporting fixture in South Africa (96,000 having watched a South Africa v Great Britain rugby international in 1955). The multitude saw Clark suffer when a bolt fell out and oil worked its way onto the exhaust. Hill's BRM emerged through the resulting smoke-screen to take the race and the championship.

Clark won the next two championship Grands Prix at East London, the first being

at the end of his superb year in 1963 and the second, on 1 January, marking the start of his next championship in 1965. There was, therefore, no South African Grand Prix falling within the 1964 Formula 1 season.

While East London had been attracting the major events, the mayor of Johannesburg and begun to make encouraging noises about restoring the status quo and building a circuit in the locality. There was an immediate response from various motor clubs, but although they had enthusiasm to burn, none of them had money. Francis Tucker, the vice-chairman of the Sports Car Club, became chairman of a committee comprising three members from each of the leading clubs. Thus, the South African Motor Racing Club (SAMRC) was born and a search for a suitable location.

Sixteen miles north of the city, on the road to Pretoria, they found the land they wanted, purchased it at a knock-down price and, with the help of Caltex, built the circuit. It was named Kyalami, from the Zulu words kaya lami, meaning 'my home'. And, thanks to the tireless efforts of Francis Tucker and Alex Blignaut, the circuit manager, it possessed a homely atmosphere from the start. The Rand Grand Prix in 1961 marked the first major meeting, the South African Grand Prix switching to Kyalami when East London began to run into financial problems six years later.

This was the first round of the 1967 World Championship and it turned out to be a curious race. Denny Hulme led for 60 of the 80 laps before brake trouble forced three pit stops. To the full approval of a crowd reported to be in excess of 100,000 (although sceptics believed 60,000 to be a more accurate figure), John Love took charge in his elderly Cooper-Climax, but a superb drive by the Rhodesian was to be interrupted disastrously by the fuel pump failing to pick up the contents of the reserve tank necessary for such a long race.

Lumbering towards the chequered flag, therefore, came the Cooper-Maserati of Pedro Rodriguez, the result causing such widespread surprise that the organisers could not find a copy of the Mexican

national anthem. With remarkable cheek and quick thinking, they played 'South of the Border' instead. Pedro, as ever, did not seem to mind.

The drivers requested improvements in the circuit's safety provision, and the SAMRC willingly complied. Kyalami was virtually closed down for a period while the track was widened and resurfaced, banks cut back, barriers and fencing introduced. When the Grand Prix teams returned for the opening round of the 1968 championship on 1 January, Kyalami was reckoned to be one of the best tracks in the world.

The effect of the improvements showed immediately. Jim Clark took pole with a time almost seven seconds faster than the previous best, although the Lotus 49 could claim a portion of the credit. This was to be the last time Formula 1 Lotus would appear in its traditional green-and-yellow colours. As Clark steered his way towards the winner's enclosure at the end of a blisteringly hot day, it marked his 25th, and last, Grand Prix victory. He had led all but the first lap, the brief moment of glory going to a combination of the future, as Jackie Stewart edged the unpainted and largely untried Tyrrell-Matra into a position which the new liaison would soon become familiar with on a regular basis.

In 1969 they led all the way, but 12 months later the political need to switch to a March chassis meant Stewart and Tyrrell had to make do with third place. This, in fact, was the first race for the fledgling March company, but the sight of their cars filling the first two places on the grid proved to be something of a false promise. After a typically measured drive, Jack Brabham scored what was his last Grand Prix win before retiring at the end of the season.

With the Springbok championship having long since lost its way on an fully international basis, the Formula 1 teams had switched their attention to the Tasman series in Australasia. To avoid a clash of dates, the South Africans had moved their race to March. An additional benefit was the extra time available for testing and Kyalami became a most popular and, for

The first-lap charge into Crowthorne was always memorable at Kyalami. The McLarens of Scheckter and Hulme lead the way in 1973.

some, expensive location. Preparation for the 1971 Grand Prix was a typical example.

In January, Jackie Stewart wrote off his new Tyrrell while, a week or so before the race, Clay Regazzoni managed a spectacular accident which tore off the front of his Ferrari and flung the onboard fire extinguisher several hundred yards down the road. The Kyalami organisers, meanwhile, had been keeping pace with requirements by building extra grandstands and a road bridge as well as supplying some lock-up garages and generally complying with safety requirements. The Grand Prix had won the award for the best-organised race in 1970 and there seemed no reason why they should not carry it off again.

Stewart took pole position in his Tyrrell but he never recovered from fuel starvation at the start. The race looked like going to Denny Hulme in the new McLaren M19 but, a few laps from the finish, a bolt dropped out of the suspension and let the Ferrari of Mario Andretti score his first Grand Prix win. Hulme made up for his disappointment by winning the following year, but only after the gearbox on Stewart's Tyrrell had lost its oil. Before that, Stewart had been under serious pressure from Mike Hailwood, but just as the former motor cycle champion looked as though he would take the lead, the suspension failed on his Surtees.

Hailwood was back in the news in 1973 when, without thought for his personal safety, he plunged into the blazing wreck of Clay Regazzoni's BRM and pulled the unconscious Swiss free. The accident, involving four cars, happened on lap 3, and Stewart was later accused of having overtaken under the yellow flags at the scene of the incident. He was later cleared of the charge and allowed to keep a victory which, a day before, seemed unlikely after he had badly damaged his Tyrrell during practice.

In 1974, South Africa in general, and Kyalami in particular, went through a torrid time thanks to the worldwide fuel crisis. The Grand Prix, no longer the first race of the season thanks to the introduction a few years before of Grands Prix in South

America, was shifted from the beginning to the end of March in a bid to ease the problems for the organisers.

Then, a week before the race, came tragedy; Peter Revson lost his life when a suspension failure pitched his Shadow into the barrier at Barbeque. The American-backed team withdrew from the Grand Prix and the race was won in very fine style by the Brabham of Carlos Reutemann.

There was a touch of *déjà vu* about the Grand Prix in 1975 when Jody Scheckter crashed during practice and then blew an engine on the morning of the race. Frantic work by the Tyrrell mechanics had the local boy in the race and he repaid them by taking the lead on the third lap and staying there until the end.

Scheckter was never in the reckoning 12 months later when Niki Lauda dominated for Ferrari, Lauda's only problem being a puncture which allowed James Hunt to close during the final laps. The 1976 season, of course, was to be the year of a thrilling battle between McLaren and Ferrari, and much had happened by the time they returned to Kyalami in March 1977.

Hunt had taken the title and Lauda had been on his death-bed. The South African Grand Prix was to provide conclusive proof that Lauda had lost none of his race-craft and speed, although his superb victory was marred by one of the most bizarre incidents imaginable.

In the early stages of the race the Shadow driven by Renzo Zorzi had caught fire, the Italian pulling onto the verge, just beyond the crest of the hill on the main straight. A marshal, anxious to do his bit, sprinted across the track just as Zorzi's team-mate, Tom Pryce, crested the rise at over 170 mph. The marshal was flung into the air and his heavy-duty extinguisher smashed into Pryce's helmet, killing him instantly.

The Shadow, however, continued on its course, the driver's foot still on the throttle pedal. The wayward car was not arrested until it hit Laffite's Ligier and careered into the wall at Crowthorne. The marshal died of his terrible injuries. His fire extinguisher was later found in a car park; the force of the

impact had flung it clean over the main grandstand. The loss of Pryce, a supremely gifted young Welshman, was keenly felt and Lauda's stunned expression, as he learned the news while on the rostrum, said it all.

Variety was the main ingredient in 1978 as Andretti led, then Scheckter then, surprisingly, the Arrow of Riccardo Patrese. The novice's day was to end in tears when his engine failed, Patrick Depailler taking

the lead. Then, with a few laps to go, the Tyrrell refused to pick up the last gallons of fuel and Ronnie Peterson closed in. On the last lap, they were side-by-side, banging wheels, Depailler unable to hold off the Lotus during the final thrilling mile.

A heavy burst of rain caused the 1979 Grand Prix to be stopped after a couple of laps, the remaining 73 being fought out by the Ferraris of Gilles Villeneuve and Scheckter. Jody had gambled by taking the

restart on slicks, but Villeneuve built up too large an advantage and the French-Canadian was able to retake the lead on fresh slicks after stopping to get rid of his wet-weather tyres.

There was little hope for Scheckter to redeem the situation the following year, placards for the *Rand Daily Mail* announcing: 'Jody way down on GP grid'. With the rise in competitiveness of turbocharged engines there was much talk of their greater

suitability to Kyalami and its altitude, 5,600 feet above sea level. That seemed to be the case as the Renault team dispensed with qualifying tyres while claiming the front row, René Arnoux dutifully taking the lead when Jean-Pierre Jabouille suffered a puncture after 61 of the 78 laps. The turbo advantage made a mockery of the race.

Renault, along with Ferrari and other 'manufacturer' teams, were absent in 1981 as Kyalami became the innocent victim of a

war between FISA, the sport's governing body, and FOCA, representing most of the teams. The FOCA teams turned up to produce a reasonable race. Carlos Reutemann performed with finger-tip grace after starting with slicks on a damp track, the Williams driver taking advantage when the rest stopped to change tyres. That Grand Prix did not count towards the championship, but the bold action by the FOCA teams prompted a quick solution before the season got under way. Peace at last.

The poor South Africans were stunned when 12 months later they unwittingly provided the setting for yet another row, this time over the wording of a super-licence contract which FISA required the drivers to sign. The drivers refused and, instead of practising, they boarded a bus, travelled to the Sunnyside Park Hotel and locked themselves in the ballroom for the night. Their unprecedented behaviour looked like forcing the cancellation of the race.

After lengthy discussions, the drivers returned and took part in one practice session on the eve of the race. In the Grand Prix itself, Alain Prost won after a brilliant comeback drive following a puncture but, once the business of the weekend had been completed, Prost and his colleagues found they had lost after all, as FISA weighed in with heavy fines and suspensions.

With the race shifting to an October date in 1983, South Africa had the privilege of settling the championship. It was a simple equation: Alain Prost (Renault), Nelson Piquet (Brabham-BMW) and René Arnoux (Ferrari) had to go for a win to make sure of the title. In the end, Arnoux was never in the hunt and, when Prost retired with turbo problems, Piquet reduced speed and happily let his team-mate, Riccardo Patrese, through to win. Piquet finished third, good enough to take the title by two points.

The teams were back six months later for the second round of the 1984 championship. The late and arbitrary date change by FISA hurt the organisers badly, for they

had already applied to run the motor cycle Grand Prix at this time so as not to clash with the original late-season Formula 1 race. Brabham were destroyed by an on-form Niki Lauda as he led home a McLaren one-two, team-mate Prost having driven a storming race from the back of the field.

The organisers, meanwhile, were covered in embarrassment. The trophy, a silver bowl valued at £14,000, could not be found and Lauda received the Rand Grand Prix trophy instead. Such a blunder was perhaps indicative of the falling standards. Kyalami had been struggling for some time to make ends meet. The Grand Prix had consistently lost money and matters had not been helped when

the circuit was sold to a group whose motivation did not seem to be purely sporting.

New pits and facilities were built for the 1985 Grand Prix, but Mansell's win was the last of an era, the rand coincidentally hitting rock bottom against the dollar. After decades of panic stories concerning a shortage of cash, this time it was for real. Two years later, part of the land was sold and the track virtually cut in two, a heavily revised version using the lower portion through Sunset and Clubhouse before swinging left at Leeukop and into a new loop. It was subsequently used for testing by the Formula 1 teams and reports were generally favourable, if not totally enthusiastic.

When racing finally got under way at Kyalami in 1982, the Renault turbos dominated.

With the best will in the world, nothing could compensate for the loss of the superb main straight and the plunge through Barbeque and Jukskei. They are just memories now, as indeed are the relaxed days by the pool at the Kyalami Ranch Hotel, the race on Saturday, and the barbecue and prize-giving at the Tucker family home on Sunday. Even the name has been changed, to the Swiftsure Grand Prix Circuit. It is no longer 'my home', and that seems appropriate. Grand Prix racing has moved on, but Kyalami has more than played its part.

Bibliography

All Arms and Elbows Innes Ireland (Pelham Books, 1967)

All But My Life Stirling Moss and Ken Purdy (William Kimber & Company Ltd, 1963)

Brands Hatch to Indianapolis Tommaso Tommasi (Hamlyn, 1974)

The Certain Sound John Wyer (Edita SA, 1981)

Challenge me the Race Mike Hawthorn (William Kimber & Company Ltd, 1958)

Champion Year Mike Hawthorn (Aston Publications Ltd, 1989)

The Chequered Year Ted Simon (Cassell and Company, 1971)

Colin Chapman: The Man and his Cars Gerard Crombac (Patrick Stephens Ltd, 1986)

Cooper Cars Doug Nye (Osprey Publishing Ltd, 1983)

Driven To Win Nigel Mansell/Derick Allsop (Stanley Paul & Company Ltd, 1988)

Fangio Juan Manuel Fangio and Roberto Carozzo (Patrick Stephens Ltd, 1990)

Faster! Jackie Stewart/Peter Manso (William Kimber & Company Ltd, 1972)

Ferrari: The Grand Prix Cars Alan Henry (Hazleton Publishing, 1984)

Formula One: the Cars and the Drivers Michael Turner/Nigel Roebuck (Temple Press, 1983)

The Formula One Record Book John Thompson (Leslie Frewin Publishers Ltd, 1974)

The F̶ ̶ ̶ ̶Grand Prix David Hodges ̶ ̶ ̶ Ltd, 1967)

̶ ̶rand Prix** Cyril ̶mple Press Ltd, 1966)

̶f Canada** Gerald ̶Books, 1984)

Say Cheese. Hawthorn, the archetypal Englishman, poses in the cockpit of a Jaguar D-Type.

The Grand Prix Drivers Editor: Steve Small (Hazleton Publishing, 1987)

Grand Prix Greats Nigel Roebuck (Patrick Stephens Ltd, 1986)

Grand Prix Racing, Facts and Figures George Monkhouse/Roland King-Farlow (G.T. Foulis & Co, 1964)

James Hunt: Against all Odds James Hunt/Eoin Young (Hamlyn Publishing Group Ltd, 1977)

Jim Clark: Portrait of a Great Driver Graham Gauld (Hamlyn Publishing 1968)

The Jim Clark Story Bill Gavin (Leslie Frewin Publishers Ltd, 1967)

Jim Clark: The Legend Lives On Graham Gauld (Patrick Stephens Ltd, 1989)

Life at the Limit Graham Hill (William Kimber & Company Ltd, 1969)

McLaren: The Grand Prix, CanAm and Indy Cars Doug Nye (Hazleton Publishing, 1984)

The Monaco Grand Prix David Hodges (Temple Press Ltd, 1964)

Nigel Mansell David Tremayne (Hazleton Publishing, 1989)

Power and Glory William Court (Patrick Stephens Ltd, 1966/1988)

A Record of Grand Prix and Voiturette Racing (Vols 1 & 6) Paul Sheldon (St. Leonard's Press, 1987)

The Sebring Story Alec Ulman (Chilton Book Company, 1969)

Speed John Surtees (Arthur Barker, 1964)

Speed Was My Life Alfred Neubauer (Barrie & Rockliff, 1960)

Springbok Grand Prix Robert Young (Kinsey, 1969)

Stirling Moss Robert Raymond (Motor Racing Publications Ltd, 1953)

Stirling Moss: My Cars, My Career Stirling Moss/Doug Nye (Patrick Stephens Ltd, 1987)

A Story of Formula 1 Denis Jenkinson (Grenville Publishing Company Ltd, 1960)

A Turn at the Wheel Stirling Moss (William Kimber & Company Ltd, 1961)

The World Atlas of Motor Racing Joe Saward (Hamlyn, 1989)

Periodicals
The Autocar, Autocourse, Autosport, Competition Car, Grand Prix International, The Motor, Motoring News, Motor Racing, Motor Racing Year, Motor Sport, Speed World International.

Index

Picture credits
We are grateful to the following sources for
the use of their photographs: Allsport,
Bruce Craig, Esler Crawford, Denis
Jenkinson, The Observer Picture Library,
David Phipps, Quadrant Picture Library,
Nigel Snowdon and Eoin Young.